CONFRONTATION OF KINGS, 1656

The Three-Day Battle of Warsaw in the Swedish Deluge, 1655-1660

Michael Fredholm von Essen & Michał Paradowski

'This is the Century of the Soldier', Fulvio Testi, Poet, 1641

HELION & COMPANY

Helion & Company Limited
Unit 8 Amherst Business Centre
Budbrooke Road
Warwick
CV34 5WE
England
Tel. 01926 499 619
Email: info@helion.co.uk
Website: www.helion.co.uk
Twitter: @helionbooks
Visit our blog https://helionbooks.wordpress.com/

Published by Helion & Company 2025
Designed and typeset by Mary Woolley, Battlefield Design (www.battlefield-design.co.uk)
Cover designed by Paul Hewitt, Battlefield Design (www.battlefield-design.co.uk)

ISBN 978-1-804516-83-6

British Library Cataloguing-in-Publication Data.
A catalogue record for this book is available from the British Library.

For details of other military history titles published by Helion & Company Limited contact the above address or visit our website: http://www.helion.co.uk.

We always welcome receiving book proposals from prospective authors.

Contents

Introduction

This book describes the three-day Battle of Warsaw in 1656. The battle was fought within the context of the devastating mid-seventeenth century wars between Sweden, the Polish-Lithuanian Commonwealth, Brandenburg-Prussia, Muscovy, Transylvania, Cossack Ukraine, the Tatar Khanate of the Crimea, and The Holy Roman Emperor. In 1655, Sweden's King Charles X invaded the Polish-Lithuanian Commonwealth – firstly, to put an end to the King of Poland, John Casimir's, claim to the Swedish throne and secondly, to gain additional territories which would enable him to maximise his gains from customs duties on the Baltic Sea maritime trade. In Poland, the war accordingly became known as the 'Swedish Deluge' (*potop szwedzki*). Yet, this conflict cannot be disentangled from the simultaneous wars between the Commonwealth and Muscovy, from 1654, and between Sweden and Muscovy, from 1656. All of these conflicts blended into one, since they took place simultaneously and on the same terrain, which stretched from Arctic Scandinavia to the shore of the Black Sea. Of the many battles fought during these wars, it was only the Battle of Warsaw that saw the direct participation of the monarchs of three belligerent states: King Charles of Sweden, King John Casimir of Poland, and Frederick William, Elector of Brandenburg and Duke of Prussia. The short-term importance of the Battle of Warsaw was slight. Yet, it carried significant long-term consequences, being the first battle fought by an army of Brandenburg-Prussia. The Battle of Warsaw accordingly proved an important stepping stone on Prussia's path to independence and, ultimately, great power status.

At the time of the war, some of the belligerent powers followed different calendars. The Gregorian calendar, named after the sixteenth century Pope Gregory XIII who introduced it, had been developed as a correction to an observed error in the old Julian calendar. The visible result of the correction was that the date was advanced 10 days, that is, 4 October 1582 was followed by 15 October 1582. The Holy Roman Empire changed calendar on this date, as did most Catholic nations. However, many Protestant countries initially objected to adopting a Catholic innovation. The Duchy of Prussia was the first Protestant nation to adopt the Gregorian calendar, in 1612. Meanwhile, Brandenburg adopted the new calendar only in 1700, while Sweden delayed even longer. Muscovy's successor Russia delayed further still – until 1918! Most of the belligerents in the war accordingly used the Julian calendar, which thus differed from the one used by Catholic nations. Old Style (O.S.) and New Style (N.S.) are terms commonly used with dates to indicate that the calendar convention used at the time described is different from that in use at present. Unless noted otherwise, the dates given in this work are all N.S.

The different calendars already caused confusion in seventeenth century Europe, and today the situation frequently causes problems for historians. Swedish archival documents relating to the war commonly use the O.S. calendar, and most Swedish-language works describing the war still follow this style. However, the Swedish field chancellery occasionally used N.S. dates while in Poland, so it is not always possible to be certain about the style employed in a given document. Meanwhile, Commonwealth documents and modern Polish-language histories naturally follow the N.S. calendar. We have yet to see a work on The Deluge without the occasional, wrongly calculated date, and no doubt there may be mistakes in the present volume.

The linguistic, ethnic, and regional diversity then as well as now does not allow for a single, fully consistent system for the spelling of seventeenth century East European names. State borders, languages, and name forms have changed, often more than once. Major parts of the region were, in the seventeenth century, dominated by speakers of non-Slavic languages, including Lithuanian, German, and Tatar. German geographical names were particularly common in Prussia but also in north-western Poland. Thus, we have Warsaw, not Warszawa; Kiev, not Kyiv; Moscow, not Moskva; Danzig, not Gdańsk; Posen, not Poznań; Bratslav, not Bracław; and Chernigov, not Chernihiv or Czernihów, et cetera.

An attempt has been made to include, in addition to English-language translations, the original names in Polish, Lithuanian, Swedish, and German, where it seemed important to do so for reasons of clarity. However, since neither language had a codified system of spelling at the time, the forms used are not necessarily those in use today. But anybody with a working knowledge of the language should be able to identify the word forms employed. The same goes for personal names, which were then spelled in a variety of ways. Moreover, names and titles were long and cumbersome, and we often do not know which of the several given names an individual preferred.

Dramatis Personae

Sweden

Adolph John (1629–1689), Duke and *Generalissimus*. Brother of King Charles.

Ascheberg, Rutger von (1621–1693), Colonel. Veteran from Courland who had risen from the ranks in Swedish service during the Thirty Years' War, which he had entered as a common cavalryman.

Bülow, Barthold Hartwig von (1611–1667), Major General. Veteran of the Thirty Years' War who had fought at Nördlingen in 1634 under Bernard of Saxe-Weimar as well as in other battles.

Charles Magnus of Baden-Durlach (1621–1658), Margrave. Veteran of the Thirty Years' War who had served in the Swedish Army for several years including at the Battle of Jankow in 1645.

Dahlbergh, Erik Jönsson (1625–1703), Lieutenant Quartermaster General. Military engineer and fortification officer with experience from the Thirty Years' War. Ennobled as Dahlbergh in 1660.

Douglas, Robert (1611–1662), Count. General of Cavalry, from 1656 Field Marshal Lieutenant. Scottish veteran of the Thirty Years' War who had distinguished himself on numerous occasions, including in the Battles of Lützen 1632, Wittstock 1636, and Jankow 1645.

Horn, Henrik Henriksson, af Marienborg (1618–1693), Major General of Cavalry. Veteran of the Thirty Years' War, commander of the Tavastehus Cavalry Regiment which fought in Poland, promoted to Lieutenant General in 1656 or 1657.

Lewenhaupt, Gustav Adolph (1619–1656), Field Marshal and commander in Livonia and Finland. Veteran of the Thirty Years' War who had distinguished himself in the second Battle of Breitenfeld 1642, in Gustav Horn's 1644 campaign in Scania, and at the Battle of Jankow in 1645.

Lewenhaupt, Ludwig Wierich (1622–1668), Colonel.

Oxenstierna, Gustav (1626–1693), Colonel.

Philip Florinus of Sulzbach (1630–1703), also known as Philipp of Pfalz-Sulzbach, Count Palatine and Major General of Cavalry. A relative of King Charles, he began his military career in the Duchy of Lorraine but in 1655 went into Swedish service with an enlisted regiment.

Wittenberg von Debern, Arvid (1606–1657), Field Marshal. Veteran who began his military career in 1622, fought under King Gustavus Adolphus in Prussia against the Commonwealth as well as in numerous battles of the

Thirty Years' War, including Nördlingen 1634, Wittstock 1636, the second battle of Breitenfeld 1642, and Jankow 1645.

Wrangel, Carl Gustav, af Salmis (1613–1676), Field Marshal and Admiral. Veteran of the Thirty Years' War who in 1646–1648 held overall command over Swedish military forces in Germany.

Wrzesowitz und Neuschloss, Johann Weyckhardt von (1623–1656), Major General. Veteran of the Thirty Years' War from Moravia in Swedish service.

Brandenburg

Goltz, Joachim Rüdiger von der (1620–1688), Major General (*Generalwachtmeister*). Prussian veteran of Imperial service in the Thirty Years' War, followed by French service until he entered into the service of Brandenburg in 1654 with the rank of colonel.

Kannenberg, Christoph von (1615–1673), Major General. Veteran of the Thirty Years' War who rose in the ranks from common cavalryman in Swedish service.

Sparr, Otto Christoph von (1599 or 1605–1668), General, from 1657 Field Marshal General (*Generalfeldmarschall*). Veteran of the Thirty Years' War in Imperial service who from 1651 served as overall chief of artillery (*Generalfeldzeugmeister*) and from 1655 was overall commander of all Brandenburg-Prussian troops.

Waldeck, Georg Friedrich von (1620–1692), Lieutenant General and Count. Veteran of the Thirty Years' War in Dutch service. Commander of the army in Prussia until 1655. Dismissed in 1658, he went into Swedish service and fought for King Charles in Denmark.

Waldeck, Wolrad von (1625–1657), Colonel, from 1656 Major General (*Generalwachtmeister*), and Count. Brother of Georg Friedrich von Waldeck.

Polish-Lithuanian Commonwealth

Butler, Wilhelm (d.1660), Major General and Colonel of the Foot Guard regiment at Warsaw. Veteran of wars against Ukrainian cossacks and Muscovites.

Czarniecki, Stefan (*c.* 1599–1665), Colonel and *regimentarz* of the Polish Army. Castellan of Kiev from 1655. Veteran of numerous wars including against Gustavus Adolphus's Swedes in Prussia, Muscovites, Ottoman Turks, Tatars, Ukrainian cossacks, and in Imperial service in the Thirty Years' War.

Gosiewski, Wincenty Aleksander Korwin (*c.* 1620–1662), Lithuanian Field Hetman. Formerly General of Artillery of Lithuania.

Grodzicki, Krzysztof (d. 1659), Crown General of Artillery since 1653. Veteran of the Thirty Years' War who fought Gustavus Adolphus's Swedes in Prussia, studied in the Dutch Republic, served in the Imperial army under Wallenstein, and in the 1640s fought Ukrainian cossacks and Tatars.

Koniecpolski, Aleksander (1620–1659), Prince and Colonel. Voivode of Sandomierz and Grand Standard bearer of the Crown (*chorąży wielki* *koronny; vexillifer regni*), a court rank. Son of Stanisław Koniecpolski who fought Gustavus Adolphus.

Lanckoroński, Stanisław (*c.* 1597–1657), Crown Field Hetman from 1654 to 1657.

Lubomirski, Jerzy Sebastian (1616–1667), noble and magnate. Crown Field Hetman from 1657 to 1664.

Połubiński, Aleksander Hilary (1626–1679), Lithuanian Field Scribe and hussar commander.

Potocki, Andrzej (1618–1663), noble and magnate. Crown Camp Master (*oboźny koronny*; *praefectus curruum*) from 1655.

Potocki, Stanisław 'Rewera' (1589–1667), Crown Grand Hetman. Veteran of wars with Muscovy, Sweden, and Ukrainian cossacks. He acquired the nickname 'Rewera' because he so often included the Latin words *re vera* ('in fact') in his speeches.

Radziwiłł, Bogusław (1620–1669; Lithuanian: Boguslavas Radvila), Prince. Veteran of the Thirty Years' War, in Dutch service 1641–1643.

Radziwiłł, Janusz (1612–1655; Lithuanian: Jonušas Radvila), Lithuanian Grand Hetman and Prince.

Radziwiłł, Michał Kazimierz (1625–1680, Lithuanian: Mykolas Kazimieras Radvila), Prince. Leader of the Catholic branch of the Radziwiłł family.

Sapieha, Jan Fryderyk (1618–1664, Lithuanian: Jonas Frederikas Sapiega), noble and magnate. Crown Field Scribe. Veteran of the French army, in which he fought under Louis, Duke d'Enghien, later Prince of Condé, and the wars against Ukrainian cossacks and Tatars.

Sapieha, Paweł Jan (1609–1665; Lithuanian: Povilas Jonas Sapiega), Lithuanian Grand Hetman. Veteran of the Smolensk War against Muscovy and wars with Ukrainian cossacks.

Zamoyski, Aleksander (d. 1656), Crown Grand Guard (*strażnik wielki koronny*). Noble and magnate.

Zamoyski, Jan 'Sobiepan' (1627–1665), Vice Cup-bearer. Noble and magnate.

Khanate of the Crimea

Subhan Ghazi Agha (d. 1663). Officer and corps commander.

Prologue: The Three Monarchs

Charles X Gustavus, King of Sweden

Charles X Gustavus (1622–1660; r. 1654–1660) was the son of John Casimir, Count Palatine of Zweibrücken-Kleeburg in Germany, and Catherine, daughter of the Swedish King, Charles IX, of the House of Vasa. Charles Gustavus was born in Sweden, where he also grew up.

Charles Gustavus joined the Swedish Army in Germany in 1642 as a 20-year-old volunteer, just before the second Battle of Breitenfeld. Serving under Field Marshal Lennart Torstensson, Charles Gustavus also fought in the war in Denmark from 1643 to 1644 and in the Battle of Jankow in 1645. He rose in rank rapidly, because of his skill no less than because of his birth. In the summer of 1643, Charles Gustavus was appointed captain in Torstensson's Life Regiment of Horse. A few months later, he was given command of the Courland cavalry regiment, which he commanded at Jankow. In this battle, Charles Gustavus served under then Major General Arvid Wittenberg, who a decade later would spearhead the Swedish invasion of the Commonwealth. But it was Torstensson who taught the young man how to handle a modern army. Years later, having become King of Sweden, Charles Gustavus concluded that 'for everything which I know [of military affairs], I should give thanks to Torstensson.'[1]

Charles Gustavus was the cousin of Queen Christina of Sweden (1626–1689: r. 1632–1654). When both were very young, the two had been sweethearts, and Queen Christina had promised to marry him. However, in 1648 Queen Christina appointed Charles Gustavus her Lieutenant General and commander-in-chief (*Generalissimus*) of the Swedish forces in Germany. Christina had planned this for several months, as a means to avoid a marriage with him. As the new commander-in-chief, Charles Gustavus was ambitious and warlike, and by no means eager for peace. Nonetheless, when the Peace of Westphalia was signed later in the year, he accepted the task of demobilising the considerable Swedish Army in Germany. This was no easy matter, but Charles Gustavus showed great ability. Without him, it

1 Försvarsstabens krigshistoriska avdelning, *Slaget vid Jankow 1645 24/2 1945: Minnesskrift* (Stockholm: Försvarsstabens krigshistoriska avdelning, 1945), p.8.

is unlikely that the agreed-upon demobilisation process would have taken place as smoothly as it did.

When Queen Christina abdicated in June 1654 (she converted to the Catholic faith and moved to Rome), Charles Gustavus became King in her stead. He married Hedwig Eleonora of Holstein-Gottorp (1636–1715) soon after his coronation in 1654, and, although as was customary among royal families it was an arranged union, there is every reason to believe that their marriage was a happy one. King Charles liked to have Hedwig Eleonora at his side, even while on campaign. Soon after giving birth to their son, the future King Charles XI, Hedwig Eleonora travelled to the Swedish field army in Poland. She was present at the three-day Battle of Warsaw and resided for a while in Marienburg, before she returned to Sweden's capital, Stockholm, in autumn 1656.

King Charles was highly educated and while he grew up speaking German with his parents, he also knew Swedish, French, Latin, and some Italian. King Charles was a Lutheran, since this was the requirement for Swedish kingship (his father had been a Calvinist). There is nothing to suggest that he was overly pious.

Although King Charles came to focus on military affairs, he was no stranger to administrative and fiscal tasks and was diligent in their execution. During the Thirty Years' War, King Gustavus Adolphus and his Chancellor Axel Oxenstierna had greatly improved Sweden's economy through the encouragement of trade and manufacturing. Yet, proceeds remained insufficient to fund a prolonged war, and the Crown had ended up owing money to a great many people, including those colonels who enlisted regiments for the war effort but also to civilian officials whose salaries could not be paid when the Crown lacked the funds. Sweden still suffered from being an impoverished state. King Charles took measures to alleviate this but his long absence abroad and unexpected early death meant that the reform would not be carried out in its entirety.

King Charles thrived at war and was personally brave – trusting in God and his good fortune, the King led from the front, often at considerable risk to his person. He was a lucky soldier, surviving personal combat against seemingly impossible odds on numerous occasions. Despite a lifetime of war, he appears never to have suffered a wound – even though his hat, coat, and even his shirt were often shot through and once he even lost a lock of hair to enemy fire. As a commander, Charles was an audacious tactician who had no match among his opponents. When young, he had read the Latin classics on the campaigns of Alexander the Great as well as other celebrated commanders of antiquity. Even at the end of his life, Charles would occasionally quote an anecdote about Alexander, suggesting that he regarded himself as a man in a similar mould.

Torstensson's influence on the King's tactical and strategic thought cannot be overstated. The notion of achieving a gainful peace through a decisive victory on the battlefield and the destruction of an enemy army was not yet part of Swedish strategic thought, and it can be argued that such notions, which emerged later, had little relationship to reality. Torstensson, who was not shy to lead his army into battle and habitually planned his actions better

Charles Gustavus, 1652 or 1653. (Sébastien Bourdon)

than most, summarised the then Swedish view on the risks of offering battle:

> There is nothing more hazardous than to chance a battle. You may lose it through a thousand unforeseen accidents, even when you have carefully taken all measures and steps available to the most flawless military expertise.[2]

King Charles followed Torstensson's advice. He was meticulous in planning his campaigns but also ready to take chances when a good opportunity called for it. He did not, however, neglect diplomacy, and sent envoys to all potential allies and adversaries, including the Khan of the Crimea and the Ottoman Empire. The King habitually kept all options open as long as he could, before committing himself to a particular course of action, so that he could make full use of any opportunity that arose. What others, then and later, may have interpreted as the instinct of a gambler was rather the result of his willingness to use every opportunity available to him. This characteristic made King Charles keep his long-term plans to himself, which incidentally makes it difficult for later historians to distinguish between what he regarded as his primary objectives and those which he merely took advantage of in an opportunistic manner. Perhaps it is fair to conclude that Charles was a competent but not brilliant strategist.

John II Casimir, King of Poland and Grand Duke of Lithuania

John II Casimir Vasa (Polish: Jan II Kazimierz Waza; 1609–1672, r. 1648–1668), King of Poland and Grand Duke of Lithuania, was a younger son who at first seemed to have no prospects within the Commonwealth. The Parliament (*Sejm*) never granted him an adequate income, despite his eligibility to the throne. As a result, the young John Casimir attempted to make a name for himself elsewhere. He took part in the war against Sweden in 1629 and in the Smolensk War against Muscovy in 1633. He also fought in the Thirty Years' War. In 1635, John Casimir was briefly in Imperial service as colonel of a regiment which fought, and lost, in the conflict with France.

2 Peter Englund, *Ofredsår: om den svenska stormaktstiden och en man i dess mitt* (Stockholm: Atlantis, 1993), p.384.

In 1638, John Casimir embarked at Genoa to negotiate an alliance with Philip IV of Spain against France and to take up a position as admiral in Spanish service and viceroy of Portugal. However, he was imprisoned by the French upon landing in Marseilles. John Casimir remained a prisoner in France until 1640. Seemingly giving up all hopes for a secular career, in 1643 John Casimir went to Rome, where in the following year he joined the Jesuit Order. He was appointed cardinal in 1646. However, he renounced this position upon the death of his elder brother, the then King of Poland, Ladislaus IV Vasa (Polish: Władysław; 1595–1648; r. 1632–1648), so that he could stand for election for the Polish throne.

Having been elected King of Poland in 1649, John Casimir soon married his brother's widow, Marie Louise of Gonzaga (1611–1667; also known as Maria Luisa di Gonzaga-Nevers or, in Polish, Ludwika Maria). Her background was as chequered as his. She was the daughter of Charles, Duke of Nevers and Duke of Mantua. Although born in France and brought up at the French court, she was an Italian by heart. In 1645, she married King Ladislaus of Poland. This was a politically motivated marriage carried out under French pressure. Moreover, since the Polish Parliament and clergy reserved the name Marie, or Maria, exclusively for the Virgin Mary, the marriage agreement forced a formal change of name from Marie Louise to Louise Marie. The marriage was not a happy one and King Ladislaus was unwilling to give her either his affections or any significant role. Upon the sudden death of Ladislaus in 1648, Louise Marie supported the candidature of John Casimir, who promised to marry her in exchange for French support for his candidature, and having become King, he honoured his promise.

John II Casimir, *c.* 1660. (Attributed to Daniel Schultz)

The marriage of King John Casimir and Louise Marie was politically motivated but the couple had first met in 1640, after John Casimir's release from French captivity. While still in France, John Casimir frequently visited Louise Marie and they then corresponded regularly until she married Ladislaus. Their still-surviving letters give the impression of mutual affection and respect.

John Casimir knew Polish, German, Latin, French, and Italian. Louise Marie knew French and Italian (indeed, her French remained influenced by Italian throughout her life, despite her being born in France). She never mastered Polish, and the couple conversed in Italian. She supported a number of worthy causes, including, in 1661, the foundation of the first Polish newspaper, *Merkuriusz Polski Ordynaryjny*.

Marie Louise of Gonzaga.
(Ferdinand Bol)

There is reason to believe that King John Casimir, despite his background which included stints in holy orders, was no fervent Catholic. However, he shrewdly realised that the Catholic faith was a symbol around which a significant number of Commonwealth subjects might rally. And he often used Catholic symbols and imagery as means to fan hatred against foreign intruders, be they Swedes, Muscovites, or anyone else.

Polish historians were often unkind to both John Casimir and Louise Marie. The King was frequently described as weak and indecisive in war and politics and as hen-pecked by his wife, who was called the real power behind the throne. Many assumed that Louise Marie, being a foreigner, put French interests above those of the Commonwealth, and perhaps even more damning, failed to understand and respect the traditional liberties of the Commonwealth nobility. In reality, John Casimir was a competent commander who enjoyed the respect of those of his soldiers who served him directly. While he was not brilliant, neither did he lack talent. As for Louise Marie, she was energetic, strong-willed, had a hot temper, and on occasion led men in battle by personal example. John Casimir never gave up womanising, and the couple often clashed on both personal and policy issues, yet there was genuine affection between them.

Frederick William, Elector of Brandenburg and Duke of Prussia

Frederick William (1620–1688, r. 1640–1688), Elector of Brandenburg and Duke of Prussia, was born to George William of the House of Hohenzollern, Elector of Brandenburg, in one of the towns which would become Berlin. Upon the death of his father in December 1640, Frederick William inherited the Margraviate of Brandenburg, the Duchy of Cleves, the County of Mark, and the Duchy of Prussia. Unfortunately, his German territories had been devastated by the Thirty Years' War. The young Frederick William's first major act of state after assuming power as Elector of Brandenburg was accordingly to negotiate a separate peace with Sweden – the Treaty of Stockholm, signed in July 1641. With most of his territories already under Swedish military control, except Prussia which formed part of the Commonwealth and remained under Polish authority, the Treaty safeguarded his territory until the end of the Thirty Years' War and the Peace of Westphalia in 1648. In a 1647 agreement with Sweden, Frederick William also acquired Minden, Halberstadt, and Magdeburg, and secured his control over East Pomerania.

Even when young, Frederick William had found himself linked to Sweden, in part because the Swedish King Gustavus Adolphus was his father's brother-in-law, but also because Swedish armies frequently marched through Brandenburg's territories. Later, Frederick William was educated in the Dutch Republic, including in Leiden and Amsterdam. His experiences in The Netherlands made a great impact on the young prince, and for the rest of his life, he regarded the economy and society of The Netherlands as a model to be emulated in his own territories. In 1646 at Den Haag, Frederick William entered into an arranged marriage with Luise Henriette of Nassau (1627–1667), daughter of Frederick Henry of Orange-Nassau.

Frederick William was a Calvinist but tolerant of other religious faiths, no doubt because of Brandenburg's unfortunate experiences during the Thirty Years' War. Frederick William based his foreign policy on the principle of safeguarding, and preferably increasing, his own territory; since this could only be done by military means and through the consolidation of his disparate territories, in hindsight his policies appear opportunistic. So they were, but Frederick William had good reasons to distrust other rulers and their armies.

Frederick William, Elector of Brandenburg, contemporary portrait although not published until 1717. (Anselmus van Hulle)

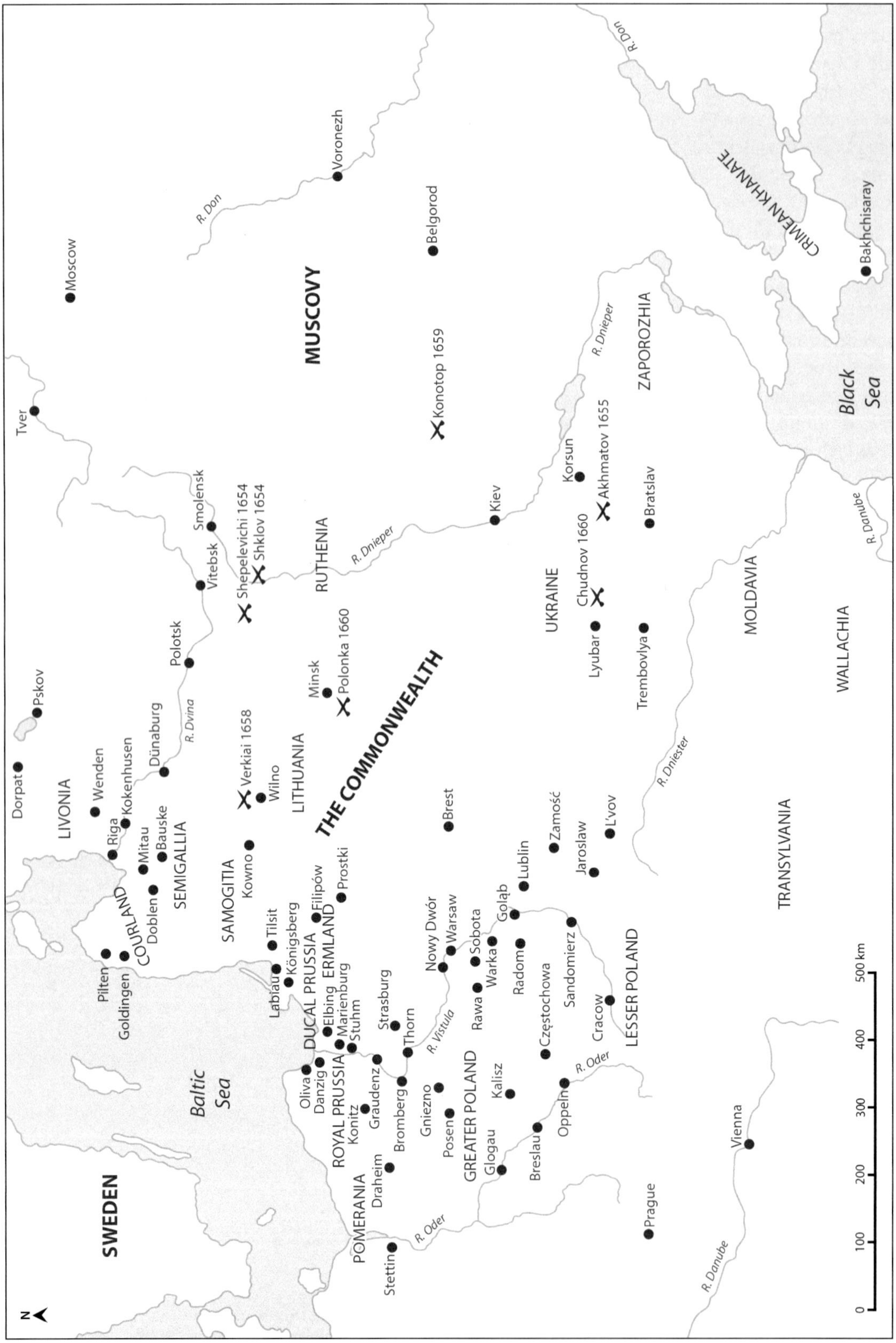

The Commonwealth

1

Background: The Wars of The Swedish Deluge

The Battle of Warsaw was fought on 28–30 July 1656 between a Swedish-Brandenburg Army, and a Commonwealth-Crimean Tatar Army.

The background was complex. The Polish-Lithuanian Commonwealth (the *Rzeczpospolita*), formally known as the Crown of the Kingdom of Poland and the Grand Duchy of Lithuania, had been at war with Sweden since 1598 because of the dynastic conflict between the Swedish and Polish branches of the House of Vasa. Although the two parties had, after much bloodshed, negotiated a truce in 1635, the dynastic rivalry made a peace treaty unattainable. John II Casimir Vasa, King of Poland and Grand Duke of Lithuania, could indeed be said to have a better claim to the Swedish throne than King Charles X of Sweden, who was only of the House of Vasa on his mother's side.

However, King John Casimir faced severe challenges in the east. The principal cause of the series of wars that broke out was the turbulent situation among the Ukrainian cossacks, who lived in the territory north of the Black Sea known as the Ukraine ('borderland'). Being of the Orthodox Christian faith and speaking a language quite different from either Polish or Lithuanian, the Ukrainian cossacks had long resented being under the dominion of the Commonwealth. As did the Ruthenian peasantry, from whom many Ukrainian cossacks derived – Ruthenia is a Latin term derived from Rus' (the same word which ultimately transformed into Russia). When the Union of Lublin formally established the Commonwealth in 1569, the Crown of Poland gained control of most of Ruthenia, which technically belonged to the Grand Duchy of Lithuania. The Ruthenian territories included Galicia, Volhynia, Podolia, Bratslav, and Kiev which together would eventually become known as the Ukraine.

In 1648, the Ukrainian-Ruthenian cossacks and peasants, under Bogdan Khmel'nitskiy, rose against the Commonwealth. Like most popular uprisings, it was a bitter and sordid affair. The rebels slaughtered their own gentry and those of the Commonwealth who fell into their hands, but also anybody deemed a Roman Catholic or a Jew. The Commonwealth armies retaliated in kind. However, the strategic context of the uprising was far from simple. Realising that his army was too small to resist the Commonwealth and simultaneously protect the Ruthenian population from the slave raids customarily carried out by the Crimean Tatars, Khmel'nitskiy before initiating the uprising met with the Khan of the Crimean Khanate. Pledging allegiance to him, and leaving his son behind as hostage, Khmel'nitskiy received the Khan's promise of sending a Tatar Army to support the cossacks. The Ottoman Sultan sanctioned the agreement later in the year. Without Crimean Tatar support, the Cossack Uprising would almost certainly have been crushed in 1649.

Yet, pledging allegiance to the Khan of the Crimea brought unintended consequences. Having answered Khmel'nitskiy's pleas for support, the Khan regarded Khmel'nitskiy and his cossacks as subjects, not allies. This was not what Khmel'nitskiy wanted or intended, so in 1650 he, instead, approached Muscovy for assistance. Although the Ukrainian cossack cause received some popular support in Muscovy, Tsar Alexis of Muscovy cautiously held back. Khmel'nitskiy's situation grew more desperate following the decisive Commonwealth victory over the Ukrainian cossacks at Berestechko in 1651, and the cossacks suddenly found themselves without Tatar support.

Khmel'nitskiy then again opened negotiations with Moscow, and this time, Tsar Alexis was more amenable. In January 1654 Khmel'nitskiy signed the Treaty of Pereyaslav, in which he withdrew his fealty to the Khan and instead acknowledged the Muscovite Tsar as his suzerain. In return, Moscow recognised Khmel'nitskiy's territory in the Ukraine as independent but under Moscow's suzerainty. In May, Muscovy invaded the Commonwealth in what eventually became known as the Thirteen Years' War of 1654–1667.

Although this war was unconnected with the Commonwealth's rivalry with Sweden (and in due time, Muscovy would declare war on Sweden, too), the repercussions soon reignited the Commonwealth-Swedish conflict as well. Learning of the news from the east, King Charles at first contemplated a joint Swedish-Commonwealth attack on Muscovy, since he regarded Muscovy as a long-term threat to Swedish territory. Expecting the Commonwealth eventually to collapse under the then ongoing Muscovite onslaught, King Charles wanted to pre-empt any Muscovite expansion to the shores of the Baltic. Stockholm assessed that Tsar Alexis wanted to gain control of parts of the same Baltic shore that Sweden coveted, something Sweden did not want to allow to happen.

However, the Commonwealth was not interested in an alliance, since King John Casimir refused to recognise Charles as King of Sweden. Rebuffed, Charles decided to invade the Commonwealth instead. A settlement of the existing Swedish-Commonwealth conflict was long overdue. Moreover, in the Commonwealth a Swedish Army could support itself, and the Swedish Crown might gain much-needed additional revenues. All facts considered, the decision to invade the Commonwealth was rational on all counts. Weakened from numerous internal divisions and the ruling strata's unwillingness to modernise either government structure or military establishment, the Commonwealth seemed ripe for the taking.

On the surface and in a seventeenth century context, it was easy to justify Sweden's new attack on the Commonwealth. Firstly, Poland's King John

Casimir refused to surrender his claim to the Swedish throne, which had caused the war in the first place, more than half a century ago. Secondly, the Commonwealth was patently unwilling to negotiate a proper peace treaty to replace the 1635 truce, which would lapse in 1661. Unsurprisingly there were ulterior motives as well, since the truce would not lapse for another six years, which gave ample time for continued negotiations. Sweden's primary objective was to conquer the entire Baltic shore. The acquisition of these territories would join the Swedish overseas possessions in the north and south and give Sweden control over the Baltic Sea. It would also enable easy redeployment of Swedish armies from Swedish Pomerania to Livonia, Estonia, Ingria, and Finland, and vice versa.[1] And it would enable additional and better naval bases than those which already existed. But even more importantly, it would allow Sweden to control the important trade routes across the Baltic Sea, and to impose tolls on this trade.

While the Muscovites rapidly assumed control over major parts of Lithuania, and the Crimean Tatars raided the Ukraine as the King of Poland's allies, the Swedish Army invaded Poland and northern Lithuania. The Swedish plan was a two-pronged attack: the main thrust would be an invasion of the Commonwealth from Swedish Pomerania in the west while the Livonian army would invade from Swedish Livonia in the north.

In spring 1655, Field Marshal Arvid Wittenberg mustered the army in Pomerania. King Charles mustered the army in Sweden, which he would accompany to Pomerania. In Livonia, a third army was mustered which would be commanded by Field Marshal Gustav Adolph Lewenhaupt. When Wittenberg attacked from the west, through East Pomerania (which belonged to Brandenburg) King Charles would follow in his footsteps and they would join forces in Poland. The Swedish Army of Livonia was ordered to take Courland and Lithuania, and would prevent the Muscovites from advancing further towards the Baltic Sea. Later, having personally arrived in Pomerania, King Charles ordered the Livonian army to move specifically against Wilno (modern-day Vilnius) or Kowno (modern-day Kaunas) so as to pre-empt their occupation by the Muscovites. However, by then it was too late to prevent Tsar Alexis from conquering central Lithuania.

The Swedes faced little resistance when, in July, they marched into the Commonwealth. Greater Poland and Warsaw soon surrendered to King Charles's armies, as did the unoccupied parts of Lithuania, which accepted Swedish protection, formally revoked its previous union with Poland, recognised King Charles as Grand Duke of Lithuania, and additionally proclaimed a union of states between Lithuania and Sweden. King John Casimir fled Poland in the search for assistance abroad. In November, the Polish Crown Army surrendered to King Charles. With all major nobles and organised military units swearing allegiance to the Swedish Crown, the

---

1 Sweden and Finland constituted the same country. Its provinces and peoples had the same rights and obligations. Hence, any reference to Swedish soldiers, nobles, and so on, can be assumed also to include those of Finland (unless specifically otherwise stated). By this time, the Swedish territories in Germany, Livonia, Estonia, Ingria, and Kexholm County also formed part of the Kingdom of Sweden, and their inhabitants were subjects of the Swedish Crown.

provincial governors quickly followed suit. Within days, representatives of several provinces appeared in Cracow to swear allegiance to Sweden. With this act, almost the entirety of Poland (except for Prussia) and most of Lithuania which had not already sworn allegiance to Tsar Alexis accepted King Charles and the Swedish Crown as their suzerain. If the Commonwealth had been a less disorganised state, the war would have been over.

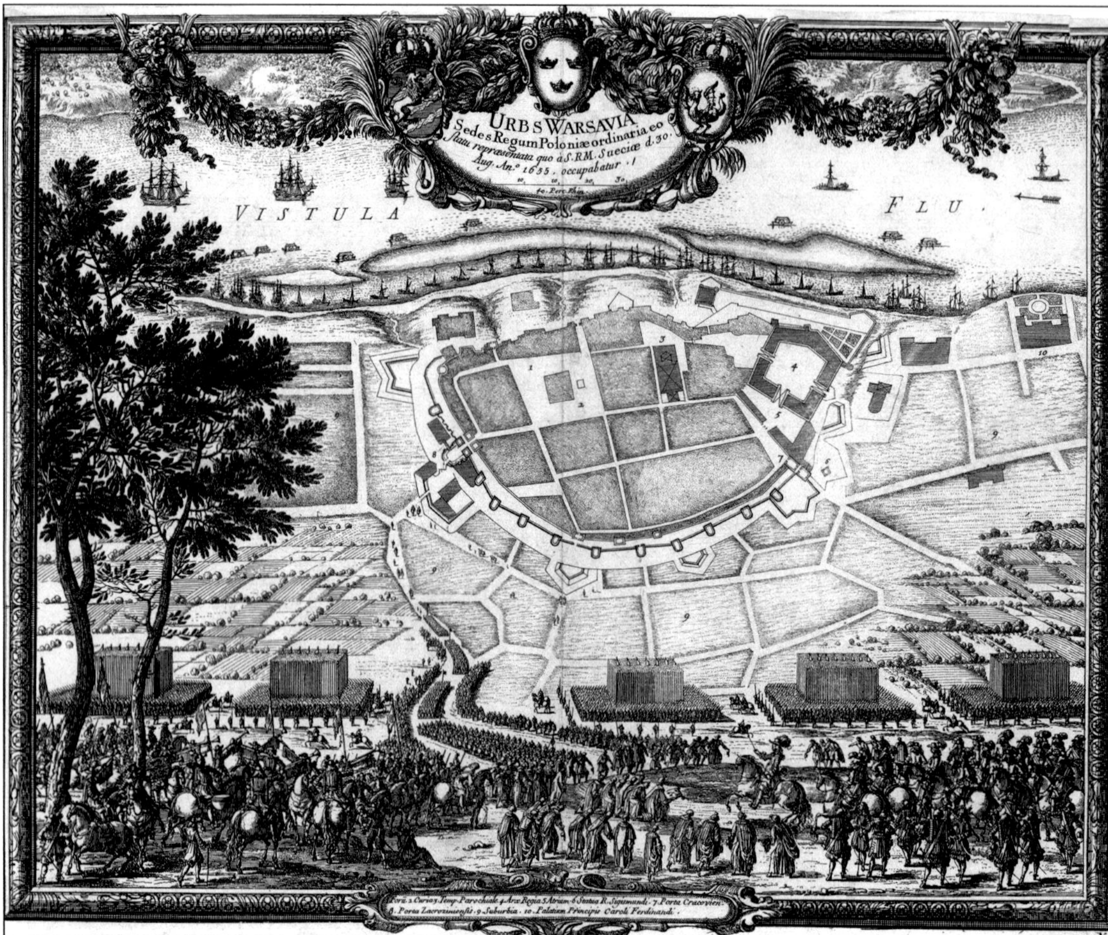

Warsaw in 1655, when the Swedes took the city, unopposed. Detail from Erik Dahlbergh's drawing for Samuel Pufendorf's *De rebus a Carolo Gustavo Sueciae rege gestis*, published in 1696. (National Library, Warsaw)

Events soon showed that it was far from over. Not all Poles and Lithuanians had surrendered and many of those who did had no intention of keeping their pledge of allegiance. Among those few notables who actually refused to swear allegiance to King Charles was the powerful magnate Jerzy Sebastian Lubomirski, and instead, he advised King John Casimir to return to fight for his throne. Another key figure who refused to swear allegiance to Sweden was Stefan Czarniecki, a veteran from the Thirty Years' War. While Czarniecki could not compare to Lubomirski in wealth and power, he had the necessary experience from domestic and foreign wars to mould his units into an efficient fighting force. Many who had sworn allegiance with no intention of keeping their oath, soon defected and switching sides began to look more advantageous than staying loyal to Sweden.

Even before the Crown army surrendered, insurgents had begun to harass the Swedish forces, and soon, disgruntled Polish nobles began to mobilise bands of irregulars. In early October, irregulars surprised the small Swedish garrison at Kosten (modern-day Kościan), near Posen. In the engagement, they killed many Swedes and also inflicted a mortal wound on Major General Frederick, Landgrave of Hesse-Eschwege, King Charles's brother-in-law. The irregulars took a rich booty from the town, which enabled them to finance further operations. In retaliation, Major General Johann Weyckhardt von Wrzesowitz und Neuschloss, a Moravian in Swedish service, six days later burnt Kosten. For both sides, the war had suddenly become much uglier. As in all guerrilla warfare, the irregulars relied on superior knowledge of the terrain and the element of surprise to ambush and defeat small enemy forces, supply convoys, and couriers. They generally took no prisoners, and did not hesitate to slaughter non-combatants, including women and children. Many Poles who had surrendered to King Charles fell victim to such raids. The Swedes retaliated in kind, as did those Poles who took their oath of allegiance to King Charles seriously and soon Poles were fighting against Poles.

Stefan Czarniecki as *regimentarz* of the Polish division in Denmark in 1659, attributed to Brother Matthiesen. (Royal Castle in Warsaw – Museum)

Playing the religious card, in late November King John Casimir issued a manifesto at Oppeln (modern-day Opole), calling for all Commonwealth citizens to rise against the Swedes in preparation for his return. What the King asked for was, in effect, a Catholic war of liberation against the heretics. In April 1656, at L'vov, John Casimir went so far as to proclaim the Virgin Mary as 'Queen of the Polish Crown and other of his countries' (the L'vov Oath). At the same time, he also promised that when he was restored to power, he would reduce the burdens on the peasantry, if they now rose against the invaders.

In January 1656, King Charles and Frederick William of Brandenburg concluded the Treaty of Königsberg (modern-day Kaliningrad). Frederick William renounced King John Casimir and instead recognised King Charles as his feudal suzerain in Prussia. He also agreed to support King Charles militarily, give Sweden half of his customs revenues from the Baltic Sea trade, and abstain from maintaining a fleet in the Baltic Sea without Swedish permission. With this Treaty, Frederick William joined the Swedish side of the war in an alliance which would last until September 1657.

King Charles then embarked upon an expedition to southern Poland in an attempt to crush the remaining resistance there. But as soon as he had moved out of Warsaw, the dispersed Commonwealth armies began to converge on the city. The first to arrive, in late April, was Grand Hetman Paweł Jan Sapieha's Lithuanian army which began to blockade the City. In early May, Czarniecki and his army joined the Lithuanians, and at the end of the month, King John Casimir arrived with his men. Finally, Lubomirski joined the others with his army on 30 May. The Commonwealth army consisted of perhaps as many as 50,000 men – an impressive force by any account. Moreover, the army contained many enlisted soldiers, in total 28,500 regulars. In addition, although of far less value in a siege operation, were between 18,000 and 22,000 noble levies plus uncounted numbers of peasant irregulars who also joined the operation. However, the heavy artillery took time to arrive, and was not in place until late in June.[2]

Warsaw was defended by the gout-ridden Arvid Wittenberg and a small Swedish garrison of men left behind from the field army. Wittenberg had reportedly defended besieged towns no less than 20 times, so he was certainly experienced. However, he had few men at his disposal, no more than a maximum of 2,484, a far from sufficient number to defend a city as large as Warsaw. Wittenberg's illness hampered him as well as he was unable to walk unassisted and his men often had to carry their commander in a litter to enable him to exercise command from the front in the customary manner.

It took time for the Commonwealth forces to achieve results. Sapieha, who arrived first, lacked artillery and a major attempt to storm Warsaw took place on 17/18 May, but the attack failed and fighting continued throughout June. A month later, the Polish siege artillery finally arrived and entered the action. After two days of bombardment, the Commonwealth armies were

Warsaw, 1656. (Pufendorf)

2 Jan Wimmer, 'Polens krig med Sverige 1655–1660: Operativ översikt', Arne Stade and Jan Wimmer (eds). *Polens krig med Sverige 1655–1660: Krigshistoriska studier* (Stockholm: Kungl. Militärhögskolan, Carl X Gustaf-studier 5, 1973), pp.325–417, on p.365.

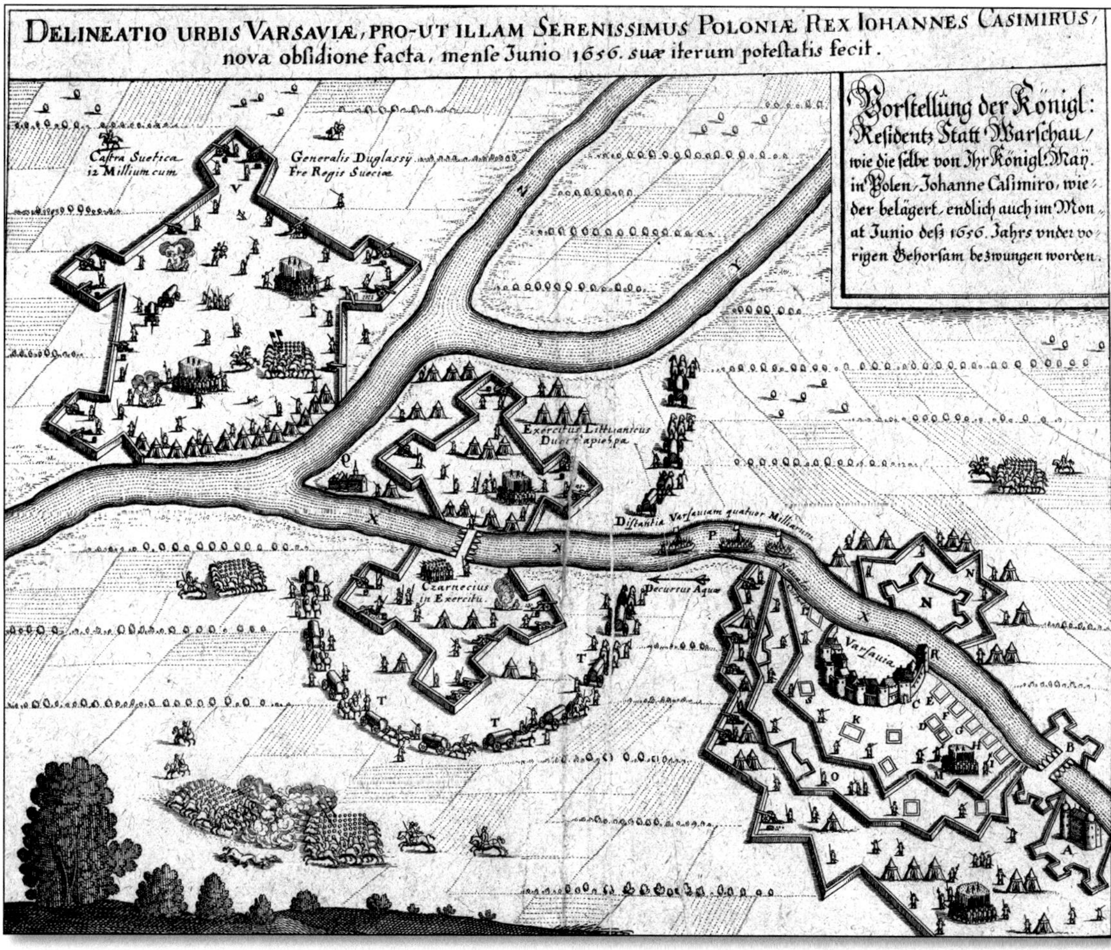

Polish and Lithuanian units lay siege to Warsaw, June 1656. At top left is the Swedish army camp under the command of Field Marshal Lieutenant Robert Douglas. (Anonymous, National Library, Warsaw)

again ready to storm the City. On 29 June, King John Casimir threatened that nobody would be spared, if Warsaw did not surrender. Wittenberg refused. On the following night, the Commonwealth army carried out a major attack, successfully penetrating the outer defences. Realising that the city could no longer be defended, on 1 July Wittenberg agreed to surrender in exchange for the freedom to depart with his men.[3] The parties also agreed that Warsaw would not be sacked, and the city's inhabitants would not be made to suffer.

Even so, some Polish units refused to acknowledge King John Casimir's ban on looting. The city's colony of Armenian merchants found themselves on the receiving end and lost all of their valuables. King John Casimir stepped in to restore order with the help of such units as were still obeying orders. According to some, perhaps embellished, sources, the Polish King had to ask

3 Samuel von Pufendorf, *Sieben Bücher von denen thaten Carl Gustavs Königs in Schweden*, vol. 3 (Nuremberg: Christoph Riegel, 1697), pp.174–175.

Wittenberg to assist with his remaining men. However, the attempt to restore order did nothing to improve the savage mood in the Commonwealth army. The capitulation of Warsaw included terms that allowed the remaining Swedish garrison to leave, under escort, bound for Thorn. The surviving garrison was not strong, only 400 fit and 1,400 ill or wounded. When the Swedes began to depart, violent protests were heard from many Poles who preferred to see the Swedes dead, and in the ensuing chaos some Swedes were massacred. Unwilling to risk a full-scale mutiny, King John Casimir at this point refused to honour the terms of the surrender and to which he had agreed, and instead ordered that Wittenberg and several other senior Swedish officers be detained. Moreover, he refused to allow any Livonians, Courlanders, or Prussians in Swedish service to depart, since claiming they were Polish subjects he did not recognise them as Swedish soldiers. As for other foreign soldiers in Swedish service, they had to enlist in the Commonwealth army – although the terms of the agreement of surrender stated that they would be free to choose whether they wanted to depart with the Swedes or to enlist in the Commonwealth army (most armies customarily enlisted captured soldiers). Soon after, Wittenberg died in captivity, likely from the illness which had already manifested itself several times since the outbreak of the war, although the harsh circumstances of his imprisonment no doubt played its part.

Days before, King Charles and Frederick William of Brandenburg had concluded the Treaty of Marienburg, by which, in effect, Sweden and Brandenburg agreed to divide the Commonwealth between them. Henceforth, Frederick William would support the Swedish army with initially 2,000 horse and 2,000 foot, to be increased later according to need. In return, Frederick William would receive hereditary sovereignty over four provinces currently held by Sweden in Greater Poland (Posen, Kalisz, Łęczyca, and Sieradz[4]). Even so, Frederick William would remain a Swedish vassal in Ducal Prussia. Sweden also promised to aid Brandenburg with 6,000 men, if needed.[5]

Then came the news that Warsaw had fallen, and that King John Casimir had retaken possession of his capital. Casimir's return to Warsaw set the stage for a major confrontation between the Swedish, Brandenburg, and Commonwealth armies – the Battle of Warsaw on 28–30 July 1656.

4 Łęczyca was known in German as Lentschitza, while Sieradz was known as Schieratz.

5 Samuel von Pufendorf, *Sieben Bücher von denen thaten Carl Gustavs Königs in Schweden*, vol. 3 (Nuremberg: Christoph Riegel, 1697), pp.171–172.

2

The Swedish Military Establishment

Sweden had the arguably most modern and up-to-date military establishment of the countries that took part in the wars of the Swedish Deluge, if for no other reason than that its innovations during the previous war had been copied by most adversaries. The systems and organisations already put in place to raise the Swedish army during the Thirty Years' War remained in operation and continued to function throughout King Charles's reign.[1]

The Swedish army was a well-trained, professional, and highly disciplined military force. Swedish soldiers entered battle with an expectation of victory, even against superior odds. In part the effect of professionalism, indoctrination, and the memory of victories in the Thirty Years' War, this expectation of victory was perhaps even more the product of the strict, even ruthless, discipline enforced within the army.

The Articles of War of the King Gustavus Adolphus still regulated Swedish military life.[2] It was forbidden, on pain of death, to desert, or not to fight to the death for the unit's standard (Article 58). Whoever first ran from a battle would forfeit his life. If he evaded capture, he would publicly be declared a traitor and an outlaw (Article 64). It was forbidden for a unit to withdraw from the battle as long as their weapons could still be used. If it was the officers who were responsible for any flight, they would be deemed to have lost all honour and would be dismissed from the camp. If both officers and men were at fault, the officers would be punished by dismissal while

1 For further details, see Michael Fredholm von Essen, *Charles X's Wars* (Warwick: Helion, 3 volumes, 2021–2023); Michael Fredholm von Essen, *The Lion from the North*, (Warwick: Helion, 2 volumes, 2020).

2 Gustavus Adolphus, *Krijgz articlar, som fordom then stormechtigste furste och herre, herr Gustaff Adolph, then andre och store, Sweriges, Göthes och Wendes konung, storfurste til Finland, hertig vthi Estland och Carelen, herre vtöfwer Ingermanland, &c. loffwerdigst i åminnelse hafwer låtit göra och författa, Anno M. DC. XXI* (Stockholm: Ignatio Meurer, 1621). Although dated 1621, when the Articles of War were issued, this print edition was published after Gustavus Adolphus's death in 1632. The King's handwritten draft version of the Articles is reprinted in Gustavus Adolphus, 'Utkast till Krigs-Artiklarna, utfärdade den 15 juli 1621', C. G. Styffe (ed.), *Konung Gustaf II Adolfs skrifter* (Stockholm: P. A. Norstedt & Söner, 1861), pp.243–253.

every tenth soldier, drawn by lot, would be hanged. The survivors then had to serve without standards or colours, sleep outside the camp quarters, and were detailed for cleaning duties in the camp (Articles 61, 62, 63). It was also forbidden, on pain of death, to surrender a bastion or redoubt until it had endured three attempted storms, there was no hope for help, and the men faced certain death (Article 66). Likewise, if the soldiers forced a commandant to surrender a fortress, all officers and under-officers who supported the proposal would be executed, while every tenth soldier would be hanged (Article 74).

There were also articles to regulate interaction with civilians. In the initial stages of The Deluge, the Swedish army operated under the severe discipline of the Articles of War, enforced by Field Marshal Arvid Wittenberg. A veteran of the Thirty Years' War, Wittenberg had distinguished himself in the second Battle of Breitenfeld in 1642 and in the Battle of Jankow in 1645, and knew how to maintain discipline in an unruly army. During the approximately six-week march from Stettin to Konin, the enlisted Scotsman Patrick Gordon noted that Wittenberg had no less than 470 soldiers executed, sometimes for what Gordon considered trivial offences, such as the case of the soldier who stole some milk from a local peasant. When the peasant's wife reported the theft, Wittenberg promptly had the soldier identified and hanged.[3] However, in the later stages of the war, when contributions and supplies had to be taken by force, there was little money with which to pay the men's wages, and civilian resistance increased, discipline grew significantly laxer. Even so, the deterioration in discipline was not for lack of trying and in 1656, King Charles issued an updated version of the 1632 edition of the Articles of War.[4]

Tactical Doctrines

The Swedish doctrine as established by Gustavus Adolphus was a combined arms model, in which the infantry acted in close cooperation with the cavalry and artillery. Gustavus Adolphus aimed for a combination of offensive power, mobility, and defensive strength. Offensive power was achieved through firepower (musketeers and regimental artillery) in combination with shock (charging pikemen and cavalry). Mobility was assured by the army's superior organisation and training. The army's defensive strength was the result of the combination of offensive power and mobility, since it allowed the army to close with the enemy rapidly and thus avoid excessive losses from its opponent's firepower.

3 Patrick Gordon, *Tagebuch des Generalen Patrick Gordon, während seiner Kriegsdienste unter den Schweden und Polen vom Jahre 1655 bis 1661, und seines Aufenthaltes in Rußland vom Jahre 1661 bis 1699* (Moscow: Prince M. A. Obolenskiy and M. C. Posselt, 1849), pp.17–18; Dmitry Fedosov (ed.), *Diary of General Patrick Gordon of Auchleuchries 1635–1699*, volume 1 (Aberdeen: AHRC Centre for Irish and Scottish Studies and Aberdeen University Press, 2009), pp.35–36.

4 Printed in 1657 by Amund Grefve, Gothenburg.

The Swedish model remained unchanged during the reign of King Charles. Because of the increased focus on cavalry in the later stages of the Thirty Years' War, and even more so, during the campaigns in the Commonwealth, the ratio of cavalry to infantry grew and cavalry became the primary offensive arm. Soon, a whole army might consist of cavalry alone. However, even then Sweden retained the combined arms model, by attaching dragoons to the cavalry units. Henceforth, many cavalry regiments included an attached company or two of dragoons. Only horse had the required mobility to cover sufficient distances to find the increasingly scarce supplies that remained available, which was particularly true of operations within the Commonwealth. Yet, in full-scale battles, the cavalry's horses constituted a limiting factor. Most could not endure for more than four or five hours, before they needed rest. Moreover, it was not always easy to replace lost horses, and on campaign the Swedish army often faced shortages in cavalry horses.

Meanwhile, Swedish infantry tactics had changed little since Gustavus Adolphus. The Swedish model continued to emphasise the offensive. Pikemen and musketeers remained drawn up in no more than six ranks, with the pikemen in the centre. The musketeers were trained to fire in volleys (salvoes), several ranks at a time. Following this volley, the pikemen would charge the enemy.

Yet, the share of pikemen in the army fell, and organisation was simplified, for practical reasons but also to accommodate men who were less well trained in comparison to previous Swedish armies. Over time, this resulted in an increased focus on infantry firepower, which came to reduce the previous emphasis on the shock provided by charging pikemen. The infantry then became a defensive arm, and it remained for the cavalry to charge the enemy. Over time, in set battles the infantry began to be seen primarily as a stable base around which the cavalry could operate. This role became particularly important during operations in the Commonwealth, since most of the army's opponents were cavalry. Even so, infantry was always needed to lay siege to towns and fortresses, and to garrison them afterwards.

The Swedish field artillery, and in particular the regimental artillery, reached its peak performance in the Thirty Years' War under the artillery expert Field Marshal Lennart Torstensson. Under his guidance, the field artillery was characterised by mobility and independence, which was fully developed in the Battle of Jankow in 1645, where the efficient use of artillery seems to have been a decisive factor in the Swedish victory. At Jankow, the Swedish artillery was constantly in action, moving from location to location and deploying in various formations. Regimental guns retained their importance in the Swedish army; they were deployed in conjunction with the units which they were designated to support, either in front of, or between, units.

Torstensson also improved the heavy artillery. By reducing the weight of the gun carriages and adding more draught horses to the teams, he significantly increased the mobility of the heavier guns. For instance, 24pdrs were moved by transporting the cannon barrels and carriages separately, each drawn by more than 20 horses, and then assembling them on the chosen site.

Under normal conditions, the heavy artillery deployed in batteries before or immediately behind the first line, or alternatively between the battalions or even occasionally on the flanks. When terrain allowed, the artillery deployed in double ranks, the rear rank firing over the front which was deployed lower.[5] Presumably, the regimental guns formed the front/lower rank, while the heavy artillery was deployed at some distance behind them and higher. During sieges, the artillery even deployed in three ranks where possible, each higher than the other.[6] Deployment in this manner also protected the heavy artillery from artillery counter-fire, since most artillery was only employed in direct fire and thus enemy artillery was less likely to hit the upper and rearward ranks.

The most commonly employed projectile against cavalry was the explosive grenade. Against other targets, round shot was employed, so that the shot after landing would continue on its course bouncing through several enemy ranks.

Swedish cavalry officers at Sandomierz, 3 April 1656. Dahlbergh was well aware of how Swedish officers dressed in the field. (Detail from Erik Dahlbergh)

5 Raimondo Montecuccoli, *Ausgewählte Schriften*, vol. 2 (Vienna: Kriegs-Archiv/W. Braumüller, 1899), p.580.

6 Jonas Hedberg (ed.), *Kungl. Artilleriet: Yngre vasatiden* (Stockholm: Militärhistoriska Förlaget, 1985), p.262.

Organisation

The Swedish cavalry was organised into provincial regiments related to where they were raised. The infantry consisted of conscripted troops, but like the cavalry were organised into provincial regiments again according to where they were raised. In addition, the Swedish military made considerable use of enlisted units, both horse and foot, primarily from the rest of Western Europe. They were organised and trained similarly to the national units. The artillery consisted of enlisted professionals.

The regiment was the primary administrative formation, but it was not used as the principle formation in the field. During a campaign, regiments were organised into temporary higher formations (right wing, centre, left wing) as needed. The cavalry retained the same organisation which had been used since 1618, and it would remain essentially unchanged throughout the Carolean era and well into the eighteenth century. Each cavalry regiment had an establishment strength of 1,000 horses, divided into eight companies of 125 horses. The cavalry, unlike the infantry, counted its strength in horses, not men. Two cavalry companies constituted a squadron, from which it thus follows that a squadron had a nominal strength of 250 horses. The squadron was the main tactical unit in both the cavalry and the dragoons. In battle, the men formed up in three ranks.

A clash between Polish and Swedish cavalry at the Battle of Wojnicz, 3 October 1655. Although some Swedish senior commanders may still have worn half-armour, at least when they had their portraits painted, this is almost certainly due to artistic licence. King Charles wore only back and breast plates in battle during the Wars of The Deluge, barely visible under his French coat. Detail from Erik Dahlbergh's drawing for Samuel Pufendorf's *De rebus a Carolo Gustavo Sueciae rege gestis*, published in 1696. (National Library, Warsaw)

Similarly, the infantry retained essentially the same organisation that had been used since 1621, and it would continue to do so throughout the Carolean era and well into the eighteenth century. Each infantry regiment was supposed to consist of 1,200 men, divided into eight infantry companies of 150 men. Four infantry companies constituted a battalion, thus a battalion had a nominal strength of 600 men – the battalion was the infantry's primary tactical unit. In the Swedish army, the battalion was for historical reasons sometimes referred to as a brigade. Battalions formed up with pikemen in the centre, flanked by musketeers, and in battle, the men formed up in six ranks.

Beige/grey felt hat, mid-seventeenth century. Marked as 'pattern for Queen Christina's infantry' and clearly intended for general issue. Brim: diameter 53cm, circumference 163cm, and width 18–18.5cm. Crown: height 16.7cm and diameter 25cm. The outer edge of the brim is protected by a sewn band of wool and linen. One of the very few surviving infantry hats of the period. (Army Museum, Stockholm; AM 11857)

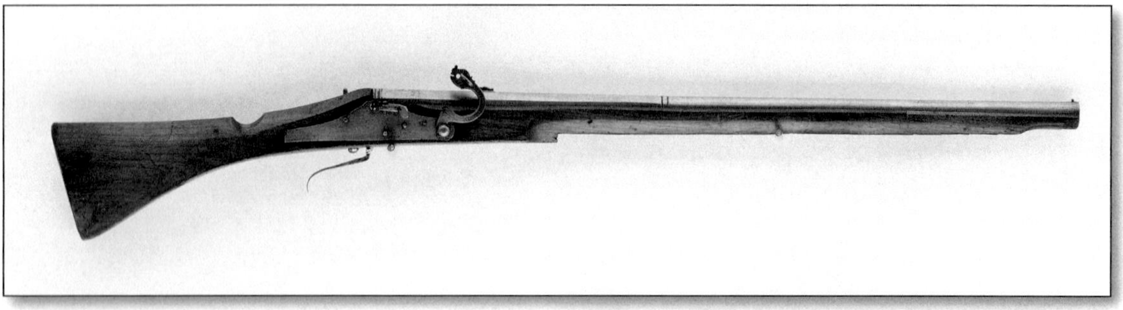

Matchlock musket, mid-seventeenth century. Total length 125.5cm, barrel length 86.4cm, weight 3.91kg, and calibre 19mm. Sufficiently short and lightweight to be used without a rest. This pattern grew increasingly common during the second half of the Thirty Years' War and is typical of Swedish muskets from the 1650s and 1660s. (Royal Armoury, Stockholm)

Pikeman's helmet, seventeenth century. (Skokloster Castle)

Infantry helmet of the mass-produced Dutch type, 1620–1660. From Vadstena Castle. (Army Museum, Stockholm)

Swedish rapier, mid-seventeenth century, identified as model of 1653. (Army Museum, Stockholm, AM 49909)

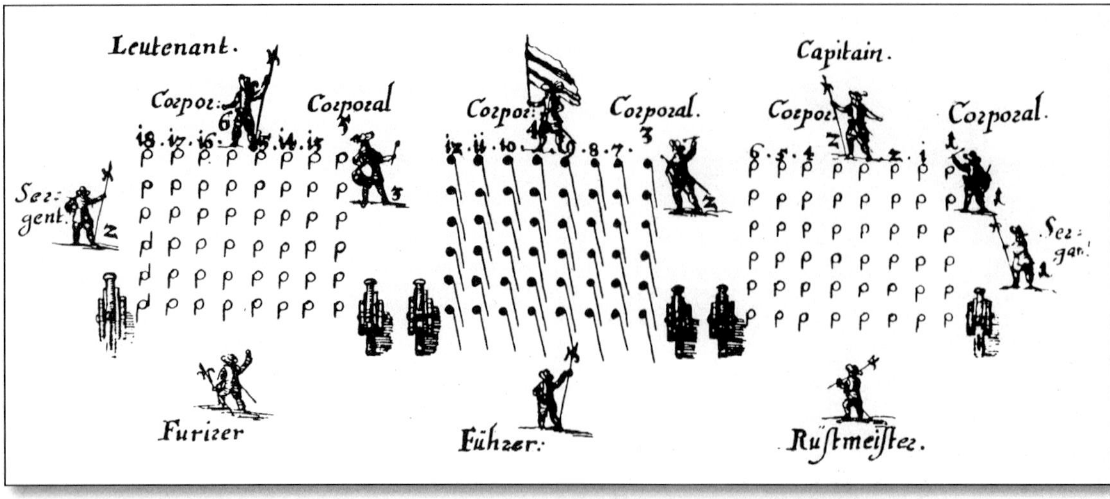

Swedish infantry company deployed in line, as described and illustrated by Lorentz von Troupitzen. (Troupitzen, *Kriegs Kunst*, 1633)

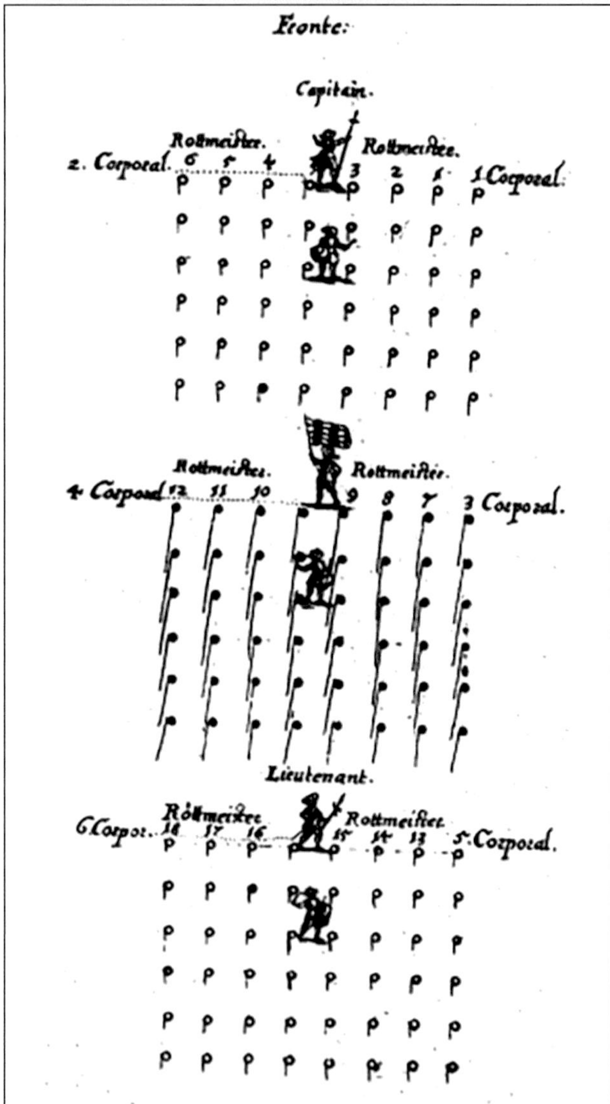

Swedish infantry company deployed in column, as described and illustrated by Lorentz von Troupitzen. (Troupitzen, *Kriegs Kunst*, 1633)

On campaign, a regiment's strength soon dwindled. When reinforcements or new recruits were unavailable, a situation which was normal during the war in the Commonwealth, the actual strength would fall to a fraction of the establishment. Depleted companies, sometimes from several regiments, would be combined into weak squadrons and battalions as needed and as conditions allowed. Swedish units in the Commonwealth were notoriously understrength.

In the first official Swedish history of the Thirty Years' War, written in German and proofread by Lord High Chancellor Axel Oxenstierna and Queen Christina before being sent to the printer, Bogislaff Philip von Chemnitz described the Swedish tactical doctrine. He also indicated what he considered most important in the infantry's organisation:

> The infantry deployed in their regiments and companies. The companies deployed in their established corporalships and files (*rotts*), each with its carefully selected senior and junior file leader (*rottmeister*), so that every common soldier, even without any order from an officer, already knew in which position he would stand and fight.[7]

In other words, the emphasis was on the corporalship and file leaders, and on the fact that each soldier had been trained in what he was expected to do in battle. The Swedish army relied on training and the existence of a sufficient number of under-officers who were able to act on their own initiative in a situation, something for which they had been trained. Training and personal initiative won the battle, not a complex organisational structure.

The artillery system established by Lennart Torstensson remained in use, with calibres identified as 24pdrs, 12pdrs, 6pdrs, and 3pdrs. A regular cannon was known as a *kartov* (from German *kartaune*), while a long-barrelled cannon was referred to as *slanga* (from German *schlange*). A regular 48pdr cannon was known as a *helkartov* ('full kartov'; German: *ganzkartaune*), while a 24pdr was a *halvkartov* ('half kartov'; German: *halbkartaune*), and a 12pdr was called a *kvartskartov* ('quarter kartov'; German: *viertelkartaune*). In the same manner, a long-barrelled 24pdr was called a *helslanga* (German: *ganzschlange*), a long-barrelled 12pdr was a *halvslanga* (German: *halbschlange*), and a long-barrelled 6pdr was called a *kvartsslanga* (German: *viertelschlange*). Mortars existed in calibres ranging from 8pdrs to 300pdrs for siege use.[8] The regimental artillery was based on the long-barrelled 3pdr (2.5m to 2.9m long; the length increased lethality at greater distances). Torstensson had compensated for the greater weight of the new type of regimental artillery with the introduction of more horses to provide mobility. The artillery within the field armies also included 12pdrs,

7 Bogislaff Philip von Chemnitz, *Königlichen Schwedischen in Teutschland geführten Kriegs*, vol. 1 (Stettin: Georg Rethe, 1648), p.475.

8 Jonas Hedberg, *Kungl. Artilleriet: Carl X Gustafs tid* (Stockholm: Militärhistoriska Förlaget, 1982, 1995), p.21.

Swedish artillery at Sandomierz, 1656. (Detail from Erik Dahlbergh)

Swedish artillery at the siege of Brest, 1657. (Detail from Erik Dahlbergh)

even though they were almost always fewer in numbers than the regimental 3pdrs.[9]

A modern army invariably needed technical specialists including quartermasters, mapmakers, intelligence officers, engineers, and sappers. The Swedish army instituted its technical specialists in the Fortification Corps (Swedish: *Fortifikationen*), under the formal command of the quartermaster general. The duties of the quartermaster general were extensive and included the provisioning of armies in the field, the construction and maintenance of fortifications, military intelligence, and mapmaking. In the field, these tasks were the responsibility of local quartermasters.

The quartermaster also controlled a field army's engineers and sappers. Their tasks included clearing any obstacles encountered on the march, and the bridging of rivers. The army's train carried ready-made field bridges which could be used to cross small rivers. River crossing equipment including field bridges were so frequently employed during the wars in the Commonwealth that King Charles saw nothing unusual in simply requesting a few field bridges to be sent post haste from the nearest supply depot. Eastern armies were not as advanced in engineering, and many of Sweden's allies needed engineering support.[10]

In addition, engineers and sappers played a vital role in the fortification of camps. Around the camp, they customarily built a dense system of outlying redoubts and artillery batteries. Field fortifications were constructed from earth, rock, and wood from the surrounding area and depended on what was locally available. Wicker baskets filled with earth and stones were used as gabions when the soil cover was insufficient for trenches and ramparts. The Swedish army was known for its fortification skills, and many of its standard practices were later adopted by the French fortification expert Sébastien Le Prestre de Vauban (1633–1707), to whose name they were linked by future generations. The Swedish engineers adapted their fortifications to the landscape. This is obvious from contemporary prints but has also been confirmed by archaeological excavations. The Swedish army relied on its engineers, but standard procedure was to complement the static defences with dynamic defence in the form of regular cavalry patrols.[11]

9 Hedberg, *Kungl. Artilleriet: Yngre vasatiden*, p.70.

10 Hedberg, *Kungl. Artilleriet: Carl X Gustafs tid*, p.119.

11 Václav Matoušek, et al., *Třebel 1647: A Battlefield of the Thirty Years' War from the Perspective of History, Archaeology, Art-history, Geoinformatics, and Ethnology* (Prague: Krigl, 2017), pp.95–96, 154, 156–157, 159–162.

3

The Commonwealth Military Establishment

The Commonwealth was the product of a meeting of Eastern and Western cultural, military, political, and religious ideas. Since the Middle Ages, the Polish nobility had grown increasingly close to their Western, primarily German, neighbours and adopted many of their customs. At the same time, major parts of the Commonwealth, in particular Lithuania and Ruthenia, remained part of Eastern traditions. This was obvious in the case of religion, which was Orthodox Christianity which looked to the east, not the west. Less obvious to the casual observer, but of no less importance, were the strong military influences inherited from the Mongol Empire and its successor states. Even so, Lithuanian nobles, and to some extent Ruthenian nobles, followed in the footsteps of their Polish peers, accepted Polonisation, often converted to Catholicism, and over time grew closer to the German West than the Tatar East.

The complex mixture of Eastern and Western traditions was obvious in the Commonwealth's military affairs. With the exception of some enlisted units which fought in the Western European manner adopted from Germany, the Commonwealth's military forces employed types of organisation and tactics which differed radically from the Swedish model. Essentially, the Commonwealth's traditional military remained greatly influenced by the Inner Asian cavalry tactics habitually employed by Eurasian steppe nomads, notably those of the medieval Mongol Empire and its successor states. Its core was formed by heavy cavalry, supported by highly mobile horse archers, or the traditional equivalents thereof in the form of Tatar, Wallachian, or 'cossack' light cavalry. The term 'cossack' (Polish: *kozak*) was the customary term for any cavalry not labelled hussar, nor identified by an ethnic label, thus most Commonwealth cavalry were called cossacks.

The Commonwealth's military forces were divided into two distinct organisations: The army of Poland, also known as the Crown army, and the army of Lithuania, also known as the Grand Ducal army. Although both were under the authority of King John Casimir, since he was simultaneously King of Poland and Grand Duke of Lithuania, the two armies had separate chains of command and often experienced coordination problems. Each army had two hetmans: a Grand Hetman in command, and a Field Hetman as second in command. The Crown Grand Hetman was always seen as senior and, as a rule, Polish troops were not supposed to be under the command of Lithuanian officers and vice versa. Not only were both armies treated separately, the structure of the Commonwealth's military establishment was complicated, as there were many elements of the armed forces, often overlapping with each other. Among them were soldiers commanded, recruited, and paid for by the King, central, and local authorities, towns and cities, and even by wealthier individuals (magnates and nobles). Some of them had a regular or semi-regular character; others could be raised only in specific situations and under strict conditions.

Structure of The Commonwealth Armies

In the middle of the seventeenth century, the regular army was known as the *komput*, from the Latin *computus*. In 1652, after the loss of a large part of the Polish standing army at Batoh, the so-called 'quarter army', previously used as the regular core of the Commonwealth military, ceased to exist and the *komput* was from then on used to describe the army that was permanently in service.

Unlike Poland, in the early seventeenth century Lithuania did not have a standing army. On occasions there were some garrison units paid by the National Treasury, while during a time of war, the regular army was raised but then disbanded once the conflict ended. From 1648 onwards, facing a series of wars against the Ukrainian cossacks, Muscovites, and Swedes, the regular *komput* was in service in Lithuania as well, increased or decreased depending on the situation. The Lithuanian army was always smaller than the Polish, normally not exceeding one-third of the Crown troops.

If the country was in serious danger – such as when facing the full might of the Ottoman Empire in 1621, the Muscovites in 1654, and the Swedes in 1655 – the King, with approval of the *Sejm*, could order the raising of the levy of nobility (*pospolite ruszenie*): this was separate for Poland and Lithuania. In theory, it was composed of all able-bodied nobles in the land, who, depending on their wealth and standing, would arrive on their own or with retinues of a variable size. Additionally, towns were to supply a levy of infantry, paid for from their own funds. During a period of peace, nobles in each voivodeship and land were obliged to take part in musters, usually annually, so that they could be counted and their armour and weapons inspected. Depending on their equipment, they arrived as hussars, cossacks, or even *reiters* (German-style cavalry), although poor nobles could even arrive on foot or barely armed. They were then grouped into banners, with prominent nobles chosen as *rotmistrz*, and all units from one region then formed into one regiment (*pułk*). As the levy of nobility could not be used as a reliable force and because the nobles serving in it were often unwilling to leave their homes for long campaigns, the Commonwealth quickly established a form of regular units that could be raised instead. These 'district troops' (*wojska powiatowe*) were set up individually by each region, and paid by special taxes agreed upon by the local *sejmik*. They were often raised for only a short period, usually for one quarter (three months), and normally just for the defence of the region. Their size, organisation, and the way they participated in campaigns varied greatly from region to region. Another type of soldier raised by districts were *łanowe* ('lan') troops. Most of them, at least during The Deluge, served as infantry. They were named from the word '*łan*', which was a Polish unit of field measurement that, depending on the region, could vary between 18 and 28 hectares.

The Cossack Uprising of 1648 ended, at least for a few decades, the so-called 'Cossack Register', as regular Zaporozhian soldiers in Polish pay were known. As such, no Zaporozhian cossack regiments (*pułki*) were in service when the war with Sweden started in 1655, although of course some individual Zaporozhians could be found in the ranks of Polish units. Another formation under central control was the so-called *wybraniecka* infantry, established by Stephen Báthory after he had become King of Poland in 1576. It was a militia raised from the peasants of royal lands. By the time of The Deluge, it was relegated to auxiliary duties, often non-combat such as engineering or assisting the artillery, and it did not play any important role in military operations.

In the seventeenth century, the Commonwealth had a rather wide array of soldiers that could be called 'private', although their specific classifications varied. First, there was the Royal Household Guard, financed from the King's own coffer. During the 1650s, as sources of royal income diminished, a majority of these guard units were incorporated into the regular army (*komput*) and were paid by the National Treasury, while retaining their Guard title. The private armies of wealthy magnates were often very large in the first half of the century, with some of the nobles at times fielding up to several thousand men, including banners of hussars and units of Western-style infantry, all supported by their own artillery. The Cossack Uprising of 1648 led to a loss of large territories and many sources of income, and thus such large private armies became rather a rare sight in the second part of the century. Nonetheless, during the wars of 1654–1667, there were still numerous examples of private soldiers of many types – both Polish and Lithuanian. Usually this was just one or two banners in the private service of a noble or magnate, but wealthy nobles, such as Zamoyski, Lubomirski, or Sapieha, were still able to afford keeping a few hundred men, with some units protecting their proprietor's lands and others taking part in fighting alongside the regular army. In some examples, private units could be converted into part of the *komput* and would cease to belong to a specific magnate or noble. The presence of such private units during a campaign is unfortunately often very hard to trace, as they are rarely mentioned in sources and are not recorded in the official treasury documents.

Other, usually irregular, forces did not play any role during the Battle of Warsaw in 1656, so reference to them here will be brief. They were volunteers, that can be broadly divided into two main types. First were the partisans (*partyzanci*), which had already started to emerge in 1655, usually fighting local actions against the Swedes. Some groups were composed only of nobles and their followers, others could be composed of the peasants from the local population. Often, they fought only in the defence of their own territory, but some groups attached themselves as an auxiliary force to the regular army or were even formed into cossack cavalry, light horse, or infantry banners. The second type of such irregular troops were those called in Polish *wolontarze* or *wolentarze*, which translates to 'volunteers'. They formed semi-regular cavalry units that could vary in size from a few hundred to a few thousand men. Useful during 'small war' campaigns, they could be a real problem once fighting ended, as they often refused to disband and became outlaws, eventually to be prosecuted and destroyed by local administration and regular army units.

Finally, there were soldiers in the service of towns. These were the militia, defending their cities, with each guild (tailors, butchers, and so on) and some minorities (e.g., Jews and Armenians) defending an allocated part of the city walls. Members of such militia units had to provide their own weapons and ammunition. In most towns, this militia would number only a few hundred, or maybe just over a thousand men. Of course, wealthier and larger towns – especially Danzig – could deploy a much stronger militia and could supplement them with mercenaries.

Erik Dahlbergh's sketch of the Battle of Wojnicz in 1655, depicting fighting between Polish and Swedish cavalry. The standards of the Polish units are clearly shown. (National Archives, Stockholm)

Recruitment and Organisation

After 1635 Commonwealth armies developed a new system of two contingents (known as *autoramenty*). The Polish section, called 'national' (*autorament narodowy*) included hussars, cossack cavalry, light cavalry (Wallachian and Tatar), and Polish-Hungarian infantry. The western section, known as 'foreign' (*autorament cudzoziemski*) was composed of foreign/German infantry, dragoons, and reiters. This system was based on the method of recruitment, organisation and types of troops. National cavalry was organised via the system of noble soldiers (known as companions – *towarzysze*) being recruited alongside their retinues (*poczty*), composed of retainers (*pocztowi*) that, at least in theory, should all have been equipped in the same manner.

The primary unit of the national contingent was the banner (*chorągiew*), under the nominal command of a *rotmistrz* (equivalent of captain). From the 1650s the larger number of *rotmistrz*-level officers, especially in units of hussars, was just an honorific title, and the actual command of the banner was held by the lieutenant. It was traditional that official sources such as army musters, and even mentions in diaries, described such units by the most important office held by its leading officer. So, for example, Stefan Czarniecki's units would be named as banners or regiments of the Voivode of Ruthenia, while Jan Sobieski's units from 1656 would be known as the Crown Grand Standard Bearer's units. Because of this, there were many units with a title of the same *rotmistrz* or colonel, even when he was not taking part in the campaign. Retinues in each banner were part of so-called *rolla*; this was the list of all retinues written down by the importance of the companions – so it starts with the *rotmistrz*'s and lieutenant's retinues, but the next place could be taken by a wealthy or some other way more important companion, not necessarily by the standard bearer. It was all a part of the rather delicate and often very confusing social structure of the unit, in which normally officers could only request their soldiers to follow the orders, since because all officers and companions were nobles, they were (at least in theory) equal. A position in a banner's *rolla* could help in future promotions, e.g., to replace a lieutenant or standard bearer. The higher an individual was in the hierarchy, the better chance he had to become deputy or the unit's representative sent out to pick up and deliver pay.

The recruitment of reiters, foreign infantry and dragoons was slightly different. The colonel of the unit, known under the German-inspired term *oberszter*, received a commission, but often such a regiment was allocated to magnates and court officials, especially to those that were at the same time the *rotmistrz* of hussar banners. As the equipping and keeping of those cavalry units in service was expensive, having at the same time the rank of the infantry or dragoon colonel – where the officer could claim some part of the unit's nominal strength as his pay (the so-called 'dead pays') – was a way of rewarding him and providing some unofficial, yet well known to everyone, way of reimbursement. Additionally, one-fifth from each soldier's pay was deducted towards the colonel's pay, a process known under the German name of *kopfgeld*.

As with many cavalry banners, the recruitment and organisation of foreign infantry and dragoons was handed over to the second in command, usually the lieutenant colonel (*oberszter lejtnant*) or major. Typically, the colonel signed a document called a 'capitulation' (*kapitulacja*) with such an individual, in which the colonel specified the conditions under which his second in command would then recruit the regiment (e.g., special pay or the period of time within which a unit needed to be created). From that point, the lieutenant colonel took over and recruited lower-ranking officers to help him raise the regiment. It was also up to each captain to raise his own company. Despite being called 'foreign', these units were normally recruited locally in Poland and Lithuania, although many officers and under-officers were indeed foreign, mostly German speaking. Volunteers for the service could officially only be looked for on royal and church lands – it was forbidden to recruit from amongst peasants living on the land owned by magnates and nobles, although many fugitives from such areas ended up in the ranks anyway. Troops were recruited by the method of 'free drum', with officers leading recruitment parties into the area designated in their commission and announcing a call for new soldiers. As with all armies of this period, a very important method of reinforcing the Polish and Lithuanian armies was the recruitment of prisoners-of-war.

Companions in cavalry banners were to provide themselves and their retinue with all necessary weapons and equipment, including horses and tabor (supply train) wagons. Only *kopia* lances for hussars were to be provided by the *rotmistrz* or the King, often leading to units serving for long period without such weapons or being forced to improvise lances, or have them made during the campaign. Commissions were often vague around actual description of the necessary equipment and armament, therefore each banner had a large range of different weapons and levels of armour in use by individual companions and retainers. In the often very harsh conditions of constant conflict, it was particularly difficult to properly equip soldiers in new units and to replace lost or broken weapons and equipment within already existing ones. It was not easy to purchase them locally or to capture enough of them from the enemy, so soldiers often had to resort to pillaging and theft. The professional soldier Hieronymus Christian von Holsten, with brutal honesty, admitted that, at the beginning of his Polish service, ex-Swedish soldiers:

> ...straight away received permission to change our horses if we see better ones, well, we could even travel to the border with Silesia or across it, in order to get some loot and clothes. It was approved by our officers. At this point whoever was the best thief, he was the best soldier.[1]

No surprise that, in a short time, three newly created companies of Lubomirski's reiter regiment were ready, with Holsten himself fully equipped

1 Hieronim Chrystian Holsten, *Przygody wojenne 1655–1666* (Warszawa: Instytut Wydawniczy Pax, 1980), pp.44–45.

and having a 'good servant and [servant] boy', and a supply wagon.[2] In Patrick Gordon's diary, there are many details about problems of supply of proper weapons and equipment for the soldiers. When creating a dragoon company from Swedish prisoners-of-war, to serve under Lubomirski's command, Gordon had to purchase weapons and clothing during the march, gradually equipping the unit. When he finally was able to present the company to Lubomirski, near Piotrków at the beginning of March 1660, he could confirm to his commander that all soldiers had muskets and powder bags but only a few of them had swords and the whole company, despite being dragoons, was without horses.[3]

While infantry and dragoons tended to, at least from time to time, receive an allocation of cloth for their uniforms, cavalry had to rely on their own resources to obtain clothes. It often led to usages not normally found in a time of peace, such as 'German' type soldiers in local Eastern style clothing or national cavalry companions using clothes and materials captured or looted during the campaign.

Cavalry banners had a 'paper strength' of 100–200 horses, from which should be deducted at least 15 percent for so-called 'dead pays' (officer's perks that were used as their additional pay). The national cavalry in both armies were grouped together into regiments (*pułki*), although such larger units did not have regimental staffs such as those that could be found in the regiments of foreign infantry, dragoons, and reiters. The number and size of the cavalry regiments could change from campaign to campaign (banners could be moved between regiments or disbanded, or new units could be added). Some regiments had up to 20 banners, while the smallest might contain only two or three. As a rule, the banner or banners that carried the name of a nominal commander of the regiment were always included in his regiment (e.g., the Grand Hetman's hussar and *pancerni*/cossack cavalry banners served in his regiment). Due to the organisation and strength of the cavalry, the majority of regiments contained only cossack cavalry banners, with just three of four regiments in the army having one or two hussar banners.

Polish-Hungarian infantry served as independent banners, without any regimental structure. 'Foreign' troops would be grouped in regiments, squadrons, but sometimes served as independent companies (so-called *freikompania*), although there was no uniform structure of those alongside either the Polish or Lithuanian army. For example, in 1653, during the Żwaniec campaign, 10 regiments of foreign infantry in the Polish army varied in strength between 402 and 1,211 portions (the term used for calculating the number of soldiers). There was also one smaller unit, designated as a squadron, which had 294 portions.[4] Next to these larger units, there were also small independent companies of 100 to 200 portions, which were mainly found in the Lithuanian army. In the campaign of 1649, the Lithuania army had a total of 1,510 portions of German infantry, divided into one squadron

2 Holsten, *Przygody wojenne 1655–1666*, p.45.

3 *Diary of General Patrick Gordon of Auchleuchries 1635–1699*, vol. 2, p.53.

4 Archiwum Główne Akt Dawnych (AGAD), Archiwum Skarbu Koronnego (ASK) 85, no. 89, f.5v.

of 600, two free companies of 200, one free company of 150 portions and three free companies of 120 portions each.[5] In September 1653, there were 4,088 portions of German infantry in the Lithuanian army, divided between nine units. These ranged from a regiment of 1,050 portions to a free company of only 100 portions.[6]

Dragoons in both armies also served in units of very different sizes. In September 1653, the Lithuanians 3,074 portions of dragoons, divided into 12 units, varying between 100 portions and 750 portions.[7] In July 1660, the Polish army had 7,400 portions of dragoons, ranging from a regiment of 1,000 portions to a free company of 200 portions.[8]

During the 1655–1660 war reiters were mainly recruited as independent companies of 100–150 horses, although there was one very large regiment under Jerzy Sebastian Lubomirski that by 1659 had 1,000 horses in 10 companies.

Noble in usual Polish dress, from a stucco relief in Tarlów dated to the 1640s showing the popular motif 'Death and the Noble'. The noble is typical of those who served in the Commonwealth cavalry, whether as hussar, cossack cavalryman, or officer in other units. He wears a *żupan* undergarment, caftan, soft leather boots, and high, fur-lined cap, all of Eastern origin. Armed with a sabre and a long-shafted warhammer which also served as a walking stick, in addition he carries a short whip (in place of wearing spurs), has a spanner for his wheellock pistol or carbine hanging from his belt, and has a sabretache at his side. The sabretache, often of red leather, was intended for carrying ammunition, but contemporary observers noted that they were equally often employed for carrying letters, documents, a comb, and money.[9] The French officer Beauplan, who served in the Commonwealth before The Deluge, noted that Polish nobles, although arrogant and rude to inferiors, were pleasant enough to foreigners. However, they were unwilling to deal with and often expressed their hatred of Turks, Tatars, Muscovites, Swedes, and Germans.[10]

5 *Korespondencja wojskowa hetmana Janusza Radziwiłła w latach 1646–1655*, vol. I, *Diariusz kancelaryjny 1649–1653* (Warszawa: Wydawnictwo Neriton, 2019), pp.355–356.
6 Andrzej Rachuba, 'Wysiłek mobilizacyjny Wielkiego Księstwa Litewskiego w latach 1654–1667', *Studia i Materiały do Historii Wojskowości*, XLIII (2007), pp.45–46.
7 Rachuba, 'Wysiłek mobilizacyjny', p.44.
8 AGAD, ASK 82, no. 9, p.71.
9 Beauplan, *Description*, p.186.
10 Beauplan, *Description*, p.181.

Army Formations

Unlike the Swedish and Brandenburg armies, where there were just a few main army formations (cavalry, dragoons, infantry, and artillery), the Polish-Lithuanian Commonwealth structure was much more complicated, with a greater number of types of units, each designed to play slightly different battlefield roles. Describing each one in detail would take too much space and has already been covered in a previous volume of the series, thus here is only a brief overview of each formation.[11]

Well-equipped Polish horseman, armed with both bow and carbine. Part of the Polish embassy entering Rome in 1633. On campaign, he would carry just one of those weapons; in case of a companion often the bow, while the carbine or musket would be carried in a supply wagon. (Stefano della Bella, 1651; Rijksmuseum, Amsterdam)

Hussars (*husaria* or *usaria*) constituted the main 'shock' cavalry, armed with a plethora of weapons including the long *kopia* lance and wearing the pelts of big cats and the famous wings, making them the centrepiece of the army and were seen as an elite force. By the time of The Deluge the number of hussars had vastly diminished. Between 1653 and 1654 the Polish army had only five banners, averaging in total between 800 and 900 horses. Some short-lived units served in 1654 and 1655, but, by spring 1659, the Polish army had six banners, with a total paper strength of 999 horses. During the late 1640s and early 1650s, the 'corps' of Lithuanian hussars varied in size but rarely exceeded 1,000 horses. As such, despite still being seen as an elite force, the small number of hussars meant that their battlefield role was not as important as it had been in previous decades as they were unable to make

11 For further details, see Michał Paradowski, *Against the Deluge: Polish and Lithuanian Armies during the War against Sweden 1655–1660* (Warwick: Helion & Co., 2022).

such a large impact on the outcome of the battles. However, even when present in small numbers, hussars could play an important role on the battlefield. The cavalry companion Jakub Łoś wrote that, during the Battle of Warsaw in 1656, 'we fought valiantly, especially the hussars who broke the [Swedish] cavalry.'[12] There were only four banners of hussars that took part in this battle, and at least one of them – Lubomirski's unit – was most likely without lances.[13] Additionally, these banners were not grouped together but fought supported by cossack cavalry, and only in the later stage of the battle would they be deployed as some sort of quasi-squadrons of two banners each.

Due to the reduced numbers of hussars, it was cossack cavalry (*jazda kozacka*) that gradually became the most important part of the Commonwealth's cavalry, fulfilling many roles from supporting hussars during battles, through being the main 'battle' cavalry fighting the Swedes and Muscovites, to taking part in reconnaissance missions and pre-battle skirmishing. In the second quarter of 1659, when the Crown army reached its largest size during the entire war, it included 122 banners of *pancerni* and cossack cavalry, with a paper strength of 13,016 horses. In comparison, there were only six banners of hussars

Another Polish horseman from the embassy entering Rome in 1633. Visible is the way in which he carries his quiver on one side, and the bow case (here empty, but he would have the bow in this case) on the other. (Stefano della Bella, 1651; Rijksmuseum, Amsterdam)

12 Jakub Łoś, *Pamiętnik towarzysza chorągwi pancernej* (Warszawa: Wydawnictwo DiG, 2000), p.66.

13 Marcin Gawęda, *Od Beresteczka do Cudnowa. Działalność wojskowa Jerzego Sebastiana Lubomirskiego w latach 1651–1660* (Zabrze-Tarnowskie Góry: Wydawnictwo Inforteditions, 2013), pp.103–108.

Noble on horseback, unarmoured but with a hussar wing fastened to his saddle in the old manner. The use of hussar wings for festive purposes was common. (Stefano della Bella)

(999 horses), 41 banners of light horse (4,387 horses) and seven units of reiters (2,246 horses).[14] Originally, this cavalry was called *jazda kozacka* (cossack cavalry), with its soldiers being known as the *kozacy* (with a lower case). It was a term in Polish used to describe free men 'serving for money' and was adopted for both military use and for household servants, often mounted. In the sixteenth century, the word started to be used to describe free men settled in Ukraine near the Dnieper River, but in Polish these men were called '*Kozacy*' (with an upper case). As such, in original Polish texts, one could find both *kozacy* and *Kozacy* serving together in one army.

This situation obviously made it very confusing when translating these terms into English, where there is usually just one form – Cossacks – in use, leading to many errors in identifying who is in fact described in the original text and attributing many military features of the Polish cossack cavalry to the Zaporozhian (Ukrainian) cossacks.

With regard to *pancerni* (which simply means 'armoured'), many modern historians tend to repeat the theory that it was a name introduced in 1648 for all cossack cavalry in order to distinguish between *kozacy* (Polish cavalry) and rebel *Kozacy* (Zaporozhian cossacks). Based on primary sources, especially army and banner muster rolls, such a theory seems to have no factual basis. It appears that through the whole of The Deluge period units of cossack cavalry mostly did not achieve the level of equipment to live up to the 'armoured' name. At least until the mid–1660s, only certain banners of cossack cavalry were named as *pancerni*. Usually, this name was used in connection to units that we might call elite – those where the nominal *rotmistrz* was the King, Grand Hetman, Field Hetman, or one of the wealthiest nobles. As such, only few units received such status, so it was cossack cavalry that made up the bulk of mounted strength in both Polish and Lithuanian armies.

Commissions to recruit normally required 'typical cossack equipment' or sometimes mentioned 'three firearms' (two pistols and a carbine, musket or arquebus). As with any other Commonwealth cavalry of the era, a sabre was treated as a standard weapon, and as such was not mentioned in documents. Companions would often use bows, treated as both a weapon and a symbol

14 Jan Wimmer, *Wojsko polskie w drugiej połowie XVII wieku* (Warszawa: Wydawnictwo Ministerstwa Obrony Narodowej, 1965), p.122.

of noble status. The presence of mail and a *misiurka* helmet was also a personal choice, more often than not dependent on the wealth of the individual companion. During the 1650s and 1660s, such elements of armour were not regulated by any written requirements or laws; therefore, within one unit, its number and quality could vary. Long campaigns, with little chance to replace lost and damaged equipment, meant that many soldiers had to go without any armour. When describing the campaign against the Muscovites in 1660, Łoś mentioned (probably with a slight exaggeration) that, except for the *pancerni* banner of King John Casimir, none of the cossack cavalry units in Czarniecki's division had armour.[15] Round, Eastern *kałkan* shields were also not a part of the 'official' requirement for equipment but were often used by both companions and retainers. Both could also use additional weapons, again chosen according to personal preferences: horseman's hammer, axe, even *palash* or *estoc* (armour-piercing sword). Despite the penchant of many modern wargaming companies to present *pancerni* and cossack cavalry as equipped with spears or short lances, there is no direct evidence of these formations using these during The Deluge, and it only became part of the equipment in the early 1670s. None of the diarists in the period of 1655–1660 mention it and there is no indication of the presence of these in known surviving documents.

Western-style cavalry, usually called *rajtaria* (and its soldiers known as *rajtarzy*) in Polish, had a long history of serving in both the Polish and Lithuanian armies. In the majority of cases, it was recruited from amongst German-speaking lands: starting with those that were a part of the Commonwealth (e.g., Royal Prussia and Livonia), through vassals (e.g., Courland and Ducal Prussia), to neighbouring regions (e.g., Silesia). There were of course also those raised from different nationalities – such as Scots, French, or Walloons – but they were fairly rare. Poles and Lithuanians were present as well, usually as part of

Polish cavalryman, equipped with mail, sabre, and pair of pistols. (Isidoro Affaitati, 1659; Nicolaus Copernicus University in Toruń, University Library)

15 Łoś, *Pamiętnik towarzysza chorągwi pancernej*, p.100.

Lithuanian soldiers in the campaign of 1651. Lithuanians fighting in the period 1655–1660 would have looked identical. On the right, an officer or companion equipped as *pancerny*, with mail and *misiurka* helmet. On the left, most likely an unarmoured cossack cavalryman, armed with *bandolet* and with *karwasze* arm-guards. Detail from a drawing by Abraham von Westervelt, 1651. (Polish Army Museum, Warsaw; photo from Michał Paradowski collection)

German-speaking units. The second part of the century did not bring many changes, with a majority of reiters being raised locally and including native Poles and Lithuanians, but thanks to opportunities to enlist former Swedish soldiers, reiters also had a larger range of German-speaking soldiers. They were armed in similar way to Swedish cavalry, with sword or sabre, two pistols, long firearm (carbine, *bandolet* or short musket). While some could use armour, in the form of back and breast plates and helmets, probably more common were just buff coats, with the head protected by a hat or cap, or sometimes a helmet.

In the first part of the seventeenth century, light cavalry units were normally not present as a separate formation in Commonwealth armies. Instead, they were included as a part of the cossack cavalry. Units composed of Tatars were especially common in Lithuanian armies, usually recruited from amongst families settled in the country, with some of them tracing their Lithuanian military service back to the fifteenth century. Private armies also included a number of such light horse units, sometimes raised from amongst the military settlers and subjects of the magnate, on other occasions recruited from foreigners such as Hungarians and Wallachians. The Khmel'nitskiy uprising, which in its initial phase led to the destruction of the standing 'quarter army', opened the door for the introduction of light cavalry as separate formations. Fairly easy and cheap to raise, equip and keep in service, banners of Tatars and Wallachians became an integral part of the Commonwealth military in the second part of the century. While the former were present in both the Polish and Lithuanian army, the latter were almost exclusively present in the Crown units, with just one 100-strong banner of Wallachians being part of the Lithuanian army in 1661. Whether fighting against Ukrainian cossacks, Muscovites, or Swedes, light horse was useful for reconnaissance, harassing the enemy, and post-battle pursuit. It was also a very flexible formation, as banners could easily be upgraded to cossack cavalry, by the simple addition of better equipment, while still retaining the skills they developed as part of a lighter formation.

In general, both types of cavalry were equipped in a similar way, with sabres, pistols, and either a long firearm or a bow; the latter more associated with Tatars. Armour, in the form of mail or at least a *misiurka* helmet, could be used by some wealthier companions but it was not part of the required equipment. During The Deluge neither Tatars nor Wallachian horse used spears or lances. Light cavalry tended to be deployed on the flanks of the Polish and Lithuanian armies, where it could harass the enemy's cavalry using typical hit-and-run attacks and could then, if the battle was won, be launched after the enemy in pursuit. Tatar and Wallachian banners were often sent out as the vanguard of a force, leading reconnaissance missions normally known as *podjazd*. They were also routinely employed during raids against the enemy's supply lines and territories, where they could employ terror tactics of burning and looting and, if the opportunity arose, of destroying smaller outposts. On occasion, they would fight in the same way as cossack cavalry: first shooting at the enemy with bows and firearms, then closing to hand-to-hand using their sabres.

Polish light horsemen, armed with bows, sabres, and *nadziak* (horseman's hammer), 1651. (Stefano della Bella; Rijksmuseum, Amsterdam)

As for foreign infantry, despite its name of 'German' or 'Foreign' infantry, these units were recruited mostly from Poles and Lithuanians, with a large proportion of officers and under-officers only being recruited from foreigners: German-speaking nobles, new arrivals from Italy, France, or even the British Isles; and also from prisoners-of-war. Unlike national cavalry, infantry was recruited by the 'free drum' method, also often reinforced by (more or less voluntary) enlistment of prisoners-of-war. Units were trained 'in Western style', that is in a similar way to Swedish or Imperial units. Most of the regiments were typical pike and shot, with a normal ratio of pike to shot of 1:2 or 1:3. However, it is likely that some units, especially free companies so often present in the Lithuanian armies, were in fact purely shot units. There was no uniform structure of the regiments in the army though, clearly indicating the rather loose approach to the issue in both the Polish and Lithuanian military establishments. The lack of a standardised organisation of the regiments can be clearly seen throughout the 1650s and 1660s, with the size of Polish army units varying between 400 and 1,600 portions. Larger regiments usually had six or eight companies, with only the Royal Guard being even larger with 10 companies.[16] The period of 1653–1655 had seen a drastic decrease in the number of these infantry units, with many regiments disbanded due to losses and lack of funding. From 1656 onwards though, the strength of the infantry 'corps' started

Musketeer from foreign infantry, here from the mercenary unit in the employ of the city of Danzig in 1659. (Detail from Peter Voget's *Wahrhafftiger und gründlicher Bericht von Belager – und Eroberung der Haupt-Schantze in der Dantziger Nährung...*, published in 1661; PAN Gdańsk Library)

16 *Stanisława Oświęcima Dyarusz 1643–1651* (Kraków: Akademia Umiejętności, 1907), pp.292–294.

Foreign infantry and dragoons from the Lithuanian Army. Their counterparts in the Polish Army would have looked identical so the only means to distinguish between units was their flags. (Abraham von Westervelt, 1651; Polish Army Museum, Warsaw, photo Michał Paradowski collection)

to increase, as such formations were needed during siege operations and in the later large-scale operations against Muscovites. In July 1660, the Polish army had 15 foreign infantry regiments, with a total paper strength of 14,600 portions.[17]

Mounted infantry known as dragoons (*dragonia*) appeared for the first time almost simultaneously in both the Polish and Lithuanian armies in 1617 and quickly became a vital part of the military establishment. Dragoons could accompany cavalry during a campaign and support it with their firepower, so were useful when fighting against the different enemies facing the Commonwealth. Units were recruited in same way as foreign infantry, and sometimes dragoons were converted into infantry and vice versa. The composition of the dragoon 'corps' varied from campaign to campaign; there were also major differences between the Polish and Lithuanian armies. In a similar way to foreign infantry, the Poles tended to focus more on a regimental structure, while the Lithuanian force had mostly free companies. In the same way as they did with foreign infantry, there was no standardised structure of units of dragoons, even within one regiment. It seems that most of these units had four companies, while only a few larger ones had six companies.

The main weapon of dragoons, in their role of fire support, were muskets, mentioned in both Gordon's diary and surviving documents concerned with the raising and equipping of units. The sidearm could vary as soldiers would receive what was locally available: sabres or any type of Western-style swords. Dragoons would often fight as skirmish screens for large formations of infantry and cavalry, securing locations like fords, hills, and forests.

In the first part of the seventeenth century, 'native' infantry, usually called 'Polish' or 'Hungarian', tended to play a fairly important role, often representing a large percentage of the whole infantry 'corps'. Gradually, this type of infantry started to be of less importance in the Polish army, often relegated to garrison duties or, in the case of hetman banners, to serve as some sort of bodyguard and military police unit. The situation was slightly different in the Lithuanian army, when – due to the smaller overall strength of the force – even a few banners with a few hundred men could make up a large part of the total infantry. Interestingly enough, in both armies, this

17 AGAD, ASK 82, no. 9, p.71.

formation was known under several names, and the terms 'Polish infantry', 'Hungarian infantry', 'Polish-Hungarian infantry', and *haiduks* are all found in contemporary sources. The Hungarian influence brought into the Commonwealth during King Stephen Báthory's reign, by the second half of the seventeenth century was mostly visible only in the clothing, such as the *magierka* cap. Banners were equipped with muskets or *rusznica* calivers. In battle, only the first rank was composed of so-called 'tenth men' (under-officers), armed with *darda* half-pikes, with all firearms-armed *haiduks* standing behind in up to 10 ranks.

Polish haiduks, part of the embassy entering Paris in 1645. (Jean Boisseau, 1645; Bibliothèque Nationale de France. Photo by Tomasz Ratyński)

The reign of King Ladislaus IV (1632–1648) brought extensive reform to the artillery in both the Polish and Lithuanian armies. Until then, 'Master of Ordnance' (*starszy nad armatą*) tended to be just a temporary title, assigned to the commander of artillery in the field. Beginning in 1637 in Poland, the master of ordnance, often called the 'general of artillery' (*generał artylerii*), became a regular army official, in charge of all artillery and engineers. He was also in control of all the armouries (*cekhauzy*) in Poland. Warsaw, Cracow, Putzig (modern-day Puck), Marienburg (modern-day Malbork), L'vov, and Kamenets Podol'skiy, the latter two in the Ukraine. The Polish artillery corps was now financed from a separate 'quarter' tax, drawn from royal lands. In peacetime, the general of artillery had under his command a small cadre of gunners, engineers, and specialists, although they rarely exceeded 100 men. The Lithuanian artillery had its own general of artillery, who was in charge of the armouries and staff in Lithuania. Each armoury was under the command of the officer known as *cejgwart*.[18] An important role in the corps was played by the *cejgmaster* or *cejgmistrz*[19] (inspector of artillery), later the lieutenant colonel of artillery, who was in fact the second in command, often leading artillery detachments in the field. The highest-ranking commanders in the artillery corps often served in the dual role of engineer/artilleryman and of officer of infantry.

18 From the German *Zeugwart*.

19 From the German *Zeugmeister*.

In the late 1630s and during the 1640s, all Polish armouries were increased in size and upgraded with larger warehouses, more staff and – most importantly – with new cannon. It is more than likely that the whole reform was closely linked with King Ladislaus's plans to wage a large-scale war against the Tatars and Ottomans, during which artillery would be useful in siege operations. Unfortunately, during John Casimir's reign, artillery had very small impact on the operations of Commonwealth armies. Constantly underfunded, lacking a proper cadre, the artillery had issues providing enough ammunition and powder for the guns and even of purchasing or hiring enough horses to transport the artillery park and supplies. During The Deluge, the logistics of the army were in very poor shape; it is therefore not surprising that help was sought from the privately owned arsenals of magnates and cities such as Danzig to provide weapons, ammunition and men. There were also not enough cannon to take the field, as the arsenals in Warsaw, Marienburg, and Cracow were seized by the Swedes when those cities were captured (in the latter, the Swedes took 96 guns).[20] When the Polish army besieged Warsaw in June 1656, it initially had to rely on smaller field pieces, including those used to support foreign infantry regiments. Only by the end of the month did the besiegers receive heavy cannon from the arsenal in L'vov and further pieces borrowed from Jan Zamoyski from his fortress in Zamość, which allowed them to set up proper batteries to support their assaults on the city.

The Lithuanian artillery was in no better shape than the Polish one, lacking properly trained crews, cannons, and ammunition – and poor funding meant that there was not enough money to hire wagons and drivers to transport artillery trains. As would be expected from this situation the Lithuanian artillery had a very minimal impact on any military actions. During the siege of Mogilyov in 1655, Janusz Radziwiłł complained about the poor skills of his artillerymen, writing in his letter that 'crews and all officials [officers] of this artillery are so poor and practically useless, as during the whole assault only one grenade [cannonball] hit the city, while other overshot or fell too short, hitting our own men.'[21] When taking part in a blockade of the Swedish field army between the Vistula and San rivers in spring 1656, the Lithuanian division under Sapieha had only two small cannon, and it was severely outclassed by the Swedish artillery.[22]

---

20 *Diary of General Patrick Gordon of Auchleuchries 1635–1699*, vol. I, p.63.

21 Konrad Bobiatyński, *Od Smoleńska do Wilna. Wojna Rzeczypospolitej z Moskwą 1654–1655* (Zabrze: Wydawnictwo Inforteditions, 2004), p.139.

22 Mikołaj Jemiołowski, *Pamiętnik dzieje Polski zawierający (1648–1679)* (Warszawa: Wydawnictwo DiG, 2000), p.192.

4

The Brandenburg-Prussia Military Establishment

Frederick William, Elector of Brandenburg, was also Duke of Prussia, however, he did not control all of Prussia. Prussia consisted of two domains: Ducal Prussia and Royal Prussia; both belonged to the Polish Crown but under different circumstances. Ducal Prussia or East Prussia was held as a fief under the Polish Crown by the Elector of Brandenburg. Royal Prussia was ruled by the King of Poland.

Although Prussia belonged to the Commonwealth, the military forces of Brandenburg-Prussia used an organisation and tactics of the Western European model, which since the end of the Thirty Years' War had been fundamentally influenced by the Swedish model. However, at the outbreak of war, the Brandenburg Army was small and insignificant. In fact, the Brandenburg-Prussian military establishment is far more notable for what it became, and for how it developed immediately after the Wars of The Deluge, than for its composition at the beginning of the war. The Wars of The Deluge marked the origin of the Prussian army, and of Prussia (together with the hitherto more established Brandenburg) as an independent state of some renown. Without Brandenburg-Prussia's participation in the wars, there would have been neither a Kingdom of Prussia under the House of Hohenzollern, nor a subsequent Prussian army.

Frederick William began the war almost without an army, and his territories did not have a functioning military establishment from which he could raise one. Following customary practices in Europe at the time, the ruler of Brandenburg did not enjoy absolute power. He had to work with the Estates through Parliament to be granted funding for extraordinary expenses, such as those incurred for military operations or the maintenance of a standing military force. Unfortunately for Frederick William, the Estates were usually unwilling to accept any new costs. In this legal reality, Frederick William's position was distinctly inferior to that of King Charles, who enjoyed widespread support which also manifested itself whenever he called a Parliament. To some extent, Frederick William's situation could be compared to that of King John Casimir.

However, Frederick William faced an additional problem. Upon the death of his father, he had inherited three widely separated territories. In the west, in the Rhine valley, lay the Duchy of Cleves and the territories of Mark, Minden, and Ravensberg. In the centre, mainly between the Rivers Elbe and Oder, was his principal possession, the Electorate of Brandenburg, but also Halberstadt, Magdeburg, and East Pomerania. To the east, on the Baltic shore and under the suzerainty of the Polish Crown, lay the Duchy of East Prussia. Each of these three territories regarded itself as separate and independent from the whole, each had its own Estates, and none accepted a duty to contribute soldiers for the defence of any of the others. Similarly, none accepted a liability to cover any monetary costs incurred by the others. This stance was influenced by regional particularism, but it was also the result of genuine, practical problems. Each of the Elector's territories (except remote Prussia) had been devastated during the Thirty Years' War. This had been largely unavoidable, since small territories of this kind simply lacked negotiating power when a major army chose to march through them. As a result, Frederick William early on realised that his small domain could only compete with the surrounding, major powers, or at least prevent them from marching through and devastating his lands, if he established a formidable army of its own.

However, this took money which the Elector did not yet have. Although Frederick William had gained additional territories through the Peace of Westphalia, which in 1648 had ended the Thirty Years' War, he had been forced to disband even his existing, quite modest army. He lacked the personal resources to support an army, and his Estates saw no reason to fund an army when the country was at peace. Frederick William managed to acquire some funding through regional agreements, such as the 1653 Brandenburg Recess between the Elector and the Estates of Brandenburg, in which the nobility, including the landed nobility of the Junker class in Prussia, provided the sovereign with funds in exchange for affirmation of extensive noble privileges. An Imperial Law of 1654 was helpful as well, since it obligated the subjects 'to provide helpful contributions to the manning and maintaining of the necessary fortresses, fortified places, and garrisons.'[1]

As a result, the Brandenburg-Prussian military establishment in the early 1650s is estimated to have consisted of no more than the Elector's personal military escort of the 63-man-strong Life Guard of Horse and the 202-man-strong Life Guard of Foot (*Leibgarde*; divided into one company each from Brandenburg and Prussia), together with a minimum number of men to garrison his more important fortresses.[2] As late as in early 1655, Frederick William's army consisted of no more than 30 companies (Table 1). This force

1 Hans Delbrück, *History of the Art of War*, vol. 4: *The Dawn of Modern Warfare* (Lincoln: University of Nebraska Press, Bison Books, 1990), p.245.

2 In 1656, the Life Guard of Horse (which consisted of 9 officers and 54 guardsmen, in total 63 men) was named the Trabant Guard in imitation of the Swedish Drabant Guard, which had itself been established in the previous century in imitation of similar German guard units. Curt Jany, *Urkundliche Beiträge und Forschungen zur Geschichte des Preussischen Heeres*, vol. 1 (Berlin: Grosser Generalstab, Kriegsgeschichtliche Abteilung II / Ernst Siegfried Mittler und Sohn, 1901), p.115.

consisted of 790 men in the East Prussian ports of Pillau and Memel which safeguarded the Baltic Sea trade and accordingly constituted a major source of revenue for the state, 596 in Colberg in Pomerania, 1,352 in Brandenburg itself, and small bodies of soldiers in the fortresses of the other territories. Altogether, the total amounted to no more than 3,907 men, dispersed in garrisons.[3] There were no resources whatsoever for manning a field army. In 1653, Frederick William had to order a third of the garrison infantry to be equipped and re-trained with pikes, so that he at least had a minimum number of units which could be converted into a field army. Following the organisational model of the Swedish army, Frederick William aimed for one-third pikemen and two-thirds musketeers.[4]

Table 1: Brandenburg's standing army, early 1655[5]

Territory	Unit	Companies
Prussia	Prussian Life Guard of Foot	1
	Garrison Infantry	5
Mark Brandenburg	Mark Life Guard of Foot	1
	Garrison Infantry	8
	Life Guard of Horse	1 (63 men)
Pomerania	Garrison Infantry	4
Halberstadt	Garrison Infantry	1
Westphalia	Garrison Infantry	9
Total		30

Even when it became increasingly obvious that war would break out again, the Estates within the Elector's dispersed territories refused to fund any more than a token military force. In September 1654, a Swedish envoy, Count Christoph Carl von Schlippenbach, visited Berlin. He suggested an alliance between Brandenburg and Sweden. Furthermore, Schlippenbach suggested, apparently on his own initiative, that the Elector swap the Prussian ports of Pillau and Memel for new territories to be taken from the Commonwealth after King John Casimir had been defeated. While King Charles certainly wanted these ports, there is no reason to believe that he wanted his envoy to show his cards to the Elector at this early stage.[6] Moreover, Pillau and Memel

3 Sidney B. Fay, 'The Beginnings of the Standing Army in Prussia' in *American Historical Review* 22: 4 (1917), pp.763–777, on p.768. Fay also lists the fundamental sources of the origin of the Brandenburg Army, notably Jany, *Urkundliche Beiträge* vol. 1, pp.84–114, which Fay cites for these figures. Jany does give similar figures, but he also notes that the Elector's army was significantly reduced in numbers in 1653, that is, between the date of these data and the raising of a new army for the Wars of The Deluge.

4 Delbrück, *History of the Art of War*, vol. 4, p.269.

5 Jany, *Urkundliche Beiträge*, vol. 1, pp.117–118.

6 Schlippenbach exceeded his authority in other diplomatic negotiations as well, including when in February 1655 he attempted to interest Bavaria in an attempt to wrest the Imperial Crown from the Habsburgs. Hearing rumours about Schlippenbach's various diplomatic initiatives, King Charles wrote to the envoy, reminding him to stay within his instructions. However, it

Otto Christoph von Sparr, by Willem van Honthorst. (Courtesy of Wikipedia)

were, next to Königsberg (modern-day Kaliningrad), the Elector's two most lucrative trading ports in East Prussia, and as a result, Frederick William turned down the proposition.

Frederick William's next action was to send his able chief of artillery (*Feldzeugmeister*), General Otto Christoph von Sparr, to Ducal Prussia to reinforce the existing fortifications there. Sparr, an Imperial officer during the Thirty Years' War, had entered into the service of Brandenburg in 1649 as a major general. In 1651, he was appointed chief of artillery, and could be trusted to defend Prussia against Swedish aggression.

Frederick William began to raise a military force from scratch, and at this point, he had no illusions about his chances of recruiting a permanent army of the Swedish type. Instead, he envisaged the customary enlisted force to be retained only while his territory was at risk and only at the sufferance of the Estates.[7] The problem was, there were no funds for what was needed. In theory, the nobles – technically, his feudal vassals – owed him military

---

seems that King Charles never learnt the full details of Schlippenbach's transgressions, so the latter suffered no serious censure.

7 Fay, 'Beginnings', p.768; citing the Elector's orders for a provisional 'militia in waiting', 20 October 1654.

service (*Rossdienst*) in times of war, in the same manner that the Swedish Retinue of Nobles and the Commonwealth's Levy of the Nobility owed such service to their respective sovereigns. However, most of the Elector's vassals were notably unfit for military service. But, feudal service was still owing to the Elector, and he accordingly exacted monetary payments in lieu of it, and then used the money to enlist professional soldiers. Frederick William knew that if Sweden invaded the Commonwealth, much of the fighting would take place in Prussia.

Having taken the measures that he could, Frederick William turned to the Brandenburg Estates, requesting money sufficient to enlist, equip, and maintain 3,000 new infantry. With the growing risk of war, the Estates were slightly less hostile to the proposal than in the past, and in spring 1655, they consented to fund the enlistment of two-thirds of the army that the Elector had requested.[8]

Meanwhile, in April 1655 Frederick William established Brandenburg's first modern ministry of war, known as the General War Office (*Generalkriegskommissariat*), with authority over all the military forces in all the Elector's territories.[9] Headed by *Generalkriegskommissar*, the department exercised some of the functions by a general staff, of a quartermaster general, and of a treasury department.[10]

War has a way of focusing parliamentary attention. In July, as Swedish units moved into the Commonwealth, Frederick William finally compelled the Estates to grant funding for raising an additional 3,000 men, citing necessity for this extraordinary measure. But far more was needed, in funding and in territorial cooperation. The military preparations of all neighbours compelled Brandenburg to follow their example. In words which foreshadowed the Elector's future attitude towards the Estates in military matters, on 12 July 1655 Frederick William declared:

---

8 Bernhard Erdmannsdörffer (ed.), *Urkunden und Actenstücke zur Geschichte des Kurfürsten Friedrich Wilhelm von Brandenburg*, Vol. 10, 315–16. The Estates had consented by 21 February 1655 (O.S.) but it took all of spring to realise the Elector's goal.

9 This office was established on 8 April 1655 (N.S.). Although it eventually acquired a reputation for professionalism due to its role as the origin of the (much later) Prussian General Staff, the *Generalkriegskommissariat* did not have broader duties, nor employ more up-to-date or efficient methods, than, say, Muscovy's Military Deployments Chancellery (*Razryadnyy prikaz*), established already in the fifteenth century, or the Swedish War Council or War Court (*Krigsrådet, Krigsrätten*), formally established in 1630 but deriving from organisational forms introduced in the sixteenth century. Generally speaking, all three handled tasks such as appointments to commands, maintenance of provincial garrisons and defences, supervision of mobilisation and recruitment, management of quartermaster functions and military intelligence, the administration of compensation entitlements, and at least in the broad sense, the planning of operations.

10 *Generalkriegskommissar* Klaus Ernst von Platen (1612–1669), the head of this department, at first was merely a member of the Privy Council assigned to look after military matters. However, he soon built up a structure of clerks and administrative boards which over time grew into a centralised military management structure, which among other tasks set standards for arms and equipment, ordered uniforms and other gear, and collected the taxes for covering these costs. Fay, 'Beginnings', 777.

> And since this army is for the benefit not simply of one, but of all our lands, we deem it proper that the cost and maintenance of the troops must be borne by all territories, and that the soldiery [German: *Soldatesque*] shall be assigned amongst them proportionally.[11]

However, even faced with imminent war the Estates refused to grant the additional powers. Frederick William therefore took the extreme step of ruling by decree and military execution, without the consent of the Estates and against their will. With such means, he collected a significant extraordinary land tax to finance his military needs. The funding thus gained was used to enlist skilled soldiers, which finally enabled the Elector to raise the required army.[12]

By mid-1655, Frederick William had enlisted a corps of 8,000 men, which he moved into Ducal Prussia in September. He united it with 5,000 newly enlisted units in Prussia and what he hoped to be a 6,000 to 7,000 men militia under Lieutenant General Georg Friedrich von Waldeck, a Thirty Years' War veteran who commanded the army in Prussia until Sparr was given command of all Brandenburg-Prussian troops later in the year.[13] This should have given Frederick William 20,000 men, but he soon found out that this figure was not actually achieved. By the end of 1655, the Brandenburg army in Prussia had, in reality, only 17,000 men at most.[14] However, Frederick William raised his military strength further, and as rapidly as he could. By mid-1656, when he joined forces with those of Sweden, his army in Prussia alone had reached a strength of almost 19,000 men (see Table 2). This army included 7,000 cavalry, 3,300 dragoons, 8,700 foot, plus artillery. Its total nominal strength was 22,000, although this included passe-volants, that is, empty posts, and various other deficiencies so the real total was lower.[15]

11 *Urkunden und Actenstücke* 10, 316.

12 Fay, 'Beginnings', 771.

13 Incidentally, Georg Friedrich von Waldeck and King Charles of Sweden knew each other because they had studied together in Paris during the winter of 1639–1640.

14 Curt Jany, Urkundliche Beiträge 7, 5; Curt Jany, *Geschichte der Königlich Preußischen Armee bis zum Jahre 1807*, Vol. 1 (Berlin: Karl Siegismund, 1928), 109–19.

15 Jany, *Geschichte* vol. 1, pp.121–122.

Table 2: The Brandenburg army in Prussia, June 1656[16]		
Regiment	**Officers & Under-Officers**	**Men**
Cavalry		
Life Guard of Horse under *Oberstwachtmeister* Christian von Klitzing	7	700
Georg Friedrich von Waldeck	12	1,200
Christoph von Kannenberg	10	1,000
Wolf Ernst von Eller	6	600
Heinrich von Wallenrodt	4	400
Georg von Schönaich	8	400
Heinrich von Halle	3	300
John George of Saxe-Weimar	6	600
Christoph de Brunell	3	300
Georg Heinrich von Wallenrodt	8	800
Dietrich von Lesgewang (under Heinrich von Kalnein)	2	200
Johann Schmidt	2	200
Putlitz	1	100
Georg Wilhelm von Massenbach	1	100
Total	**73**	**6,900**
Dragoons		
Life Guard Dragoons	1	200
Georg Friedrich von Waldeck	5	555
Elias von Canitz	4	400
Christian Ludwig von Kalckstein	5	500
Heinrich von Halle	3	300
Hans Georg von Auer	3	300
Christoph von Kannenberg	1	100
Heinrich von Wallenrodt	1	100
Georg von Ritterforth	8	800
Total	**31**	**3,255**
Infantry		
Life Guard of Foot	6	1,279
Otto Christoph von Sparr	12	1,200
Georg Friedrich von Waldeck	6	600
Wolrad von Waldeck	12	1,200
Joachim Rüdiger von der Goltz	8	800
Johann Georg von Sieberg	12	1,200
Jonas Casimir zu Eulenburg	10	1,000
Adolph von Götz	10	1.000
Heinrich von Halle	4	400
Total	**80**	**8,679**
Grand Total	**184**	**18.834**

16 Jany, *Urkundliche Beiträge* vol. 7, pp.65–66

Note that many regiments were still in the process of recruiting men. Moreover, the number of officers and under-officers in most cases seems to correspond to the number of companies, meaning that the figure is either too low, or the company strength is exaggerated, perhaps because the establishment strength was not yet reached. Many Brandenburg units never reached establishment strength.

The Battle of Warsaw was the real baptism of fire for Frederick William's army. For the first time, units from Brandenburg, Cleves, and Prussia fought side by side for a common purpose.

Organisation and Tactical Doctrines

The Brandenburg-Prussian army employed the Western model of organisation, which was based on regiments of horse and foot enlisted by colonels who, in most cases, also commanded the regiment in battle. The one significant departure from this pattern was Prussia, where the Elector could also call out a territorial defence force (German: *Landmiliz*) of levies, of both cavalry and infantry. Known as *Wibranzen* or *Vybranzen*, a Slavic word which derived from Polish *wybraniecka* ('chosen' which in this case meant 'conscripted'), these soldiers were little different from the equivalent Polish levies. Unimpressed by this system, in 1655 Frederick William reorganised and combined the existing territorial defence companies as regular cavalry, dragoon, and infantry regiments.

The cavalry company was organised in essentially the same manner as a Swedish cavalry company, although in reality, many cavalry companies failed to reach establishment strength. Under normal conditions, two full companies, or three or four weak companies, formed a squadron of around 200 men, who deployed for battle in three ranks in the Swedish manner.

Dragoon companies tended to be attached to cavalry regiments in the Swedish manner, to increase the capacity for defensive firepower.

The infantry company was also essentially based on Swedish precedents. Each infantry regiment had its own integral regimental artillery on the Swedish model. However, the establishment strength of an infantry company was smaller than in the corresponding Swedish regiments (although as noted above Swedish regiments quickly fell far below establishment strength when on campaign). Enlisted Brandenburg infantry regiments comprised two-thirds musketeers and one-third pikemen, the same as in the Swedish infantry regiments. In reality, many had fewer pikemen than laid down. Additionally, the regiments formed by *Wibranzen* (levies) seem to have consisted only of musketeers. Each regiment nominally formed two battalions, but as with the cavalry, often several weak units were combined to form a battalion.

Brandenburg regiments were only seldom complete and cavalry and infantry regiments tended to vary in strength from 3 to 12 companies. Dragoon regiments were smaller still and seldom deployed as complete regiments.

Most field artillery was light pieces, primarily consisting of regimental guns, introduced in imitation of the Swedish pattern. These pieces were fewer in number than in the Swedish army, however, and mostly distributed at about three per infantry regiment. Heavier guns were deployed in artillery batteries.

Since many senior officers had spent years in Swedish service during the Thirty Years' War, the tactics employed were essentially identical to those of the Swedish army. At the time that Brandenburg supported Sweden, some Brandenburg units were permanently moved into Swedish service, which was obviously made easier by the fact that they were organised and trained in the Swedish manner.

Soldiers firing matchlock muskets, *c.* 1660. (Johann Philip Lemke, drawn while in Germany)

5

The Crimean Khanate's Military Establishment

As noted significant influences from the old Mongol model of warfare still lingered in Eastern Europe, particularly in Muscovy but also within the Commonwealth and among the Ukrainian cossacks. However, the Mongol tradition was nowhere more obvious than within the Crimean Khanate, which, like Muscovy, was a successor state of the Mongol Empire but retained even more of its traditions.[1]

At the time of The Deluge, the Crimean Khanate remained a major regional power, and it still received tribute from the Commonwealth and from Muscovy, but these tribute obligations were the result of historical grandeur, not imperial might. The Khanate was no longer expanding its power, and although the Crimean Tatars remained a serious military threat to their neighbours, this was because the Crimean economy depended on the acquisition, by raiding, of captives which were then sold as slaves. While nomad raiders were eminently suitable for such endeavours, the Khanate no longer had an ambition to conquer and hold territory. Nor had it been able to adopt more up-to-date types of weapons, tactics, or forms of organisation.

This was also obvious in the Crimean Khanate's relations with the Ottoman Empire. For quite some time, the Khanate had served the Ottoman Empire as a client state. While this status had not yet prevented the Khanate from following an independent political course, even this relative freedom was rapidly coming to an end, and it would not be long before the Khanate was no more than a vassal of its Ottoman overlords.

The military establishment of the Crimean Khanate ultimately derived from the Mongol military model of the Middle Ages. Traditionally, the military's primary component was highly mobile horse archers, stiffened by heavy cavalry. At the time of The Deluge, light cavalry remained common, although the Khanate still fielded some heavy cavalry, based on the Tatar nobility, but their proportion of the total strength of the army was much

1 For further information with notes on additional literature, see Fredholm von Essen, *Charles X's Wars*, vol. 1, pp.242–261; Michał Paradowski, *The Khotyn Campaign 1621: Polish, Lithuania and Cossack Armies Against the Ottoman Empire* (Warwick: Helion, 2023), pp.63–68.

lower than in Muscovy, because the Khanate's warfare focused on raiding, not conquest.

This meant that the Khanate's military forces employed forms of organisation and types of tactics which differed radically from the Western model.

Organisation

The Crimean Khanate was ruled by the Khan of the Crimea, who was also the supreme commander of the Tatar army.[2] Between the origin of the Khanate in the early fifteenth century until its annexation by Russia in 1783, it was ruled by the House of Geray.[3] The Khan had two deputies, a senior and a junior. The first in the line of succession and command of the army was known as *Qalgha* Sultan, usually the Khan's brother – he also administered the Khan's estates in the eastern region of the Crimean Peninsula. Second to the *Qalgha* Sultan in rank and the third most important commander, also often a brother of the Khan, was the *Nurredin* Sultan. In addition to his military duties, he administrated the estates in the western region of the Crimean Peninsula.

Both the *Qalgha* Sultan and *Nurredin* Sultan often commanded large contingents of the Crimean army, either as an independent force or as wings of the main army when the Khan himself was present. Smaller expeditions or raids would be normally led by a *murza* or *mirza* (derived from *emir-zadeh*, 'emir's son' or 'chief's son' in Arabic-influenced Persian), from one of the noble families of the Khanate, or a noble of the allied Noghai Horde.

The military forces of the Crimean Khanate could be divided into several categories or formations:[4]

The Khan's household cavalry, known in the Ottoman style as palace guards (Ottoman Turkish: *qapiqulu*, 'door guards'). The household cavalry was a corps of between 1,500 and 3,000 well-equipped horsemen, armed mostly as horse archers. They accompanied the Khan, serving both as a bodyguard and as an elite cavalry unit.

Household infantry, armed with arquebuses or light muskets of the Ottoman type and for this reason often known, in Ottoman Turkish, as

2 Since the Khanate's archives were destroyed or dispersed in the eighteenth century, we have to rely on the few surviving documents, together with the descriptions of foreign visitors, for our knowledge of Khanate titles and organisation. This is further complicated by the fact that most or all surviving archival documents are written not in Crimean Tatar, but Ottoman Turkish, which in turn borrowed extensively from Arabic and Persian. For this reason, some uncertainty remains with regard to the names of many Tatar institutions. Modern secondary literature often uses modern Turkish forms, which sometimes differ significantly from Ottoman Turkish. This also complicates the transliteration of Tatar names, since some scholars base the transliteration on Ottoman records, while others follow one of several Tatar orthographic styles.

3 The name Geray was of Mongolian origin but was by this time pronounced in Turkicised form and written with Arabic letters. The Mongolian form was Karay, and since sixteenth century Muscovite chronicles occasionally use the variant Kirey, the Turkicised form may not yet fully have departed from the original. In modern Crimean Tatar, the form commonly used is Geray.

4 Amet-chan A. Szejchumierow, *Armia Chanatu Krymskiego. Organizacja i taktyka (XV-XVIII w.)* (Zabrze-Tarnowskie Góry: Wydawnictwo Inforteditions, 2021), pp.26–99.

tüfenkchi (from *tüfenk*, 'hand-carried gun').[5] The infantry consisted of Crimeans, but they were not ethnic Tatars. They were accordingly known as *seghban*, a Tatar term for soldier that derived from Persian, but also was adopted into Ottoman Turkish as *sekban* with the meaning of irregular soldier. The Crimean musketeers, usually from 600 to 1,200 in strength and divided into small companies of only platoon size, were raised from the agricultural villages in the Crimean Peninsula under the control of the Khan. At times, the Ottomans provided janissaries to support the Crimean army with yet more infantry, when it operated on behalf of its Ottoman masters. There were probably never more than 1,000 of them in the service at any given time. Both *seghban* and janissaries were used mostly as garrison units, although sometimes they could accompany the Khan on campaign.

A small corps of Ottoman style field artillery (*zarbuzan* or, for somewhat heavier cannon, *top*). As with the infantry, the artillerymen were mostly used for garrison duties, tending to cannons in the Crimean fortresses and outposts.[6] The artillery corps was rarely employed during campaigns.

Household troops or retainers of the Khan's relatives, officers, and the princes (known as *beghs*) of the constituent tribes of the Tatar Horde. Recruited from nobles and proven fighting men, each was known as a *nöker* (a Tatar term that ultimately derived from Mongolian, meaning 'companion', pl. *nökerler*) or, less formally, *oghlan* (another Tatar term derived from Mongolian, meaning 'young man' or 'lad'). This was probably the best part of the Tatar cavalry. They should perhaps be considered as the regular army, since warfare was their main occupation. Both their equipment and horses were provided by their noble patron, and as such their armament could be of the better quality than those used by ordinary warriors; it could even include some armour and firearms. They were used as bodyguards of *beghs* and *mirzas* and during raids or campaign they formed the core of their armed force. Some *mirzas* could have just a few retainers, while the Khan's brothers might employ several hundreds. The number depended simply on the wealth of the noble.

Levy of the able-bodied population, known in Ottoman Turkish as *seferlu* ('conscript', from *sefer*, 'campaign'). Although in time of need a large part of the armed force, the levy was normally raised on a quota system, that is, several households would put together and provide horses and equipment for one *seferlu*. Even when the Khan with a large part of the 'standing' units left the Crimea for a campaign, the major part of the levy had to be left behind, to defend the country.

Camp servants, known in Ottoman Turkish as *qazganchi* ('cauldron-cleaners').[7] Poorly armed and equipped, they could sometimes be used to support regular troops and levies in combat, but their main role was taking care of the horses, gathering and preparing food, and guarding and watching captives during the return from a raid.

5 In modern Turkish, *tüfekçi* ('musketeer').

6 In modern Turkish, *topçu* ('artilleryman').

7 In modern Turkish, *kazancı* ('cauldron-cleaner'), from Ottoman Turkish *qazgan* ('cauldron').

In the same way that the Khanate of the Crimea was a client state of the Ottoman Empire, the *Noghai* Tatar Horde usually functioned as a client state of the Khanate of the Crimea.

Noghai Tatars did not have *qapiqulu* units, instead they relied on household retainers, supported by levies and servants. They were known as good horsemen, honing their skills in constant raids and skirmishes.

In theory, the Crimean Tatar army organisation was based on the old Inner Asian division into units of nominally 10, 100, and 1,000 men. A recent survey identifies units of four sizes:[8]

The smallest was the section which consisted of between 5 and 10 men. It was known as a *qazgan* ('cauldron', meaning a group of Tatars that would eat from a communal cooking pot)[9] or *qosh*. The original meaning of the Tatar term *qosh* is unclear; it may literally have meant 'basket', although in modern Tatar the word means 'bird'. Originally, the term may have signified a family or migratory group, or indeed any group of people.

Bölük was an Ottoman Turkish term that in the case of Tatar infantry signified a unit of 50 men but in case of cavalry could means anything from few dozens to more than 100. It was roughly the equivalent of a company or banner in other armies.

Bayraq (Ottoman Turkish, *Bayrak*) meant a physical 'banner', and accordingly signified a tribal banner unit, that is, all soldiers of one clan/family led by a *begh*. As such its size could vary, depending on the wealth and power of each *begh*, from several hundred to more than 1,000 warriors.

The largest organised body was a regiment known as *alay*, an Ottoman Turkish term for squadron. While some could be the size of a *bayraq*, others could be much larger, consisting of several thousand men. For example, all the Khan's household troops, who accompanied him on campaign, were grouped into one *alay*. Several *bayraqs* could be grouped together to act as a wing of the Crimean army or to fulfil some missions as detached forces.

Tactical Doctrines

On the battlefield, Crimean Tatar cavalry still fundamentally relied on Mongol tactics. Highly mobile horse archers were used for harassing slow-moving enemy forces. When confronted with enemy cavalry, the Tatar cavalry first aimed to engage with archery, then withdrew in feigned flight until the pursuing enemy could be attacked in the flank by another Tatar cavalry unit.

Traditional nomad tactics remained useful – up to a point. In 1656, the Tatar leader Subhan Ghazi Agha advised King John Casimir, on the eve of a battle against the Swedes, that they should avoid a frontal attack, instead 'keep probing them, and exhaust them with sudden, sharp attacks'.[10] This

8 Szejchumierow, *Armia Chanatu Krymskiego*, pp.83–97.

9 The Ottoman Turkish term was *qazan*, a derivation from the earlier *qazgan*.

10 Leslie J. D. Collins, 'The Military Organization and Tactics of the Crimean Tatars During the Sixteenth and Seventeenth Centuries' in Vernon J. Parry and Malcolm Edward Yapp (eds), *War,*

was typical of Tatar tactics, or indeed the tactics of any equestrian steppe nomads, which emphasised the disorganisation of enemy formations by the use of skirmishers, simultaneous attacks at various points, feigned flights, and other means to soften up the enemy. Skirmishers were also used to drive off opposing scouts, thus denying the enemy information on the deployment, movement, and activities of the Tatar army. By this means, the Tatars could make sudden and unexpected attacks where the enemy was most vulnerable.

When finally charging the enemy, the Tatars would deploy in a half-moon formation, about 40 men broad, with their leaders placed at the front, rear, and flanks. During the charge, the Tatars would yell and ululate.

Like many other equestrian nomads, the Tatars feared musket fire and, in particular, artillery fire. By the time of The Deluge, they had grown accustomed to musket fire. However, artillery remained a problem, since the range of even field artillery greatly exceeded the range of Tatar archery. As a result, field artillery could be used to deny a Tatar army the opportunity to attack.[11]

The composite bow remained the chief Tatar weapon. The French officer Guillaume Le Vasseur de Beauplan, who between 1630 and 1648 served in the Polish army, noted that the similar Polish bow had a range of over 100 paces.[12] Most shooting would take place at close range, with the Tatar horse galloping past the enemy line. However, there was a way to achieve a greater range than this. While travelling across the Ukrainian steppe, Beauplan was attacked by Crimean Tatars. He reported that the Tatars could shoot accurately up to 60 or 100 paces (by which he most likely meant about 50 to 90 metres). Beauplan also made the following observation:

> I have encountered them many times in the country to the number of a good five hundred Tatars who wished to attack us in our tabor [wagon fort], and even though I was accompanied by only fifty or sixty cossacks, they could do nothing to us nor could we best them because they would not approach within the range of our weapons; but after making numerous feints to attack us and trouble us with clouds of arrows on the head because they shot in arcade easily at twice the range of our weapons, they retired…[13]

Shooting in arcade is to shoot at a steep angle, of about 45 degrees, to extend the range as far as possible. The result is that the arrows drop almost

---

Technology and Society in the Middle East (London: Oxford University Press, 1975), pp.257–276, on p.269.

11 The Tatar inability to withstand artillery fire was a factor at the Battle of Berestechko in 1651, in which a Commonwealth army decisively defeated a combined Tatar-Ukrainian cossack army. Anon. [Pierre Chevalier], *A Discourse of the Original, Countrey, Manners, Government and Religion of the Cossacks, With Another of the Precopian Tartars, and the History of the Wars of the Cossacks against Poland* (London: Hobart Kemp, 1672), 147; Sait Ocakli, *The Relations of the Crimean Khanate with the Ukrainian Cossacks, the Polish-Lithuanian Commonwealth and Muscovy during the Reign of Khan Islam Giray III (1644–1654)* (dissertation, University of Toronto, 2017), pp.208–210.

12 Guillaume Le Vasseur, Chevalier de Beauplan, *Description de l'Ukranie depuis les confins de la Moscovie jusqu'aux limites de la Transylvanie* (Paris: J. Techener, 1861), p.48.

13 Beauplan, *Description*, pp.95–96.

vertically on the target, as Beauplan makes clear. Such shooting is, of course, very inaccurate; however, a massed enemy of the type that the horse archers often confronted was very vulnerable to such archery.

A sixteenth century Arabic treatise on archery confirms the range of archery mentioned by Beauplan, pointing out that while the extreme range for accurate fire is 45 bow lengths, the range for effective (in penetrative power), although frequently inaccurate, fire is more than twice this.[14] In the fourteenth century, the Egyptian Mamluks were expected to hit a circle somewhat less than 1 metre in diameter at a range of 60 bow lengths.[15] Again, we can assume that the range for effective but inaccurate fire was longer.

Interesting observations about Tatars, their way of life, and the way that they waged war, can be found in the works of Evliya Çelebi (1611–1682). While Çelebi, an Ottoman traveller and scholar, is prone to huge exaggerations when describing Ottoman and Tatar campaigns, as in claiming that during the 1650s and 1660s Crimean raiders reached The Netherlands and Sweden, at the same time he provides interesting details of things that he witnessed when spending time in the Crimea between the 1640s and early 1660s. Çelebi highlighted the raiding nature of Tatar campaigns, as

> they are nation of heroes and fighters for the cause of Islam.... They raid against the lands of *giaurs* [infidels], pillage them, defeating their enemies without mercy [but] with the sword of their violence and sharpness of their sabres. Those *giaurs* that survived the sword, alongside their children and families, they drag and drive to the Muslim lands, where they convert them to Islam.[16]

He praised their armies, even though – as was often the case with his accounts – he clearly inflated the numbers.

> Khans have the army that they can be proud of indeed. There are no pack horses, tabor, pantry or kitchen, nor do they have wagons, camels, caravans, cannon, muskets, tents or heavy burdens. There are just eighty thousand soldiers – all of them horsemen, eager to fight, with bow cases in their hands,[17] also six or

14 N. A. Faris and R. P. Elmer (eds), *Arab Archery: An Arabic Manuscript of About A.D. 1500: A Book on the Excellence of the Bow and Arrow and the Description Thereof* (Princeton: Princeton University Press, 1945). The translators interpret 45 bow lengths as about 75 metres, which seems excessive. Cf the following note.

15 J. D. Latham and W. F. Paterson, *Saracen Archery: An English Version and Exposition of a Mameluke Work on Archery (ca. A.D. 1368)* (London: The Holland Press, 1970), p.138. The translators interpret 60 bow lengths as about 75m, which suggests a bow length of 1.25m. However, elsewhere the Mamluk bow is recommended to be of the same length as the arrow and correspond to the length which the archer is able to draw, which suggests a bow length of roughly 1m.

16 *Księga podróży Ewliji Czelebiego (wybór)* (Warszawa: Książka i Wiedza, 1969), pp.222–224. Only parts of his works exist in English. Most easily accessible are the two volumes of Evliya Efendi [Evliya Çelebi] (Joseph Hammer-Purgstall tr.), *Narrative of Travels in Europe, Asia, and Africa, in the Seventeenth Century* (London: Oriental Translation Fund of Great Britain and Ireland, 1834 and 1850).

17 Most likely he meant bows, not bow cases.

> seven times of one hundred thousand horses and stallions, divided into baskets [groups] and connected by their tails.[18]

Çelebi also provides ethnographical insights into the Tatars' diet during wartime. Whether these observations were his own or something he had read in the ancient classics remains unknown:

> They do not have any tabor with them, so besides *talkan*,[19] dried curd,[20] horseflesh and old horses [for slaughter], they do not take any other food with them on the campaign. If those supplies are not enough, then they kill horses that became lame during the journey, or those that are sick, tired, losing strength and slow. They do it immediately, so they will not be captured by infidels, then they quarter them with hide and divide between all. Some of them will boil this meat, others will place it under the shabraque (known as *serki* by some, *cherki* by others), get on the horse and ride for some time. Once all juice leaks out from the meat, they see it as ready to be eaten, and they eat this horseflesh, that was under the shabraque, and they satisfy their hunger.[21]

Another ethnographical observation of unknown provenance focuses on horse forage and the way that Tatars dealt with it while on the warpath:

> What is more peculiar is that they have no special fodder for the horses. As soon as they get off the horses, they drive them into the fields under the supervision of their boys, and once they roll, kick and swing, they begin to graze. If the expedition takes place in winter, the horses dig out the grass from under the snow, so they pull out and eat the dry grass left from last summer. The Tatars do not feed their horses with barley, but when they prepare them for a military expedition, they do not give them either straw or hay for forty or fifty days, but they leave them with bags full of barley for all day and all night.[22]

In February 1656, Daniel Żytkiewicz, in his account of the war and the state of current affairs, presented in front of the King and nobility in L'vov, wrote some interesting information about the role of 'small war' tactics against the Swedes and the way that Tatars excelled in it. It is also another piece of evidence that the Poles were eager to ensure the Khanate's support against invaders, seeing them as useful allies:

> [The Swedes] are very afraid of Tatars and their tactic which is [attacking] from the flanks, from the rear, and [the Swedes] have already seen from our men what weapon the bow is and how quickly and how easy and from further range one can kill with it both man and horse, [so the Swedes] are very much afraid of such way of fighting, especially to be cut off in the field, and first them and their horses to be

18 *Księga podróży Ewliji Czelebiego (wybór)*, p.232.
19 Flour made from roasted millet.
20 Possibly made from sheep milk.
21 *Księga podróży Ewliji Czelebiego (wybór)*, p.224.
22 *Księga podróży Ewliji Czelebiego (wybór)*, p.282.

> defeated by hunger than by [strength of] arms. Therefore they want to have them on their side, so there are already Swedish and our [envoys] despatched there [the Crimea], maybe even with money [for bribes].[23]

Royal secretary Mikołaj Szulga highlighted the Tatars' hit-and-run tactics, writing that 'they fled on purpose, luring [the enemy] to chase after them and then hitting them one by one.'[24] There are also many details about the composition of Tatar raider forces in Beauplan's writings, based on his observation during his time in Polish service. He mentioned their specific order of march, used during attacks on the Ukraine and Podolia, which gives some idea how such raiding forces could travel during campaigns in Poland and Prussia:

> Thus the Tatars travel with a front of 100 horses, that is to say 300, because each Tatar leads two by the hand as his relays, as we already said. Their front can be 800 to 1,000 paces, and in depth they are 800 to 1,000 horses, taking up a good three great leagues [French *grandes lieues*; about 10km] when squeezed in four files. Because otherwise they make a column more than 10 leagues long [above 30km]. For someone who did not see it with his own eyes, it is an amazing spectacle, as 80,000 Tatars means more than 200,000 horses and even trees in the forest do not grow as close as those horses marching there. And if you see them from the distance, they look like a huge cloud rising on the horizon, getting larger as they approach, which strikes fear in even the bravest. I speak of those who are not used to seeing such number of legions [troops] together.[25]

Arms, Armour, and Dress

Crimean Tatars did not look very different from other Turco Mongol nomads. The French observer Beauplan noted that they were not very tall, and even the tallest among them were no taller than Europeans of average height. Additionally, Beauplan described them as still Oriental in appearance, with a round face, short nose, and black hair.[26] Certainly, there was a Turco-Mongol strand among the Tatars, in particular among the allied *Noghai* whom Beauplan may have confused with Crimeans. In reality, the inhabitants of the Crimea included many of Mediterranean and even distant Germanic origin because of the Peninsula's long, settled history.

Common Tatars wore shirts and breeches of woven flax. Over this, a Tatar who had the means would wear a caftan or, if not, a jacket of sheepskin which could be reversed in winter, when the fleece was worn inwards. In

23 *Pisma polityczne z czasów panowania Jana Kazimierza Wazy, 1648–1668. Publicystyka, eksorbitancje, projekty, memoriały. Volume 1. 1648–1660* (Wrocław-Warszawa-Kraków-Gdańsk-Łódź: Wydawnictwo Polskiej Akademii Nauk, 1989), p.148.

24 AGAD, Archiwum Warszawskie Radziwiłłów (AR) II, vol. 21, p.190.

25 Beauplan, *Description*, pp.85–86.

26 Beauplan, *Description*, p.73.

Noghai Tatar family, illustrating the sheepskin clothing of the Tatar rank and file. (Adam Olearius, 1656)

heat or rain, the wool was instead worn outside, the garment then functioning as a raincoat. Wealthy Tatars followed Ottoman styles in both apparel and armour. This meant a shirt and breeches of cotton, a caftan, and a fur-lined coat. The cap, often made of quilted cloth, could be fur-lined as well. Tatars generally shaved their heads and only seldom wore beards, unless of high rank. Moustaches were common.

Those who had the means wore armour, commonly a mail shirt and an iron helmet. Those who had armour also generally carried round shields, of a similar type to those still in use within the Commonwealth and, in the previous century, had been common in Muscovy. Armament included the composite bow, a long, curved sabre, and a curved dagger. Beauplan describes quivers for 18 to 20 arrows.[27] Some Tatars carried pistols, arquebuses, or muskets. Firearms and powder containers were Ottoman in style, and most were manufactured within the Ottoman Empire. However, armourers operated workshops in the Crimean capital of Bakhchisaray, and some of them manufactured muskets, including a limited few of high quality. However, these were generally not used by Khanate soldiers but were exported, in most cases to the Circassians of the North Caucasus, from which the Crimeans in turn imported high-quality arrows.

Crimean Tatar envoys to Sweden, 1650. Mustafa Agha, the delegation's leader, is portrayed on the extreme left. The Khan requested an alliance against Muscovy, however, Queen Christina of Sweden turned the offer down, stating that Sweden enjoyed peaceful relations with Muscovy. (*Theatrum Europaeum*)

27 Beauplan, *Description*, p.76.

Although the occasional wealthy Tatar might use a lance, akin to a bear spear (a heavy spear with a leaf-shaped head, known in Slavic lands as a *rogatina*), these were unusual before the 1660s.

Cannon and artillerymen were commonly provided by allies: Ottomans or Ukrainian cossacks. The few Tatars who served as artillerymen would have dressed similarly.

Tatars rode in the Mongol style, with a saddle and short stirrups, and guided their horses with a short whip, in the same manner as other easterners who based their military on the Mongol system and nomad customs. The saddle was placed over a felt saddlecloth which also could be used as a blanket, or even as a simple tent. However, the Tatars also used actual tents of the yurt type, as traditionally employed by Eurasian equestrian nomads.

Wealthy Tatars wore a hussar-style wing on their back, in the manner of the Polish hussars.

Tatar with a hussar-style wing on his back, in the Polish hussar manner. (Detail of a painting of the Battle of Warsaw 1656, made under the direction of the eyewitness Erik Dahlbergh; Drottningholm Castle)

Mirza Ali Geray at the Battle of Vienna, 1683, with the single wing used by some Crimean Tatars. (*Theatrum Europaeum*)

Crimean Tatar noble, from a drawing in the Album of Costumes acquired in Constantinople in 1657–1658 by the Swedish envoy, Claes Brorson Rålamb. Dressed in a blue caftan, brocade sash, fur-lined vermillion overgarment, and the characteristic fur-trimmed cap. (Collection of the Royal Library, Stockholm)

Crimean Tatar retainer, from a drawing in the Album of Costumes acquired in Constantinople in 1657–1658 by Swedish envoy, Claes Brorson Rålamb. Note the short whip, used instead of spurs when mounted. (Collection of the Royal Library, Stockholm)

Crimean Tatar, from the Album of Costumes, *c.* 1620, known as *The Habits of the Grand Signor's Court*. (Collection of the Royal Library, Stockholm)

Crimean Tatar round shield, with a replacement boss probably made later by a Ruthenian craftsman. (Museum-Arsenal, L'viv Historical Museum)

Crimean Tatars crossing a river, as depicted in an Ottoman miniature of 1579. They are wearing caftans in a variety of colours, including vermillion, light blue, dark blue, green, yellow, pink and white. Some caftans, including a yellow one and a pink one, are obviously made of brocade. The miniature depicts two standards, one red with a single tail and another green with swallow-tails. Both standards are decorated in gold with what probably are Arabic letters. (*Tarih-i Sultan Süleyman*, also known as the *Zafarnâma*). (Collection of Chester Beatty Library, Dublin, reproduced with thanks)

Beauplan mentioned that a Tatar was armed with sabre, bow, arrow case with 18 to 20 arrows, a firelock musket, and a knife. An important part of their equipment was 'five to six fathoms of leather lasso that they use to bind prisoners.' Only the wealthiest were equipped with mail, with the majority fighting in whatever clothing they had available. Beauplan also commented on the way they rode horses, admitting that Tatars were 'very agile and brave on their horses' but criticised the way that the raiders sat on horseback, 'with their legs totally crouched and themselves very much leaning', leading to the remark that they looked like a 'monkey on a hound'. He praised the skill of the raiders though, mentioning that they are able to jump from one horse to another at full gallop. Beauplan added that if confronted by an enemy, Tatars would often withdraw from melee. However, they would continue to shoot with their bows during the retreat and after this feigned retreat gather together and attack again. Tatars would continue employing such tactics until the enemy grew tired and was forced to retreat. They also tended to avoid the fight if they did not have a good numerical advantage over their opponents. 'In other situations they just shoot from a distance, without closing too much.'[28] While bows were closely associated as the main weapon used by Tatars, perhaps not all were that well-armed. In 1648, an anonymous companion serving in the cossack cavalry banner of the Polish 'quarter army' described rather poorly equipped Crimeans that arrived to support the mutinous Zaporozhian Cossacks. 'Horde rather poor and shy and inconspicuous, all [wearing] sheepskins and a small siermięga[29] without sabres, without bows; most of them with masłak, which is a bone attached to supple piece of wood,[30] which is worse than sabre.'[31] While his comments sound very contemptuous, and no doubt were intended as such, we need to remember that Tatars could be a very dangerous enemy, especially when facing their enemies on their own terms. Fast moving, very skilled riders, they continued shooting at the opponents from their bows, no matter if they were advancing or retreating.

Banners and Music

Crimean Tatars used a variety of standards. Following old Mongol tradition, the Khan used a horse-tail standard (*tugh*), which was a staff with horse tails arranged circularly at the top. Each tribe would also bring a tribal banner (*bayraq*) when going to war. There were also officers' flags (*sanjaq*) since they were needed to keep the formations in order while moving across the steppe. However, there seems to be no reliable contemporary information on the appearance of the various standards and colours.

In addition to standards, kettle-drums were used to keep the formations in order. Again, this was part of the old Mongol tradition. The members of each *qosh* reportedly would also bring a drum and the aforementioned communal cooking pots (*qazgan*) to the army.

28 Beauplan, *Description*, pp.76–77 & pp.99–100.

29 Outer garment made from cheap cloth, commonly used by Polish peasants. Here used as synonym for poor and cheap clothing.

30 Other descriptions of this weapon usually mentioned that it was horse jaw bone.

31 Mirosław Nagielski (ed.), *Relacje wojenne z pierwszych lat walk polsko-kozackich powstania Bohdana Chmielnickiego okresu "Ogniem i Mieczem" (1648–1651)* (Warszawa: Wydawnictwo Viking, 1999), p.103.

6

Orders of Battle at Warsaw

The two armies that prepared for battle at Warsaw were different from one another both in numbers and tactics. The Allied Swedish-Brandenburg army, under King Charles and Frederick William, had a combined strength of around 18,000 men. The united Commonwealth-Crimean army, commanded by King John Casimir, was larger, although different sources give different numbers. As far as we know, the united army of King John Casimir was at least twice the size of the army of King Charles and Frederick William.

It seems clear that King Charles and Frederick William fielded more infantry than King John Casimir, although that difference was not large. The Swedish-Brandenburg army also included more field artillery than the Commonwealth army. However, it seems equally clear that King John Casimir fielded far more regular cavalry than King Charles and Frederick William. Even if we discount the noble levies altogether, King John Casimir enjoyed a huge advantage in cavalry.

However, both Swedes and Brandenburgers were better trained than their Commonwealth counterparts. Moreover, their commanders were experienced leaders who had fought in the Thirty Years' War. Quite a few of the common soldiers in both the Swedish and Brandenburg armies were veterans as well, and many of the Brandenburgers had previously fought under Swedish banners. Among Lithuanians who remained true to their oath to King Charles was Prince Bogusław Radziwiłł, another veteran of the Thirty Years' War who had been in Dutch service between 1641 and 1643 (during which time, incidentally, Georg Friedrich von Waldeck served in his command).[1] Within the Commonwealth Army, Czarniecki and a few others had fought in the same war and shared the outlook, training, and experience of these veterans, but most Commonwealth commanders had no comparable experience.

1 Bogusław Radziwiłł was an educated man who had mastered French, German, Polish, Latin, and Ruthenian.

The Swedish Army

The Swedish army consisted of around 9,500 men (7,500 horse and 2,000 foot). The Swedes also brought 31 guns onto the field.[2]

Table 3: The Swedish army in the Battle of Warsaw, 28–30 July 1656[3]	
Regiment	**Squadron / Battalion**
Cavalry	
Life Guard of Horse (including the Drabant Guard under Lieutenant Colonel Hans Georg Mörner af Morlanda), under Lieutenant Colonel Barthold de Mortaigne	1 squadron, or more likely a company-sized unit incorporated into another squadron
Uppland Cavalry Regiment, under Lieutenant Colonel Erik Planting (formally under Johan Mauritz Wrangel who was imprisoned in Warsaw)	2
Västgöta Cavalry Regiment, under Major Per Hierta (since the death of regimental commander Lars Cruus)	2
Åbo Cavalry Regiment, also known as Fabian Berndes's Finnish Cavalry Regiment after its colonel, under Berndes and Lieutenant Colonel Carl Bäck	2
Småland Cavalry Regiment, probably under Major Zacharias Sabelfelt	2 On 24 July had 473 men, but according to another source, 397 men
Tavastehus Cavalry Regiment (until recently also known as Henrik Henriksson Horn's Cavalry Regiment), under the recently promoted Colonel Johan Galle	1 (possibly 2)
Östgöta Cavalry Regiment (formally under Ludwig Wierich Lewenhaupt who was imprisoned in Warsaw; actual commander unknown)	2
Duke Adolph John's Cavalry Regiment (constituted from several existing companies enlisted in Germany; from January 1656 also known as the *Generalissimus*'s Cavalry Regiment), under Lieutenant Colonel, by this time possibly Colonel, Andreas Probst	1
Her Royal Majesty the Queen's Life Regiment of Horse (enlisted in Germany; also known as Duke John George of Anhalt-Dessau's Cavalry Regiment), under Lieutenant Colonel Georg Henrik Lübecker	1
Duke Charles of Mecklenburg-Schwerin's Cavalry Regiment (enlisted in Germany), under the Duke and Lieutenant (?) Colonel Dietrich von Rosen	2 (400 men)

2 J. Levin Carlbom, *Tre dagars slaget vid Warschau den 18, 19 och 20 juli 1656: Samt de föregående mindre fältslagen 1655 och 1656 – Ett tvåhundrafemtioårigt minne* (Stockholm: Varia, 1906), pp.96 & 113.

3 Carlbom, *Tre dagars slaget*; Hedberg, *Kungl. Artilleriet: Carl X Gustafs tid*, pp.93–94.

Count Palatine Philip von Sulzbach's Cavalry Regiment (enlisted in Pomerania), under Lieutenant Colonel Johan Printzenskiöld	1
Margrave Charles Magnus of Baden-Durlach's Cavalry Regiment (enlisted in Germany)	1
Field Marshal Hans Christoph von Königsmarck's Cavalry Regiment (enlisted in Bremen-Verden; also known as Königsmarck's Life Regiment of Horse), under Lieutenant Colonel Jobst Caspar von Reitzenstein; when he was wounded in the battle, command was assumed by Major Friedrich Ulrich von Rossow	3
Field Marshal Carl Gustav Wrangel's Cavalry Regiment (enlisted in Germany), under Lieutenant Colonel Anders Planting-Bergloo	1
Field Marshal Arvid Wittenberg's Cavalry Regiment (enlisted in Pomerania; under Lieutenant Colonel Peter von Kiesell since Wittenberg was in Polish captivity)	1
Major General Hans Böddeker's Cavalry Regiment (enlisted in Bremen)	1
Colonel Jacob Johan Taube's Cavalry Regiment (mostly enlisted in Finland)	1 (200 men)
Count Johann von Waldeck's Cavalry Regiment (enlisted in Germany), possibly under Major Casper von Bleckmann	1 (or possibly 2)
Colonel David Sinclair's Cavalry Regiment (mostly enlisted in Sweden; when Sinclair was wounded, Lieutenant Colonel Claes Ekeblad assumed command)	1
Colonel Per Hammarskiöld's Cavalry Regiment (mostly enlisted in Sweden), probably under Major Axel Spens (since Hammarskiöld was imprisoned in Warsaw)	1
Colonel Christian von Pretlach's Cavalry Regiment (enlisted in Bremen)	1 (200 men)
Colonel Jacob von Yxkull's Cavalry Regiment (enlisted from Swedes and Germans in Bremen and Pomerania, with one company from Livonia)	1
Colonel Wenzel Sadowski's Cavalry Regiment (primarily Poles; Sadowski was a Bohemian who had spent almost 20 years in Swedish service)	1
Colonel Israel Isacsson Ridderhielm's Cavalry Regiment (mostly enlisted in Sweden)	1
Colonel Georg Friedrich von Canitz's Regiment of Horse (converted Brandenburg dragoons transferred into Swedish service)	1
Lieutenant Colonel Rutger von Ascheberg's Cavalry Regiment (enlisted in Germany)	1 weak, reduced by disease
Lieutenant Colonel Kehrberg's Horse	Obscure weak unit of at most 80 horse
Total	34 (average of 200 men each)

Dragoons	
Count Palatine Philip von Sulzbach's Dragoon Regiment, under Lieutenant Colonel Lorenz Naumann	1
Prince Bogusław Radziwiłł's Dragoon Regiment (enlisted in Lithuania), under Lieutenant Colonel Eberhard Puttkammer	1
Colonel Fabian Berndes's Finnish Dragoon Regiment (decimated by much fighting and dispersed into garrison. Almost certainly not at Warsaw as a unit, although perhaps a handful of men had been merged into another squadron)	
Total	2 (average of 200 men each)
Infantry	
Uppland Regiment, probably under Major William Nisbet	1
Skaraborg Regiment, under Colonel John Nairn	1
Södermanland Regiment, under Colonel Christer Jönsson Svinhufvud	1
Hälsinge Regiment, under Colonel Carl Larsson Sparre	1
Västgöta-Dal Regiment, under Lieutenant Colonel Carl von Scheiding (formed together with men from Skaraborg Regiment)	1
Kalmar Regiment, under Colonel Gustav Cruus	1
Total	6
Artillery	
Field artillery, probably 7 x 12pdrs, 6 x 6pdrs, 18 3pdrs, under Colonel Gustav Oxenstierna	

Comments on the Swedish Order of Battle

There are virtually no surviving contemporary documents that record the Swedish order of battle, and we also lack much of the detailed information for this period, such as the muster rolls.[4] Another problem is that even reliable eyewitness accounts of the battle often contradict one another. Even the well-informed Swedish intelligence officer and quartermaster Erik Dahlbergh, who participated in the battle, sometimes contradicts himself in the narratives, orders of battles, and drawings he later made to describe the Battle of Warsaw. The same goes for the plans and drawings by Johann Gregor Memhardt, Frederick William's primary engineer and architect, who was a contemporary but did not participate in the battle. This means that we can seldom get closer to the Swedish numbers and deployments than

4 Most relevant preserved records (except those pertaining to enlistment in Bremen-Verden) can be found in Swedish National Archives (Riksarkivet, RA), SE/KrA/0022 Rullor 1620–1723: primarily SE/KrA/0022/1656/1; SE/KrA/0022/1656/2; SE/KrA/0022/1656/3; SE/KrA/0022/1656/4; SE/KrA/0022/1656/5; SE/KrA/0022/1656/6; SE/KrA/0022/1656/7; SE/KrA/0022/1656/8; SE/KrA/0022/1656/9; SE/KrA/0022/1656/10; SE/KrA/0022/1656/11. See also SE/KrA/0022/0/10 Katalogband med register till samlingen Rullor 1620–1723.

estimates and descriptions based on what can be gleaned from literary and pictorial sources and archival documents that describe the units at best a few months before or after the battle. The near-contemporary Samuel von Pufendorf, who wrote the official Swedish history of the wars, suggests 9,000 Swedes. The early twentieth-century military historian Johan Levin Carlbom amends this to 9,500 without quoting archival sources.[5] However, Carlbom worked with archival documents, and all subsequent Swedish historians repeat his estimates, as do most non-Swedish historians, including the Polish historians Stanisław Herbst, Jan Wimmer, and Mirosław Nagielski.[6]

It is particularly difficult to identify the role, if any, played by the Life Guard of Horse which by this time included the Drabant Guard. We know that Lieutenant Colonel Barthold de Mortaigne participated in the battle as commander of the Garde de Corps. However, there are also references to a Life Regiment of Horse, which at this time was likely an altogether different unit, if so probably Philip of Sulzbach's Cavalry Regiment. In short, we cannot identify the other units, if any, in the battle under Mortaigne's command. Incidentally, Her Royal Majesty the Queen's Life Regiment of Horse was enlisted in Germany separately from the unit which had previously carried this name.[7]

Another difficulty is that many cavalry regiments lacked a sufficient number of horses. As an example, we can look at the Åbo Cavalry Regiment, at the time of the battle also known as Fabian Berndes's Finnish Cavalry Regiment after its new colonel. On 26 April, the muster roll already noted that 111 out of 444 cavalrymen lacked horses and accordingly fought on foot. At the same time, 71 men were sick. Possibly, the fit men who lacked horses rode the horses of the men who were too sick to serve although the roll actually suggests otherwise. Be that as it may, the total of 444 cavalrymen and about 104 officers and under-officers was then formed in eight companies. After the Battle of Warsaw, the muster roll of 8 August recorded a total of 210 mounted and fit men (excluding officers and under-officers) in the same eight companies, and in addition 87 men who had to fight on foot because their horses were 'useless'. Casualties were then reported as 9 men killed in action, 10 horses killed in action, 9 men dead from disease, 37 men who were too sick to serve, and one deserter.[8]

Finally, it has not always been possible to identify the officer who was actually in command of a given unit during the battle. The Åbo Cavalry Regiment was led by Fabian Berndes, but he received an assignment as

5 Carlbom, *Tre dagars slaget*, pp.118–120.

6 Stanisław Herbst, 'Tredagarsslaget vid Warszawa 1656', Arne Stade and Jan Wimmer (eds). *Polens krig med Sverige 1655–1660: Krigshistoriska studier* (Stockholm: Kungl. Militärhögskolan, Carl X Gustaf-studier 5, 1973), 255–293, on 265; Wimmer, 'Polens krig med Sverige', 368; Mirosław Nagielski, *Warszawa 1656* (Warsaw: Bellona, 2009), p.138.

7 Some have noted Carl Mauritz Lewenhaupt's Cavalry Regiment as present at the battle, so this unit was included in the army list presented in Fredholm von Essen, *Charles X's Wars* Vol. 3, p.138. While Lewenhaupt fought in the battle, further research suggests that his regiment, although contracted by the Crown, was never actually raised as a combat-ready unit and did not participate in the campaign.

8 Muster rolls reprinted in Carlbom, *Tre dagars slaget*, 56–57. Originals in Swedish National Archives (Riksarkivet, RA), SE/KrA/0022/1656/3, pp.66–67; SE/KrA/0022/1656/10, p.143.

commander of a line of battle, and we do not know who then led his regiment. The colonel of the Östgöta Cavalry Regiment was imprisoned in Warsaw, and the name of his deputy does not seem to have been recorded. The Södermanland Regiment had previously been commanded by Colonel Johan von Vietinghoff (1580–1685), a veteran who had finally retired in April, and was then replaced by his deputy, Christer Jönsson Svinhufvud, who was promoted to colonel.

The Brandenburg Army

The most accurate reconstruction of the Brandenburg army taking part in the summer campaign of 1656 is provided by Polish researcher Sławomir Augusiewicz in his work describing the army in Prussia in the period 1655–1660. Using archival documents and the work of researchers such as Curt Jany, August Riese, and Johann Gustav Droysen, he was able to correct some mistakes present in previously published studies; he also gathered information about the officers who were actually in command of a number of regiments.

Frederick William's army was newly created, with the 'oldest' units raised in spring 1655. Regiments were recruited in Brandenburg, Ducal Prussia, and some neighbouring German states (Reich lands). At least a part of the officer cadre was composed of experienced veterans, who had previously served in Polish, Imperial, or Swedish armies. According to Augusiewicz, the Elector brought the following units in his field army:[9]

Brandenburg Cavalry and Dragoons

unless where noted, units raised in Brandenburg and in Reich lands.

The Elector's Drabant Company under Ludvig de Wees (von Weiss) – 67 men.

The presence of this unit at Warsaw is uncertain, but the company accompanied the Elector on the campaign.

The Elector's Life Regiment of Horse (*Leibregiment zu Pferde*) under the nominal command of Colonel Alexander von Spaen. During the campaign, the unit was led by Lieutenant Colonel Georg von Polentz – eight companies.

The Regiment was formed in summer 1655, with most of the men recruited in Brandenburg and Reich lands, and at least one company raised in Ducal Prussia.

9 Sławomir Augusiewicz, *Przebudowa wojska pruskiego w latach 1655–1660. U źródeł nowożytnej armii* (Oświęcim: Wydawnictwo Napoleon V, 2014), pp.203–208.

Count Georg Friedrich von Waldeck's Cavalry Regiment, under the command of Lieutenant Colonel Georg Henning von Barfuss – 12 companies.

The majority of this regiment (seven companies) was raised in Ducal Prussia in April 1655.

Major General Christoph von Kannenberg's Cavalry Regiment, under the command of Lieutenant Colonel Bucht – 10 companies.

Duke John George of Saxe-Weimar's Cavalry Regiment – six companies.

Colonel Wolf Ernst von Eller's Cavalry Regiment – six companies.

Colonel Georg von Schönaich's Cavalry Regiment – four companies.

The presence of this unit at Warsaw is uncertain. The regiment was raised in Ducal Prussia.

Colonel Heinrich von Kalnein's Cavalry Squadron – two companies.[10]

Colonel Christoph de Brunell's Cavalry Squadron – three companies.

Count Georg Friedrich von Waldeck's Dragoon Regiment, under the command of Lieutenant Colonel Aulack – five companies.

The unit was raised in Ducal Prussia in the winter of 1655/1656.

Colonel Elias von Canitz's Dragoon Regiment under command of Lieutenant Colonel Georg Friedrich von Canitz – four companies.

Colonel Christian Ludvig Kalckstein's Dragoon Regiment under command of Lieutenant Colonel Christian Stephan von Grumbkow – four companies.

The unit was raised in Ducal Prussia, probably in late 1655.

Total: approximately 4,000 cavalry and 1,000 dragoons.

Brandenburg Infantry

Major General Joachim Rüdiger von der Goltz's Regiment, under the command of Lieutenant Colonel Dietlof Friedrich von Barfuss – eight companies.

In June the regiment mustered 722 men. The regiment was created from garrison companies stationed in Brandenburg.

10 Until June 1656, this was the unit of Dietrich von Lesgewang, explaining why many authors put Lesgewang's squadron at Warsaw.

Major General Wolrad von Waldeck's Regiment – 12 companies.

Part of this unit was the former regiment (or squadron) of Gerhard von Bellicum which had been raised in late 1655 in Ducal Prussia.

General Otto Christoph von Sparr's Regiment, under command of either Lieutenant Colonel Heiden or Lieutenant Colonel Moll – 11 companies.

In June the regiment mustered 1,218 men. The regiment was created from garrison companies stationed in Kolberg (Kołobrzeg), Minden, and Lippstadt.

Colonel Johan Georg von Sieberg (Syburg)'s Regiment – 11 companies, with a twelfth company detached as the garrison of Johannisburg (Pisz).

The regiment was raised from spring 1655 in the Rhineland and Westphalia.

Despite many researchers stating that The Elector's Life Guard of Foot under Colonel Pierre de la Cave, or at least a part of it, was present at Warsaw, it was not. At the time of the battle, the whole unit was in quarters in Königsberg, Pillau, and the surrounding areas.

Total approximately 3,500 infantry

The artillery train was under command of Colonel Christian von Hochkirch and in June 1656 it had two 12pdrs, two 8pdrs, and 10 regimental 3pdr cannon, with a supply of 100 cannonballs for the 12pdrs (on one wagon), 100 for the 8pdrs (on one wagon) and 100 for the 3pdrs (on two wagons). There were 38 artillery staff, including drivers, with 19 wagons and 128 horses (including 48 used for pulling the cannon).[11] According to Curt Jany, at the time of the Battle of Warsaw, the artillery train was reinforced, as during the muster at Zakroczym on 27 July 1656 it comprised 30 cannon and five howitzers.

Altogether, the Brandenburgers mustered around 8,500 men (5,000 horse and 3,500 foot; Table 4).[12] The Brandenburg army also had 30 cannon and 5 howitzers.[13]

11 Kurd Wolfgan von *Schöning, Historisch-biographische Nachrichten zur Geschichte der Brandenburgisch-Preussischen Artillerie, Volume 1* (Berlin: Ernst Siegfried Mittler, 1844), 57.

12 Carlbom, *Tre dagars slaget*, 118–120. Carlbom amends Pufendorf's 9,000 Swedes and 8,000 Brandenburgers without quoting archival sources. It is known that Carlbom worked with archival documents, and all subsequent Swedish historians repeat his estimates, as do most non-Swedish historians, including the Polish historians Stanisław Herbst, Jan Wimmer, and Mirosław Nagielski. Herbst, 'Tredagarsslaget', p.265; Wimmer, 'Polens krig med Sverige', p.368; Nagielski, *Warszawa*, p.138.

13 Carlbom, *Tre dagars slaget*, pp.96, & 113.

Table 4. The Brandenburg army in the Battle of Warsaw, 28–30 July 1656[14]	
Regiment	Companies
Cavalry	
The Elector's Life Regiment of Horse	8
Duke John George of Saxe-Weimar's Cavalry Regiment	6
Count Georg Friedrich von Waldeck's Cavalry Regiment	12
Christoph von Kannenberg's Cavalry Regiment	10
Wolf Ernst von Eller's Cavalry Regiment	6
Georg von Schönaich's Cavalry Regiment	4
Heinrich von Kalnein's Cavalry Squadron	2
Christoph de Brunell's Cavalry Squadron	3
Dragoons	
Count Georg Friedrich von Waldeck's Dragoon Regiment	5
Elias von Canitz's Dragoon Regiment	5
Christian Ludwig von Kalckstein's Dragoon Regiment	4
Infantry	
Wolrad von Waldeck's Regiment	12
Otto Christoph von Sparr's Regiment	11
Joachim Rüdiger von der Goltz's Regiment	8
Johann Georg von Sieberg's Regiment	11
Artillery	
30 field pieces, mostly regimental guns, 5 howitzers	

Senior Swedish and Brandenburg Generals at the Battle of Warsaw

Many Swedish and Brandenburg regimental commanders were simultaneously senior generals who commanded wings and lines within the Allied army. Although they seem to have been assigned positions in command of the respective lines of battle, most were apparently not bound by these assignments and there was some movement by general officers as demanded by the developing circumstances. Nonetheless, most of their positions can be pinpointed, at least during the initial stages of battle.

Duke Adolph John (1629–1689), King Charles's brother, had already been appointed *Generalissimus*, or supreme commander, over the Swedish

14 Augusiewicz, *Przebudowa wojska pruskiego*; Carlbom, *Tre dagars slaget*; Jany, *Urkundliche Beiträge*; Hedberg, *Kungl. Artilleriet: Carl X Gustafs tid*, p.93.

Duke Adolph John, portrayed here in the dress of a Roman officer which he wore during a carousal, which in the seventeenth century was a festive parade of nobles on horseback. (David Klöcker Ehrenstrahl)

Robert Douglas, 1651. (Jeremias Falck, after the portrait by David Beck)

Philip Florinus of Sulzbach. (Abraham Wuchters, Gripsholm Castle)

armies in the Commonwealth by the King, thus making him the commander-in-chief in the King's absence. King Charles assigned Duke Adolph John a position next to himself, where he served as the King's deputy.

Count Robert Douglas (1611–1662), recently promoted to Field Marshal Lieutenant, was a Scottish veteran of the Thirty Years' War who had distinguished himself on numerous occasions, including at the Battles of Lützen in 1632, Wittstock in 1636, and Jankow in 1645. His position was next to King Charles and Duke Adolph John on the Swedish cavalry wing.

Philip Florinus of Sulzbach (1630–1703; also known as Philipp of Pfalz-Sulzbach), Count Palatine and Major General of Cavalry; a relative of King Charles who began his military career in the Duchy of Lorraine but in 1655 went into Swedish service with an enlisted regiment. He commanded the first line of cavalry on the Swedish wing, or at least the part closest to the centre.

Margrave Charles Magnus of Baden-Durlach. (Artist unknown; National Museum, Stockholm)

1.

2.

Plate A.

1. King Charles X of Sweden; 2. Frederick William, Elector of Brandenburg and Duke of Prussia

(Illustration by Sergey Shamenkov © Helion & Company)

See Colour Plate Commentaries for further information.

1.

2.

Plate B.
1 Swedish Cavalryman; 2 Swedish Dragoon
(Illustration by Sergey Shamenkov © Helion & Company)
See Colour Plate Commentaries for further information.

Plate C.
1 Swedish Musketeer; 2 Brandenburg Musketeer
(Illustration by Sergey Shamenkov © Helion & Company)
See Colour Plate Commentaries for further information.

1.

2.

Plate D.
1 King John II Casimir of the Polish-Lithuanian Commonwealth
E.2 Queen Louise Marie of the Polish-Lithuanian Commonwealth
(Illustration by Sergey Shamenkov
© Helion & Company)
See Colour Plate Commentaries for further information.

Plate E.

1 Polish Hussar; 2 Polish *Pancerny*
(Illustration by Sergey Shamenkov © Helion & Company)
See Colour Plate Commentaries for further information.

Plate F.

1 Unarmoured Noble Cavalryman; 2 Wallachian Cavalry Officer

(Illustration by Sergey Shamenkov © Helion & Company)

See Colour Plate Commentaries for further information.

Plate G. Lithuanian Cossack Cavalryman
(Illustration by Sergey Shamenkov © Helion & Company)
See Colour Plate Commentaries for further information.

1.

2.

Plate H.
1 Polish Dragoon; 2 Polish Haiduk
(Illustration by Sergey Shamenkov © Helion & Company)
See Colour Plate Commentaries for further information.

Plate I. Crimean Tatar
(Illustration by Sergey Shamenkov © Helion & Company)
See Colour Plate Commentaries for further information.

Plate J. Commonwealth standards and colours

(Illustration by Olof Hoffman)

See Colour Plate Commentaries for further information.

Plate K. Commonwealth standards and colours
(Illustration by Olof Hoffman)
See Colour Plate Commentaries for further information.

Plate L. Swedish colours, Brandenburg-Prussian guidons
(Illustrations by Tomasz Nowojewski, Anderson Subtil)
See Colour Plate Commentaries for further information.

Margrave Charles Magnus of Baden-Durlach (1621–1658), a veteran of the Thirty Years' War had served in the Swedish army for many years including at the Battle of Jankow in 1645, and commanded the second line of cavalry in the Swedish wing.

Major General of Cavalry Henrik Henriksson Horn (1618–1693) commanded the third line or reserve on the Swedish wing closer to the centre. He was a veteran of the Thirty Years' War and seems to have held overall responsibility for the third line.

Colonel Fabian Berndes (1610–1678), a veteran of the Thirty Years' War, commanded the third line on the outer part of the Swedish wing. However, he was ill on both 28 and 29 July, so did not participate in the battle at least for these two days. It is not known who commanded his regiments in his absence, nor if any of his officers served as his deputy as commander of the third line. Berndes had a reputation as a violent man and on one occasion had to flee Sweden because of a killing; the peasants and workers in his service frequently filed complaints with the courts over his habit of responding with whippings and abuse when contradicted.

Major General Barthold Hartwig von Bülow (1611–1667) commanded the Swedish infantry. He was a veteran of the Thirty Years' War who had fought at Nördlingen 1634 under Bernard of Saxe-Weimar as well as in other battles. He was in charge of the third line of the infantry centre, that is, the infantry reserves.

Colonel Gustav Oxenstierna (1626–1693) commanded the Swedish artillery.

Count Carl Gustav Wrangel af Salmis (1613–1676), Field Marshal and Admiral, was a veteran of the Thirty Years' War who in 1646–1648 held overall command over Swedish military forces in Germany. He was positioned next to Frederick William of Brandenburg on the Brandenburg wing. This was in line with the traditional Swedish practice of always appointing a reliable and experienced Swedish deputy next to any German prince who served with the Swedish army. At Warsaw, Frederick William was, of course, a sovereign ruler, but the Swedes knew the value of placing a senior Swedish commander in a position where he simultaneously could advise and keep an eye on the prince so that he did not act contrary to Swedish interests. It is notable that at Warsaw, King Charles also deployed several Swedish cavalry regiments and Major Generals Tott and Böddeker on the Brandenburg wing.

Carl Gustav Wrangel, 1652. (David Klöcker Ehrenstrahl).

Major General Count Claes Tott (1630–1674) commanded the second line of the Brandenburg wing.

Claes Tott. (National Museum, Stockholm)

Major General Hans Böddeker (d. 1659) was already an old soldier. He appears to have commanded the second line of cavalry on the Brandenburg wing.

Duke Charles of Mecklenburg-Schwerin (1626–1670) at least on 29 July commanded a part of the Brandenburg third line as major general.

Prince Bogusław Radziwiłł (Lithuanian: Boguslavas Radvila) (1620–1669) was a veteran of the Thirty Years' War. He was positioned on the Swedish cavalry wing, together with one or two lieutenant generals, near King Charles.

The Brandenburg army had fewer senior generals than the Swedish. The most senior was General Otto Christoph von Sparr (1599 or 1605–1668), a veteran of the Thirty Years' War in Imperial service who from 1651 served as overall chief of artillery (*Generalfeldzeugmeister*) and from 1655 was overall commander of all Brandenburg-Prussian units. He commanded the infantry centre, including the Swedish units.

Lieutenant General Count Georg Friedrich von Waldeck (1620–1692) was assigned a position next to Frederick William of Brandenburg. Waldeck was a veteran of the Thirty Years' War in Dutch service, he had commanded the army in Prussia until 1655.

Major General Christoph von Kannenberg (1615–1673) commanded the first line of the Brandenburg wing. He was a veteran of the Thirty Years' War who had risen in the ranks from a common trooper in Swedish service.

Major General (*Generalwachtmeister*) Count Wolrad von Waldeck (1625–1657) was a brother of Georg Friedrich von Waldeck. Wolrad von Waldeck commanded the first line in the infantry centre.

Major General (*Generalwachtmeister*) Joachim Rüdiger von der Goltz (1620–1688) possibly commanded the second line in the infantry centre. A Prussian veteran of Imperial service in the Thirty Years' War, he then entered French service and ultimately entered into the service of Brandenburg in 1654 with the rank of colonel.

Swedish-Brandenburg Deployment

Although the broad events during the Battle of Warsaw are well known, there are major difficulties in reconciling the various sources when it comes to specific details. It is known that the Swedish-Brandenburg army was divided into a Swedish wing, a centre, and a Brandenburg wing. The initial order of battle can tentatively be set out as follows (all lines are described from left to right):

Swedish Wing: Cavalry

Commanded by King Charles, Duke Adolph John, and Field Marshal Lieutenant Robert Douglas

First line, commanded by Count Palatine Philip of Sulzbach.
Count Palatine Philip von Sulzbach's Dragoon Regiment
Count Palatine Philip von Sulzbach's Cavalry Regiment with the Life Guard of Horse
Her Royal Majesty the Queen's Life Regiment of Horse
Uppland Cavalry Regiment
Småland Cavalry Regiment
Östgöta Cavalry Regiment
Duke Adolph John's Cavalry Regiment
Colonel Jacob Johan Taube's Cavalry Regiment
Count Johann von Waldeck's Cavalry Regiment

Second line, commanded by Margrave Charles Magnus of Baden-Durlach.
Prince Bogusław Radziwiłł's Dragoon Regiment

Åbo Cavalry Regiment
Field Marshal Arvid Wittenberg's Cavalry Regiment
Margrave Charles Magnus of Baden-Durlach's Cavalry Regiment
Colonel David Sinclair's Cavalry Regiment
Colonel Per Hammarskiöld's Cavalry Regiment
Lieutenant Colonel Rutger von Ascheberg's Cavalry Regiment
Colonel Christian von Pretlach's Cavalry Regiment

Third line, commanded by Major General Henrik Horn together with (on the third day) Colonel Fabian Berndes.
Tavastehus Cavalry Regiment
Field Marshal Hans Christoph von Königsmarck's Cavalry Regiment
Colonel Jacob von Yxkull's Cavalry Regiment
Duke Charles of Mecklenburg-Schwerin's Cavalry Regiment
Colonel Wenzel Sadowski's Cavalry Regiment

Centre: Infantry

Commanded by Brandenburg General Otto Christoph von Sparr and Artillery Colonel Gustav Oxenstierna

First line, commanded by Brandenburg Major General Wolrad von Waldeck.
Södermanland Regiment
Västgöta-Dal Regiment
Kalmar Regiment
Uppland Regiment

Second line, possibly commanded by Brandenburg Major General Joachim Rüdiger von der Goltz.
Skaraborg Regiment
Hälsinge Regiment

Third line, commanded by Major General Barthold Hartwig von Bülow.
Colonel Johann Georg von Sieberg's Regiment
Major General Joachim Rüdiger von der Goltz's Regiment
Major General Wolrad von Waldeck's Regiment
General Otto Christoph von Sparr's Regiment

Brandenburg Wing: Cavalry

Commanded by Frederick William of Brandenburg, Field Marshal Carl Gustav Wrangel, and Lieutenant General Georg Friedrich von Waldeck.

First line, commanded by Major General Christoph von Kannenberg.
Major General Christoph von Kannenberg's Cavalry Regiment
Count Georg Friedrich von Waldeck's Cavalry Regiment
The Elector's Life Regiment of Horse

Second line, commanded by Major General Claes Tott and Major General Hans Böddeker.
Count Georg Friedrich von Waldeck's Dragoon Regiment
Major General Hans Böddeker's Cavalry Regiment
Colonel Israel Isacsson Ridderhielm's Cavalry Regiment
Field Marshal Carl Gustav Wrangel's Cavalry Regiment
Västgöta Cavalry Regiment
Colonel Elias von Canitz's Dragoon Regiment

Third line, commanded by Swedish Duke Charles of Mecklenburg-Schwerin.
Colonel Christoph de Brunell's Cavalry Squadron
Colonel Heinrich von Kalnein's Cavalry Squadron
Colonel Georg von Schönaich's Cavalry Regiment
Duke John George of Saxe-Weimar's Cavalry Regiment
Colonel Wolf Ernst von Eller's Cavalry Regiment
Colonel Christian Ludwig von Kalckstein's Dragoon Regiment

Some details remain uncertain: we do not know where Lieutenant Colonel Kehrberg's small cavalry unit was deployed, although it was presumably incorporated into one of the other cavalry squadrons. The position of Colonel Georg Friedrich von Canitz's Regiment of Horse, in Swedish service, is also uncertain.

The Commonwealth Army

It is no easy task to estimate the strength of the Commonwealth armies that participated in the Battle of Warsaw. As is often the case with researching the strength of the Polish and Lithuanian armies during a campaign or battle, the task is very difficult due to the number of contradictory sources and the rather wide range of figures given by different authors. In his study of the battle published in 1870, August Riese pointed out how arduous the task was to compile and compare such numbers. He examined eight different accounts, mostly written in German, showing that they clearly contradict each other, adding a great deal of confusion to the research on this subject.

The strength of the Polish regular army varied in the sources from 8,000 to 50,000; the Lithuanian army between 5,000 and 30,000; the Polish levy of nobility between 16,000 and 60,000; while the allied Tatar contingent was described as anything from 6,000 to 85,000 men. Interestingly, the estimates of the foreign infantry (most likely including dragoons) was pretty accurate, in the range of 4,000 to 6,000 men. Two accounts also mention armed camp servants, with one claiming their number as 15,000 and the other as 80,000. Such huge discrepancies in the strength of the elements of the Commonwealth army gives the total number of soldiers and armed servants (including Tatars) as from 39,000 to 197,000 men.[15] One of the most interesting accounts, containing information from inside the Polish camp, can be found in the despatches of Georg Barkmann, who was envoy of the City of Danzig to the Royal Court of King John Casimir. He seems to have had access to informants in the councils of war, providing him with access to campaign planning and information directly from the King's inner circle. At the same time, it is worth noting that his estimates of the strength of the Polish-Lithuanian army seems to be greatly exaggerated, and one has to wonder if he was intentionally fed incorrect data, to make a better impression on the Danzig City Council. For example, according to him, in mid-July three 'divisions' of the Polish army (Potocki and Lanckoroński, Czarniecki, Lubomirski) were supposed to have 60,000 cavalry, divided into three contingents of 20,000 each, while the Lithuanian army was 12,000 men strong.[16] With such a level of inconsistency with accounts of the battle, in order to capture more accurately the strength of King John Casimir's army, we need to look more closely into surviving documents describing the structure and organisation of both the Polish and Lithuanian armies of 1656. These should provide a more accurate base for the analysis, which can be then further filtered and reinforced with other primary sources.

Polish Troops

In the second quarter of 1656 the national cavalry in the Polish army was composed of seven banners of hussars (1,025 horses), 123 banners of *pancerni* and cossack cavalry (13,264 horses), 11 banners of Tatar light cavalry (1,343 horses) and 15 banners of Wallachian light cavalry (1,411 horses). They were divided into 17 to 19 regiments (*pułki*) of different size and strength, from large ones of up to 20 banners to very small ones with only three or four banners.

Of these regiments, two – Jerzy Lubomirski's and Jacek Szemberk's – were not present at Warsaw, as they were part of the division sent to besiege Cracow. It is estimated that they had at least 19 banners, with a paper strength of 2,275 horses; they included one banner of hussars (Lubomirski's own), at least one banner of Wallachian light cavalry (Szemberk's), and the rest of the units were made up of cossack cavalry. Lubomirski also had with him his other own units of the regular army: a regiment of reiters (307 horses), a regiment of German infantry under Mikołaj Konstanty Giza (1,476 portions), and a dragoon banner (100 horses). There were also at least four banners of Polish-Hungarian infantry (520 portions). So in total 2,685 horses and 1,996 portions of infantry of the regular army were detached under the command of

15 August Riese, *Die dreitägige Schlacht bei Warschau 28., 29. und 30. Juli 1656* (Breslau: Verlag von Max Mälzer, 1870), pp.72–74.

16 Johann Gustav Droysen, *Die Schlacht von Warschau 1656* (Leipzig: S. Hirzel, 1863), p.145.

Lubomirski and were unavailable to take part in battle at Warsaw. These units were also supported by the levy of nobility from Cracow and Sandomierz Voivodeships and some irregular troops.[17]

While we do not know the exact structure of the cavalry regiments present at Warsaw, it is at least possible to provide identification for 15 of them. Regiments were customarily known by the name or official title of their commander. The list also includes those units that were detached under Czarniecki's command during the first two days of the battle and were only present during the final day of battle:

King John II Casimir (the so-called Royal regiment), under the command of Stefan Czarniecki, Castellan of Kiev
Crown Grand Hetman Stanisław 'Rewera' Potocki, under the command of Lieutenant Sebastian Machowski (in charge of the hetman's hussar banner)
Crown Field Hetman Stanisław Lanckoroński, under the command of Lieutenant Jakub Rokitnicki (in charge of the hetman's hussar banner)
Aleksander Koniecpolski, Voivode of Sandomierz
Stanisław Witowski, Castellan of Sandomierz
Jan Fryderik Sapieha, Crown Field Scribe
Jan Zamoyski, Crown Vice Cup-bearer
Aleksander Zamoyski, Crown Guardian
Jan Sobieski, Crown Standard Bearer
Andrzej Potocki, Crown Camp Master
Mariusz Jaskólski, possibly under command of Michał Zbrożek
Prince Dymitr Wiśniowiecki
Seweryn Mikołaj Kaliński, *starosta* of Bracław
Stefan Piaseczyński
Jerzy Bałaban, *starosta* of Trembowla

In total, the Polish cavalry at Warsaw had 137 banners, with a paper strength of just over 14,700 horses. Amongst them were five banners of hussars: the Royal banner (199 horses), Grand Hetman Potocki's (202 horses), Field Hetman Lanckoroński's (88 horses), Jan Zamoyski's (137 horses), and Władysław Myszkowski's (165 horses). Of two other units that were in service during the second quarter of 1656, the banner of Adam Działyński (only 44 horses) had probably already been disbanded by the time of the battle, as it was certainly no longer on the army roster by the third quarter of the year. The last unit, under Lubomirski, accompanied him in the Cracow campaign. According to Jakub Łoś, Polish hussars were not equipped with lances.[18]

From the paper strength of the available units, we need to reduce at least 10 percent for 'dead pays' in officers' retinues; and additionally an unknown and unspecified number for combat and non-combat (i.e. sickness) losses taken during the campaigning prior to the battle – probably reducing

17 Jarosław Stolicki, 'Oblężenie Krakowa przez Jerzego Lubomirskiego w latach 1656–1657', *Studia i Materiały do Historii Wojskowości*, vol. 40 (Białystok: Ośrodek Badań Historii Wojskowej Muzeum Wojska w Białymstoku, 2003), pp.95–100.

18 Łoś, *Pamiętnik towarzysza chorągwi pancernej*, p.68.

overall strength by at least another 10 percent. We need to remember that all cavalry had seen its share of fighting in the months preceding the events at Warsaw: the Battles of Warka on 7 April, at Gniezno (Kłeck) on 7 May and Exin (Kcynia) on 1 June. While there may have been some opportunities to recruit new men and replace some losses during July and August, it is fairly certain that many banners were far from their full strength. So it is safe to assume that Polish regular cavalry units at Warsaw did not exceed 12,000 men, and it is possible that the actual number was even lower than that. It is interesting that Patrick Gordon, who during the battle was in the Polish camp, mentioned only 8,000 *quartianers*, by which he means soldiers of the 'quarter army'.[19] While this formation was disbanded in 1652, after the Battle of Batoh, the term *kwarciani* was still used in Poland as the name for regular soldiers, so it is hardly surprising that the Scottish mercenary picked up the word and used it in his diary (the term frequently appeared for Polish regulars in Swedish reports, too, even though they knew that the formation had been disbanded). While 8,000 seems to be a very low estimate, it could indicate that such numbers were mentioned amongst the soldiers in the Polish camp. The Polish army was in a particularly bad shape, both due to losses taken so far in the campaign and, especially, due to severely lacking their pay. which was overdue. There was growing discontent amongst the troops, as, despite capturing Warsaw, soldiers had not received their promised share of the loot; with the majority – as it was believed – taken by the King and Queen.[20] This can in some way explain why regular soldiers were not so eager to follow John Casimir's orders during the battle.

With regard to the 'foreign' units, at Warsaw there were four regiments of German infantry, with their paper strength based on the second quarter of 1656, together 3,871 portions, so probably no more than 3,500 soldiers:

Royal Guard of Foot regiment under Major General Wilhelm Butler – 963 portions
Regiment of Crown Artillery General Krzysztof Grodzicki – 743 portions
Regiment of Colonel Ernst Magnus Grothusen (former unit of Jan Sapieha) - 997 portions
Regiment of Jan Zamoyski, Voivode of Sandomierz – 1,168 portions (new unit, created at the beginning of 1656)

As for the rest of the German infantry units, Lubomirski's regiment marched with him to Cracow, while three smaller regiments were deployed as garrison units, so were not present at the battle.

Another part of the 'foreign' troops were the dragoons, with the largest unit at Warsaw being the Royal Guard regiment under Johann Heinrich von Alten-Bockum, with eight companies and a paper strength of 967 horses. Attached to this dragoon unit was a small company of reiters under Captain Franciszek Bieliński (96 horses) that served as the King's bodyguard. There

19 *Diary of General Patrick Gordon of Auchleuchries 1635–1699,* vol. 1, p.111.
20 Jemiołowski, *Pamiętnik dzieje Polski zawierający (1648–1679)*, p.208.

was an unspecified number of other dragoon units, estimated as between 500 and 700 horses. It is highly probable that among the units present were the squadron of Hetman Stanisław Potocki (238 horses), the squadron of Aleksander Koniecpolski (158 horses), and the newly-raised banner of Jan Zamoyski (144 horses). It is also possible that the private unit of Konstanty Lubomirski (80 horses) was part of these troops as well. Patrick Gordon wrote about '4,000 foot and dragouns' at Warsaw, although it seems that his estimate is on the low side, as, even excluding 'dead pays' and previous losses, 5,000 seems to be more accurate.[21] It is unclear whether Stefan Czarniecki's dragoon regiment was present at Warsaw. The unit was being rebuilt and reinforced since late 1655 and in the second quarter of 1656 had, on paper, 894 horses. As the recruitment process took a long time and, in spring 1656 some companies were detached to the garrison of Przemyśl, it is possible that the regiment did not operate as a whole in July 1656. Only Barkmann mentioned its presence in his account, when he wrote that some of Czarniecki's dragoons were detached to reinforce Grothusen's infantry.[22] No other Polish source listed this unit as being present at Warsaw. It is possible though, that some companies of the regiment, probably no more than few hundred men, fought in the battle.

With regard to the Polish-Hungarian infantry, none of the primary sources mention any specific unit of such infantry as being present at Warsaw. At the time, there were 12 banners with a total of 1,626 portions in service but the majority were stationed as garrison units or, as already mentioned, had been sent with Lubomirski to take part in the siege of Cracow. It is still possible that units of main officials, such as Hetman Potocki (130 portions) and Hetman Lanckoroński (120 portions) were present, although alongside some private units of Polish magnates. In total all such units would probably have been no more than a few hundred men. There is no information about their activities during the battle so it is possible that they were relegated to protecting the camp or were left inside Warsaw. However, when writing about the siege of Warsaw, Łoś mentioned that '[our] infantry was good, both Hungarian and German', suggesting that at least some banners of Polish-Hungarian infantry were present with the army.[23]

As it was often the case with Polish armies, the artillery accompanying the army was neither very strong nor very well prepared to properly support the troops: lacking sufficient numbers of guns and supplies. It is possible that foreign infantry regiments had a few regimental cannon attached and which were used to support the troops during the defence of the field fortifications. The heavier pieces were deployed in three main batteries protected by infantry, but with probably no more than 20 guns in total. Barkmann wrote that during the muster in mid-July the army had 30 cannon, most of them heavy and 'none below 12 pounds', although it is not known if they were all deployed during the Battle of Warsaw.[24]

21 *Diary of General Patrick Gordon of Auchleuchries 1635–1699*, vol. 1, p.111.

22 Droysen, *Die Schlacht von Warschau 1656*, p.149.

23 Łoś, *Pamiętnik towarzysza chorągwi pancernej*, p.68.

24 Riese, *Die dreitägige Schlacht bei Warschau 28., 29. und 30. Juli 1656*, p.72.

Between 25,000 and 30,000 of the levy of nobility were present during the siege of the capital, where of course they did not play an important military role, although their presence was a clear indication of the support for King John Casimir. Amongst those present were levies from Voivodeships of Greater Poland (Wielkopolska), Sieradz, Łęczyca, Mazowsze, Cracow, Sandomierz, Lublin, Podlachia (Podlasie), Ruthenia, Volhynia, and Bełż.[25] A large part of them returned home after the capture of Warsaw, and it is estimated that around 10,000–13,000 were present during the battle on 28–30 July 1656.[26] Patrick Gordon provides a higher number though, mentioning '16,000 of the country gentry'.[27] The vast majority of the levy would serve as cossack cavalry, although even within each banner there would be a wide variety of equipment, e.g. many men would be without mail or firearms, or were mounted on poor horses. A percentage of the levy would have been equipped as hussars, grouped into their own banners, although there is no detailed information about numbers of such equipped nobles, so there is no basis for even rough estimates of their strength.

As always, the army was accompanied by a large number of armed camp servants, especially those serving the cavalry – known as *luźna czeladź*. During the battle they could provide cavalry with fresh mounts, take care of wounded and of prisoners, and were always eager to plunder the battlefield. However, they would be of no use against regular troops of the Swedish and Brandenburg armies in open battle. In the Polish army's camp there were also several thousand armed peasants who had taken part in the siege of Warsaw. While they were of some use during 'small war', utilising guerrilla tactics, they would be, as with camp servants, of no importance in a battle.

Lithuanian Troops

It is much more difficult to even estimate the size of the Lithuanian army at the time of the Battle of Warsaw. Paweł Jan Sapieha, who since autumn 1655 had been reorganising loyalist Lithuanian forces, was in March 1656 nominated as the new Lithuanian Grand Hetman. His soldiers were a mixture of former units serving under the command of Janusz Radziwiłł and newly created units, with many of the latter raised in the first half of 1656. Additionally, since Field Hetman Wincenty Aleksander Korwin Gosiewski managed in spring 1656 to flee from captivity and re-joined the army, he had also started recruiting new units. It led to a split of the Lithuanian army into two divisions: the right wing under Sapieha and the left wing under Gosiewski. By mid-1656 the total paper strength of the regular Lithuanian Army was:

3 banners of hussars – 600 horses
37 banners of cossack cavalry – 5,148 horses

25 Mirosław Nagielski, *Bitwa pod Warszawą 1656* (Warszawa: Bellona, 2007), pp.242–243.
26 Nagielski, *Bitwa pod Warszawą 1656*, p.243.
27 *Diary of General Patrick Gordon of Auchleuchries 1635–1699*, vol. 1, p.111.

16 banners of Tatar light horse – 1,920 horses
2 regiments/squadrons and five banners/companies of dragoons – 1,760 horses
3 companies of German infantry – 380 portions
3 banners of Polish-Hungarian infantry – 440 portions

In total 10,248 horses and portions, which gives approximately 8,500 to 9,000 men (after allowing for dead pays et cetera). Sapieha's division was much the stronger, with close to 8,000 horses and portions; the remainder were under Gosiewski's command, although he was gradually strengthening his division in the second part of 1656.[28] There were also further units that supported the regular army: private units of the Lithuanian magnates, district troops, and unpaid volunteers. Although, as it is highly unlikely that any of these were present at Warsaw, they would not affect the overall headcount of the Lithuanian soldiers.

Five Lithuanian cavalry regiments under command of Hetman Sapieha can be identified at Warsaw. As with Polish troops, these units were known from the name of the nominal commander of the regiment:

King John II Casimir (so-called Royal regiment), under command of Aleksander Hilary Połubiński
Lithuanian Grand Hetman Paweł Jan Sapieha, under command of Władysław Jerzy Chalecki
Michał Kazimierz Radziwiłł
Krzysztof Franciszek Sapieha
Filip Kazimierz Obuchowicz, Voivode of Smolensk (Obuchowicz himself had died earlier in the campaign)

It is possible that other regiments of Sapieha's command – like those of Jerzy Karol Hlebowicz or Zygmunt Adam Słuszko – were also a part of the army gathered at Warsaw, although no sources confirm this. As such, it is not possible to confirm if the Grand Hetman had managed to assemble all of the troops of his division, which in part explains why estimates of Lithuanian strength at Warsaw varies, from the 5,000 men given by Patrick Gordon to the 7,000 men based on the overall calculation of the units that could have been present.[29]

An interesting indication of how understrength Lithuanian units were comes from a document that presents the size of banners that in May 1656 arrived in the vicinity of Warsaw. The Royal hussar banner under Połubiński had 147 horses (against a theoretical strength of 200 horses), while Hetman Sapieha's hussar banner had 193 horses (out of a theoretical strength of 200). Much worse was the situation of cossack cavalry banners: Hetman Sapieha's with 84 horses (out of a 200 establishment), Jerzy Karol Hlebowicz's with 53 (out of 150 establishment), Filip Kazimierz Obuchowicz's with 53 (of a paper

28 Rachuba, 'Wysiłek mobilizacyjny Wielkiego Księstwa Litewskiego w latach 1654–1667', pp.49–52.
29 *Diary of General Patrick Gordon of Auchleuchries 1635–1699,* vol. 1, p.111.

strength of 123), Mikołaj Samuel Szemiot's with 55 (establishment of 120), Bobrownicki's with 60 (this unit remains unidentified) and Zygmunt Adam Smuszka's with 80 (out of a paper strength of 175); only Połubiński's banner was shown at a full strength of 120 horses.[30] While it is a fairly small sample, it clearly shows that even the 5,000 Lithuanian troops at Warsaw may be too high an estimate.

The Lithuanian contingent was mostly a cavalry force, predominantly composed of cossack cavalry and light horse, supported by some dragoons. As in the Polish army, there were also armed camp servants attached to the cavalry units. Amongst Sapieha's division were just two banners of hussars: the royal banner under Połubiński, and Sapieha's banner under Władysław Jerzy Chalecki. As mentioned, each of these units had a paper strength of 200 horses, although due to 'dead pays' and previous campaigning losses, in total they probably had around 300 men. Unlike their Polish counterparts, Lithuanian hussars seems to have been equipped with lances.[31] Field Hetman Gosiewski and his division (at least 1,500 men) were operating outside of the main army, as since mid-July they had been despatched on a reconnaissance mission to Tykocin. It is very possible that Gosiewski took his own hussars banner with him as well, and so this unit was not present at Warsaw.

To summarise, the Polish regular army probably had around 10,000–12,000 cavalry and up to 5,000 infantry and dragoons, while the Lithuanian contingent did not exceed 6,000 men (mostly cavalry). They were supported by the Polish levy of nobility, probably between 10,000 and 13,000 men, of which the vast majority served as cossack cavalry. Artillery support consisted of between 20 and 30 guns. A summary is given below. The strength of the allied Tatars contingent is discussed below.

Summary of known units of the Commonwealth Army at the Battle of Warsaw, 28–30 July 1656

(see main text for further details)

Crown Army

His Royal Highness's Regiment, commanded by Stefan Czarniecki
Crown Grand Hetman Stanisław 'Rewera' Potocki's Regiment
Crown Field Hetman Stanisław Lanckoroński's Regiment
Aleksander Koniecpolski's Regiment
Stanisław Witowski's Regiment
Jan Fryderyk Sapieha's Regiment
Jan Zamoyski's Regiment
Aleksander Zamoyski's Regiment

30 Biblioteka Książąt Czartoryskich (BCzart.), no. 2749, 352, Andrzej Rachuba, 'Wysiłek mobilizacyjny Wielkiego Księstwa Litewskiego w latach 1654–1667', p.49.

31 Łoś, *Pamiętnik towarzysza chorągwi pancernej*, p.68.

Jan Sobieski's Regiment
Andrzej Potocki's Regiment
Mariusz Jaskólski's Regiment, commanded by Michał Zbrożek
Dymitri Wiśniowieckis's Regiment
Seweryn Mikołaj Kaliński's Regiment
Stefan Piaseczyński's Regiment
Jerzy Bałaban's Regiment

His Royal Highness's Guard Dragoon Regiment, under Johann Heinrich von Alten-Bockum
His Royal Highness's Royal Guard of Foot, under Wilhelm Butler
Krzysztof Grodzicki's Regiment of Foot
Colonel Ernst Magnus Grothusen's Regiment of Foot
Jan Zamoyski's Regiment of Foot

Other dragoon or infantry units, including those of:
Hetman Stanisław Potocki
Aleksander Koniecpolski
Jan Zamoyski

Lithuanian Army

His Royal Highness's Lithuanian Regiment, under Lithuanian Field Scribe Aleksander Hilary Połubiński
Lithuanian Grand Hetman Paweł Jan Sapieha's Regiment
Prince Michał Kazimierz Radziwiłł's Regiment
Krzysztof Sapieha's Regiment
Filip Krzysztof Obuchowicz's Regiment (Obuchowicz himself had died earlier in the campaign)

The Crimean Tatar Army

The Tatar army from the Crimea was independent and did not form a part of the Commonwealth army, and the Crimean Khanate was not at war with Sweden. Actually, Swedish–Tatar relations were usually friendly, since both states often faced common enemies. Nonetheless, Mehmed Khan had sent a Crimean Tatar force, commanded by Subhan Ghazi Agha, to assist King John Casimir. It is not known if Mehmed Khan realised that this involved fighting the Swedish army. King Charles in his diplomatic correspondence chose to regard the participation of the Crimean contingent in the subsequent battle not as a declaration of war by the Khanate but as the result of Subhan Ghazi Agha exceeding his orders.

The strength of the auxiliary contingent provided by Mehmed Khan is highly debatable, as sources provide us with a rather confusing and very contradictory picture. Pierre des Noyers, secretary of Queen Louise Marie mentioned in some of his letters very high numbers of Tatars, based on the rumours that arrived at the Royal Court. On 13 April 1656 he noted that it can be confirmed 'without a doubt' that 10,000 Tatars were marching to Mazowsze, to support the uprising of the Polish nobles and to prevent the Swedish units there from joining King Charles. Another 20,000 Tatars were to arrive with King John Casimir and 'march wherever they are ordered'.[32] On 18 May 1656 he went even further, clearly indicating that the news that arrived at the Polish Court in exile was highly exaggerated. This time, based on the letters received from Poland, there were supposed to be 30,000 Tatars marching in the vanguard, with an even stronger army, led by the Khan himself, following them, 'with a hope that they can pillage Pomerania and Livonia'.[33] By the beginning of July 1656 Pierre des Noyers mentioned that Tatars were not so willing to leave the Khanate and march to Poland, as they were concerned that in the absence of the larger part of their military force, cossacks might use the opportunity to attack Crimea. As the overall situation in Poland was improving, the Poles were not overly keen to see such a troublesome ally. Tatars, 'as a sign of their willingness [to help], were sending 15,000–20,000 men instead of 80,000'.[34] But his estimate of the Tatar auxiliaries at Warsaw is completely unreliable, as in the letter dated 27 July 1656, written from Warsaw, there is a note that the Tatars are just three leagues (about 10km) from the city and that their strength is '35,000 warriors alone and [with them] 50,000 servants, who are as good fighters as their masters.'[35] For their presence in the battle itself, Noyers provided a much more realistic figure, writing about 5,000 Tatars taking part in the fight.[36]

Noyers was not the only one who overestimated the strength of the Crimean contingent. According to the highly exaggerated opinion of Mikołaj Jemiołowski, there were 20,000 Tatars.[37] Joachim Jerlicz gave an even larger number, mentioning that, in early July 'a horde of 40,000 men' was marching through Volhynia towards Warsaw.[38] Stanisław Wierzbowski, who based his description on the relation of his father, Łukasz, wrote that the Polish-Lithuanian army was supported by 10,000 Tatars.[39] The seventeenth century historian Wawrzyniec Jan Rudawski, in his work describing the reign of King John Casimir, mentioned 20,000 Tatars.[40] The latter number seems to be based on the letter from Mehmed Khan to King John Casimir, in which the Crimean Khan said that he despatched 20,000 *Noghai* Tatars from the

32 Pierre des Noyers, *Lettres de Pierre des Noyers* (Berlin: B. Behr, 1859), p.133.

33 Noyers, *Lettres*, p.166.

34 Noyers, *Lettres*, p.195.

35 Noyers, *Lettres*, p.208.

36 Noyers, *Lettres*, p.215.

37 Jemiołowski, *Pamiętnik dzieje Polski zawierający (1648–1679)*, pp.208–209.

38 Joachim Jerlicz, *Latopisiec albo kroniczka*, vol. 1 (Warszawa: Kazimierz Władysław Wóycicki, 1853), p.184.

39 Stanisław Wierzbowski, *Konnotata wypadków w domu i w kraju zaszłych od 1634 do 1689 r.* (Lipsk: Księgarnia Zagraniczna, 1858), p.102.

40 Wawrzyniec Jan Rudawski, *Historja Polska od śmierci Władysława IV aż do pokoju oliwskiego*, vol. 2 (Petersburg-Mohylew: Nakładem Bolesława Maurycego Wolffa, 1855), p.141.

Budjak Horde.[41] Barkmann wrote about '20,000 Tatar boyars [nobles] and their servants', clearly relying on the rumours spread in the Polish ranks.[42] An anonymous Swedish or Brandenburg description of the battle, published in German in 1656, seems to be on the more cautious side, with the Tatars mentioned as 6,000 men.[43] Another anonymous account, this time published in Polish, estimated the contingent at 8,000 Tatars.[44]

Figures provided by soldiers present on the battlefield would seem to be much more accurate and tend to be used as a reliable base by modern researchers. Johan Martitz, secretary and valet to the Elector, was present at the battle and according to his notes, there were 8,000 Tatars present.[45] The Elector in his own account of the battle mentioned the attack of 2,000 Tatars, although that of course does not rule out that this was not the whole contingent.[46] Łoś described the Tatar contingent as 'several thousand chosen men'.[47] The Polish soldier and historian Wespazjan Kochowski wrote about 6,000 Tatars,[48] with the same number given by Patrick Gordon[49] and Samuel Pufendorf.[50] Yet, even experienced eyewitnesses may be wrong in their estimates. In his drawings and notes, the Swedish quartermaster and intelligence officer, Erik Dahlbergh, variously mentions 6,000, 10,000, and 18,000 Tatars, which shows that he did not actually know how many were present. Perhaps significantly, however, Dahlbergh estimated those Tatars who actually fought at any given moment as 6,000, with the higher numbers supposed to be the total strength of the Tatar contingent.

In his article published in 1957, Bohdan Baranowski acknowledges information provided by different sources but decided that numbers were too high and arbitrarily reduced the Tatar contingent to '2,000 [men] valiant but prone to pillage'.[51] For years his estimate was used by others, such as Mirosław Nagielski's monograph on the Battle of Warsaw. In 1997, based on estimates of the population of Budjak, Wiesław Majewski criticised such a reduction of the Tatar contingent at Warsaw and provided his own suggestion of 3,000–4,000 men[52] Considering that in 1620s the *Budjak* Horde was able to field

41 Ludwik Kubala, *Wojna Brandenburska i najazd Rakoczego w roku 1656 i 1657* (Lwów: H. Altenberg, G. Seyfarth, E. Wende i Sp, 1914), p.275.

42 Riese, *Die dreitägige Schlacht bei Warschau 28., 29. und 30. Juli 1656*, p.72; Droysen, *Die Schlacht von Warschau 1656*, p.145.

43 Droysen, *Die Schlacht von Warschau 1656*, p.122.

44 'Relacyja co się dzieje w Polszcze aż ad diem 23 augusti 1656' [in:] Mirosław Nagielski, *Bitwa pod Warszawą 1656*, p.230.

45 Johan Martitz, 'Gründliche Nachricht' [in:] Ernst Friedlaender 'Zur Schlacht bei Warschau', *Hohenzollern-Jahrbuch*, issue 2 [Berlin-Leipzig: Giesecke & Devrient,1898], p.246.

46 Droysen, *Die Schlacht von Warschau 1656*, p.110.

47 Łoś, *Pamiętnik towarzysza chorągwi pancernej*, p.69.

48 Wespazjan Kochowski, *Lata Potopu 1655–1657* (Warszawa: Wydawnictwo Ministerstwa Obrony Narodowej, 1967), 200.

49 *Diary of General Patrick Gordon of Auchleuchries 1635–1699,* vol. 1, p.111.

50 Pufendorf, *Sieben Bücher* vol. 3, p.180

51 Bohdan Baranowski, 'Tatarszczyzna wobec wojny polsko-szwedzkiej w latach 1655–1660' in *Polska w okresie Drugiej Wojny Północnej 1655–1660. Vol. 1. Rozprawy* (Warszawa: Państwowe Wydawnictwo Naukowe, 1957), p.479.

52 Wiesław Majewski, 'Działania wojenne w Prusach Książęcych, wrzesień 1656-luty 1657', *Komunikaty Mazursko-Warmińskie,* no. 4 (Olsztyn: Ośrodek Badań Naukowych im. Wojciecha

armies of 10,000 to 12,000 men and between the 1670s and 1690s regularly sent contingents of 4,000 *Noghai* Tatars on campaigns, it is possible that the Tatar contingent at Warsaw could be in fact stronger than 2,000 men.[53] Even the estimate of 6,000 men may not be far from the truth, with part of the strength composed of *nöker* warriors (household troops of Tatar nobles) and the rest of the force made up by the *seferlu* (levy of able-bodied men) and *qazganchi* servants. The Tatar contingent was led by Subhan Ghazi Agha (d. 1663), an experienced commander whom the Poles titled as 'Voivode of the Budjak Horde'. He had previously fought against the Commonwealth, supporting the Zaporozhian cossacks in 1648 and in 1649 taking part in the siege of Zbarazh. He was a supporter of 'small war' tactics, seeing it as much more beneficial and useful against the Swedes than an open battle.

Because of the many conflicting accounts and estimates, it is impossible to give a detailed Tatar order of battle. Following Kochowski, Gordon, Dahlbergh, and Pufendorf, it is likely that they had a combat strength of 6,000 Tatars.

Commonwealth Army Command

One of the issues that played a very important role in the Battle of Warsaw was the high command of the joint Polish-Lithuanian army. As King John Casimir was present, it was the usual custom that he would be commander-in-chief of the whole army. He had had some previous military experience in the Thirty Years' War and from the campaigns against Ukrainian cossacks; was personally brave and did not avoid leading his men from the front. At the Battle of Warsaw he commanded 'with fire in his eye and voice (it was heard that he was giving orders with 'In God's name' on his lips).'[54] As the French volunteer Antoine de Gramont described him during the subsequent 1663/1664 campaign against Muscovy, the King 'was kind, full of humanity, brave as his sword, and counted in his life many valiant deeds in which he always stood out personally.'[55] John Casimir seemed to rely on the advice of Sir John Henderson,[56] a Major General of the Imperial army, sent as military adviser by Emperor Ferdinand III. This Scottish Roman Catholic was a very experienced officer, with a long service record from the Thirty Years' War, during which he spent time in the ranks of the Danish, Swedish, and Imperial Armies. As well as his military career, he also dabbled as a spy, for both Charles II of England's court in exile and for Oliver Cromwell. This veteran officer of dragoons and infantry was definitely at odds with Polish officers, who had a completely different military experience and were used to

---

Kętrzyńskiego, 1997), pp.580–583.

53 Amet-chan A. Szejchumierow, *Armia Chanatu Krymskiego. Organizacja i taktyka (XV-XVIII w.)*, pp.101–102.

54 Kochowski, *Lata Potopu 1655–1657*, p.198.

55 Antoine de Gramont, *Iz istorii moskovskogo pokhoda Yana Kazimira, 1663–1664 g.g.* (Yuriev: Tipografiya *K. Mattisena, 1929), p.*16.

56 Polish sources often misspelled him as Anderson or Aderson.

an 'Eastern' style of warfare. Under Henderson's suggestions, John Casimir decided to order his infantry to build field fortification and use them as a central part of the battle plan.

Both main commanders of the Polish army: Grand Hetman Stanisław 'Rewera' Potocki (1589–1667) and Field Hetman Stanisław Lanckoroński (1590–1657), were present at Warsaw but their influence over the army was severely diminished. The King had not forgotten that in 1655 they had changed side and joined the Swedes, taking practically the whole regular army with them. While after the Tyszowce Confederation they came back to serve King John Casimir again, there was definitely a problem with his lack of trust of them. Furthermore, both were mediocre commanders, who, while personally brave, were neither talented strategists nor inspiring leaders. They spent the battle in the entourage of the King, neither eager to lead soldiers personally nor to play an important part in the events unfolding in the battle.

In a rather odd situation, two of the most talented Polish commanders were away from the army during the battle. Jerzy Sebastian Lubomirski (1616–1667) was leading his division against Cracow, while the King's *protégée*, *regimentarz* Stefan Czarniecki (1599–1665) for the first two days of the battle was despatched with some units upon a reconnaissance mission to Zakroczym.[57] His absence can be easily explained though, as he was strongly opposed to facing the Swedish-Brandenburg army in open battle, preferring to focus on a 'small war', sapping the strength and manpower of the invaders. The King, annoyed by Czarniecki's comments during the council of war that took place on 27 July 1656, sent him away to take him 'out of the picture' for a period. One has to wonder whether the presence of Czarniecki would have changed the situation during the crucial second day of the battle, especially during the organising of the follow-up to Połubiński's hussar charge. He led Polish cavalry during the final day of the battle and managed to extract most regiments without heavy losses.

The situation with the Lithuanian command was even more complicated. Grand Hetman Paweł Jan Sapieha (1609–1655) was present at Warsaw but prior to battle he had been injured. His horse fell on him and Sapieha suffered a sprained shinbone, which prevented him leading his troops during the battle. The injury seemed to bother him for quite some time, as after the battle he travelled to Brest (a town presently better known as Brest-Litovsk – that is Lithuanian Brest), to recover.[58] Field Hetman Wincenty Korwin Gosiewski (1620–1662) was, as mentioned above, absent with a large part of his division, and his troops were unable to reach Warsaw in time. Without those two main commanders, the Lithuanian army was under the command of Aleksander Hilary Połubiński (1626–1679), Lithuanian Field Scribe, lieutenant of the prestigious Royal hussar banner, and colonel of the Royal

57 In the seventeenth century Polish-Lithuanian Commonwealth, *regimentarz* was a temporary rank for the commander who was in charge of the army during the hetman's absence (due to death, captivity, or vacant office). Czarniecki, in a rather unique way, held this rank between 1656 and 1665, despite the presence of both Grand and Field Hetman.

58 Jan Antoni Chrapowicki, *Diariusz. Część pierwsza: lata 1656–1664* (Warszawa: Instytut Wydawniczy Pax, 1978), p.97.

regiment in the Lithuanian army. Despite his relatively young age, he was already a veteran officer and was known as a talented cavalry commander. At this stage of this career however, he lacked experience in leading larger group of soldiers, so was probably better suited to commanding a regiment than a whole division of the Lithuanian Army.

Another issue that affected the Commonwealth army was discord between high commanders. King John Casimir was eager to face the Swedes and Brandenburgers in battle, certain that his army was ready for the open fight. Barkmann mentioned an argument between the King and Stefan Czarniecki during one of the councils of war, probably on 27 July. While the King was pushing for battle, Czarniecki was suggesting a more cautious approach, claiming that *wojna szarpana* (hit-and-run tactics) were the best approach. The enraged King reportedly answered that 'you gentlemen do not wish to fight in the honest way, you have too much liking for these hit-and-run tactics'. Undeterred, Czarniecki answered that this way of waging war so far had 'thrown at his Majesty's feet 12,000 [defeated] enemies'. However, King John Casimir did not want to listen to this sound advice and ended the discussion with the strong warning that 'those who will not follow my orders will lose their heads.'[59] One can of course argue, that Danzig's envoy probably was not present during this council meeting, so his story could be just based on a hearsay and court rumours. But it provides an interesting explanation for the absence from the Battle of Warsaw of the ablest Polish cavalry commander.

As was pointed out by Czarniecki's biographer, Adam Kersten, the Polish *regimentarz* knew his troops very well, with all of their both positive and negatives aspects. So far in 1656, experience of campaigns was not good, with defeats at Gołąb, Gniezno (Kłeck) and Exin (Kcynia) proving that, when facing a prepared enemy, supported by infantry and artillery, Polish cavalry had little chance of achieving victory. The morale of the army was not good and any able commander should have been able to realise that the levy of nobility would not be of great use in the battle.[60]

While the King might have been encouraged by the victory at Warka, it is worth remembering that it was achieved under specific conditions, with overwhelming Polish force facing poorly led Swedish units, lacking proper infantry support and without artillery. It is interesting to add that the only other senior commander who sided with Czarniecki in supporting a reliance on 'small war' was Subhan Ghazi Agha. The Tatar was rather surprised that the Poles had given such lenient surrender terms to the garrison of Warsaw, allegedly saying, 'How could you send those soldiers back to the King of Sweden, when he [had previously] so many times broken his oaths to you?'[61] As he knew that his horsemen were of no use in an open battle, he strongly suggested keeping the Polish infantry and artillery on the left bank of the Vistula, with only regular cavalry and Tatars deployed to the right bank,

---

59 Droysen, *Die Schlacht von Warschau 1656*, 148.

60 Adam Kersten, *Stefan Czarniecki 1599–1665* (Lublin: Wydawnictwo Uniwersytetu Marii Curie-Skłodowskiej, 2006), 354.

61 *Portfolio królowej Maryi Ludwiki*, volume 2 (Poznań: Drukarnia i księgarnia Nowa, 1844), 57.

where they could harass the Allies, in order to 'surround the enemy, starve him, and thus force him to retreat.'[62]

King John Casimir could not be convinced to change his plans and the council of war had to follow his decision. Moreover, it appears that despite their massive advantage in numbers of cavalry and a strong contingent of light horse (both regular army and Tatars), the Commonwealth command was practically blind to the movement of the Allied army and was unaware that King Charles and Frederick William were already planning their own offensive – 28 July 1656 was to be day full of surprises for both sides…

---

62 Noyers, *Lettres*, 221.

7

The Three-Day Battle

Road to Battle

The period of spring and summer of 1656 brought a lot of changes in the military and political situation in Poland. While the majority of the country had fallen to the Swedes, resistance against invaders was growing, often limiting their area of control to towns and fortresses. More and more of the Polish regular soldiers, previously serving the Swedes, were changing side and returning to the service of King John Casimir.

At the end of March 1656, the Swedish field army, led by King Charles, was trapped at Gorzyce, between the Vistula and San rivers, but managed to slip past the Lithuanian army and continue towards Warsaw. At the same time, Polish troops, under Stefan Czarniecki and Jerzy Sebastian Lubomirski, destroyed a Swedish relief force at the Battle of Warka on 7 April 1656. It was the first major Polish victory over the Swedes in a formal battle during this war and, while it helped King Charles evade the Polish-Lithuanian trap because of the absence of the main Polish army, it also provided a great boost to the morale of the Commonwealth army.[1] On 21 April, the Polish army, under the command of John Casimir, opened the siege of Warsaw, which was defended by a Swedish garrison under Arvid Wittenberg. At the same time, part of the Polish army – again under the joint command of Czarniecki and Lubomirski – campaigned in Greater Poland, but was defeated at the Battle of Gniezno (also known as the Battle of Kłecko) on 7 May. Warsaw surrendered on 1 July to the combined Polish and Lithuanian armies.

However, the Swedes were not idle. As the Polish soldier and historian Wespazjan Kochowski wrote in his description of the war, 'To cut the story short, [the Swedish King] Charles neglected nothing to increase his strength. He moved heaven and earth, and even hell.'[2] At the end of June

1 By attacking the relief force, a lesser threat, Czarniecki and Lubomirski spoiled their chances of neutralising the greater – the Swedish main army under King Charles, and at a time when that army was almost out of powder.

2 Kochowski, *Lata Potopu 1655–1657*, p.195.

1656, Frederick William and King Charles met in Preussisch Holland (Pasłęk) where they discussed planned military actions. On 14 July 1656, two corps of the Brandenburg army, that included both Brandenburger and Prussian troops, concentrated at Szreńsk, 100km north-west of Warsaw. The Elector had under his command almost 10,000 men: 60 companies of cavalry (4,800 men), 13 companies of dragoons (1,000 men) and 42 companies of infantry (4,000 men), supported by at least 14 guns.[3] After the muster, the army marched to the Swedish camp at Nowy Dwór from where both armies planned to attack the Lithuanian units deployed on the right bank of the River Vistula. Once that threat was neutralised, the Allies then planned to capture a bridgehead at Praga,[4] in order to destroy the bridge there, and afterwards move the army across to the left bank of the Vistula at Zakroczym and, in a surprise attack, strike into the vulnerable rear of the Polish and Lithuanian Armies.

As mentioned, in the early summer of 1656, the Commonwealth command was practically blind to the movement of the Allied army and was unaware that King Charles and Frederick William were already planning their own offensive. The Commonwealth commanders did not have a real plan of action prior to the Swedish-Brandenburg offensive, only a rather general idea about what to do next with their own forces.

The Swedes had two fortified camps near Warsaw: one at Nowy Dwór near Modlin under the command of Duke Adolph John, and the other at Pomiechów at the River Wkra under the command of Robert Douglas. Some Swedish units were also involved in a relief mission to Tykocin, which since May had been besieged by a mixed force of Lithuanian regulars, Polish levy of nobility, and irregulars. In June 1656, the Poles sent scouts towards Nowy Dwór, but the resultant skirmishes with the Swedes did not escalate into larger military actions. In early July, due to the torrential rain, the River Vistula flooded and destroyed bridges at Warsaw and Zakroczym, while the one at Nowy Dwór, over the River Bug, was destroyed soon after as well.

In mid-July, upon learning about the Swedish relief operation to Tykocin, King John Casimir decided to send Lithuanian Field Hetman Gosiewski and his men to the fortress, to engage the Swedish units there. Gosiewski was late, however, and could not prevent Douglas and his cavalry from scattering the besiegers at Tykocin. The Hetman therefore decided to change his plans, on 22 July attempting to besiege Pułtusk, north of Warsaw. However, after a few days he had to order a retreat in the face of the Swedish King leading a cavalry force against him, and the Lithuanians crossed the River Narew to avoid the Swedes. King Charles mustered his troops at Nowy Dwór, with the Elector and his army stationed 30km away.

By late July, the Commonwealth headquarters finally prepared a plan for an offensive. Some units were to cover the left bank of the River Vistula and protect Warsaw from possible attack, with a few Polish infantry banners deployed as a garrison of the capital. The main army, under command of

3 Augusiewicz, *Przebudowa wojska pruskiego w latach 1655–1660. U źródeł nowożytnej armii*, pp.206–208.

4 Currently the right (eastern) bank district of Warsaw, until 1791 it was a separate town.

King John Casimir, was to cross to right bank of the river, join the Lithuanian army already deployed there and, after crossing the River Narew, strike against the Swedish army camp at Nowy Dwór. It was hoped that the Swedish troops stationed there could be defeated before the arrival of reinforcements led by King Charles and the Elector. Part of the Tatar auxiliary contingent was to cross the River Bug at Nieporęt and outflank the camp at Nowy Dwór to its north. As they could be potentially vulnerable to the heavy fire of the Swedish soldiers, 'some Lithuanian troops were attached to them as fire [firearm armed] men (as Tatars require such assistance).'[5] Czarniecki and his Polish cavalry were to be sent to the left bank of the Vistula, in order to operate near Zakroczym and block the crossing on the River Bug there from being used by Swedes and Brandenburgers. The plan was devised by King John Casimir, and as we have seen, it faced opposition from Czarniecki, who was against meeting the Allies in open battle. Czarniecki argued that the Commonwealth Army should avoid open battle, since the Swedes had the superior firepower; Subhan Ghazi Agha made the same observation. However, King John Casimir overruled them both.

In short, having taken Warsaw and restored a semblance of order among his men, King John Casimir wanted to move north, cross the River Bug, and advance on the Swedish and Brandenburg armies before they could join forces. North of the Bug, King Charles had the same idea: to move south with the Swedish Army alone, without awaiting the arrival of the Brandenburgers, so that he could defeat the Commonwealth armies one at a time. However, the water-level of both the Vistula and the Bug was too great to immediately allow a safe crossing for either party. King John Casimir had first to rebuild a bridge across the Vistula at Warsaw, and his men seem to have been ill-prepared for engineering work. The bridge was only ready for use on 27 July.

While awaiting completion of the new bridge, John Casimir had parts of the Crown army ferried across the Vistula, intending to confront the Swedish army on the right (east) bank of the river. These Crown units joined with the Lithuanian army already on the right bank. Then they dug in, following the expert advice of John Henderson, who had joined the King's staff as an adviser sent by the Emperor and who like many Imperial officers was a skilled military engineer. Meanwhile, following the orders of his King, Czarniecki moved north along the left (west) bank with perhaps 2,000 men under his command. His orders were to monitor the progress of the Allied armies. Just as at Sandomierz earlier in the year, the Commonwealth armies proved unable to coordinate their movements and as a result King John Casimir's forces became widely separated from one another. The King himself with the Crown army and Czarniecki's cavalry army deployed on the left bank of the Vistula, but at some distance from each other, while the Lithuanians and Crimean Tatars took up positions on the right bank. Their opponents were not, however, so separated; on the same day that King John Casimir's bridge was ready, Frederick William joined forces with King Charles at Nowy Dwór, where the Swedes had erected a bridge across the River Bug.

5 Nagielski, *Bitwa pod Warszawą 1656*, p.223.

As a result, King Charles seized the initiative. Crossing the Bug on 28 July, he marched down the right (east) bank of the Vistula, confronting the Commonwealth troops.

The Swedish-Brandenburg plan required a fast march to surprise their enemies, so it was decided that most of the supply train and the heavy artillery would be left in the camp. Left with them, to guard against possible incursions of Tatars, were approximately 2,000 Swedish soldiers. As the Allied command expected to return to Nowy Dwór quickly, the soldiers took with them only three days of provisions. In July the sun rises early (around 4:51–4:54 a.m. on each day of the battle), which facilitated the crossing. King Charles ordered Major General Claes Tott ahead with a vanguard that would ultimately consist of both Swedish and Brandenburg horse. Between 7:00 and 8:00 a.m., the Swedish vanguard, 300 cavalry under Tott, began slowly to advance towards Praga. The Brandenburgers set out later, meaning that the total number of men in the vanguard depends on the time of the morning, and as a result, accounts give its strength from 600 to 1,000 cavalry.

The march took longer than anticipated because of the narrow road and the hot summer weather. To compound the problem, a section of the bridge over the Bug collapsed, and while Swedish engineers were at hand to repair the damage, it took four hours to fix it, further delaying the main body of the Brandenburg cavalry that constituted the rearguard.

Swedish soldiers facing Sandomierz, 2 April 1656. Two officers wear coats, a musketeer in the foreground carries a rest, and several trumpeters are signalling. (Detail from the original by Erik Dahlbergh)

The First Day of Battle: 28 July 1656

By noon on 28 July, when the Swedish-Brandenburg army had reached about halfway to Warsaw, a trumpeter arrived with a letter to Frederick William from King John Casimir. Although described as full of threats and recriminations, the King of Poland apparently hoped for the Elector to mediate negotiations with King Charles. The army stopped for rest and a meal, and the King of Sweden had a tent erected on the outskirts of Jabłonna, in which he and the Elector had breakfast while discussing the letter. King Charles did not wish for mediation and his resolve was strengthened yet further at the end of the breakfast, when Antoine de Lumbres, the French Ambassador to Warsaw, arrived from the Polish camp with the news that King John Casimir did not want peace and that the Polish army was crossing the bridge across the Vistula with the intention to attack the invaders. The orders in Warsaw, he said, were not to take any prisoners but the Swedish King and the Elector. Apparently, the French Ambassador also told the two monarchs that King John Casimir had said to him that he would give the Swedes to his Tatars for breakfast, while he would put the Elector in a prison where neither sun nor moon would shine. He probably also informed the Allies about the dispositions and preparations of the Commonwealth forces – certainly, the Poles strongly believed that he did so.

It seems uncertain whether the King and his commanders knew that the Swedes and Brandenburgers had joined forces on the previous day. Possibly, the Commonwealth commanders thought that the Swedes still remained at Nowy Dwór, north-west of Warsaw, and that the Brandenburgers were at Płońsk, yet further away.

Between 2:00 and 4:00 p.m. Tott's vanguard encountered the first banners of Lithuanian cavalry deployed as pickets. During the initial skirmishes, the Swedes were reinforced by 300 Brandenburg cavalry. The Allied army had to march through the narrow corridor between the Vistula and wooded dunes, which was no more than 800 to 900 m wide. Tott's vanguard was followed by one wing of the army, composed of Swedish cavalry and dragoons. Then marched the main body of infantry, artillery, and some more cavalry. At the rear travelled the other wing of the army, composed of Brandenburg cavalry. The Lithuanian cavalry focused on fighting against the vanguard, and made no attempts to engage the long Allied marching column. Already at this early stage of the battle, the Commonwealth command was surprised by the turn of events and did not react quickly enough to the changing situation.

The fact that the Allies launched an offensive caught King John Casimir completely unprepared, as it was the main Polish army that was due to attack the Swedish positions, hoping to trap the enemy in an area by now mostly devoid of food for men and fodder for horses. During the night of 27/28 July the Polish infantry and artillery was already crossing to the right bank of the Vistula, as part of the planned attack towards Nowy Dwór. Suddenly, however, facing an enemy on the move, this plan had to be changed and new decisions made. It was agreed that the army would prepare defensive positions in which to await the arrival of the enemy. The Commonwealth commanders hoped that such a defence line would delay and sufficiently blunt the Allied attack, allowing the regiments of Polish cavalry to cross to the right bank of the Vistula and assemble for massive charges against the Allies. Under the influence of General Henderson, King John Casimir ordered his foreign infantry to prepare field fortifications between the Vistula and the dunes. Soldiers from three regiments: Butler's Guard, Grodzicki's and Grothusen's, were soon busy with erecting three redoubts, including some artillery emplacements for the meagre Polish artillery. Additionally, on the hill north-east of the redoubts, they raised an earthwork fort with four bulwarks.

When the Swedes and Brandenburgers approached Warsaw later the same day, they encountered the Commonwealth infantry, over 3,100 enlisted pike and shot supported by artillery, dug in across a narrow corridor of open plain beside the river.

At around 5:00 p.m. on 28 July the three-day Battle of Warsaw began with skirmishes around the Lithuanian redoubts. The sun set at 7:34 p.m., but the skirmishing continued until around midnight.

The open area along the road, between the River Vistula and the forest, did not enable the Swedish-Brandenburg army to march in battle formation. Moreover, Allied units arrived at different times, depending on when they had set out. Nonetheless, King Charles, FrederickWilliam, Field Marshal Lieutenant Robert Douglas, Field Marshal Carl Gustav Wrangel, Lieutenant General Georg Friedrich von Waldeck, and Count Palatine Philip of Sulzbach all pressed on with the cavalry. As a result, the level of fighting was occasionally intense, and both sides suffered casualties from musket and artillery fire. The fact that the Allied units appeared at different times gave the Commonwealth commanders the impression that reinforcements were constantly arriving.

Tott's cavalry vanguard managed to push back the Lithuanian cavalry screen and force it to retreat behind the fortifications. Gordon described this part of the fight, 'About a mile and a halfe from the leaguer [camp] the Polnish guards and voluntiers engaged with the Swedish foretroupes or skoutes, the Polls retireing and the Sweds advancing and pikiering, with the losse and wounds of diverse of the most couragious.'[6] Between 6:00 and 8:00 p.m., after receiving further reinforcements, the Swedes and Brandenburgers pushed forward some probing attacks against the Polish infantry's position; during the attacks Tott's cavalry was supported by more units of cavalry under Philip of Sulzbach. While troops from the main Allied army were arriving at the area of the fighting, they did not have enough space to attempt anything more than direct attacks towards the fortifications. As Jan Leszczyński, Voivode of Poznań, wrote to royal confessor Georg Schönhoff in his account of the battle, '[the enemy] marched towards our redoubts, that were well manned with infantry and cannon; moved lightly, but happily with trumpets and other military music [playing], firing from their own cannon'.[7] The foreign infantry regiments of the Polish army, at least three regiments and possibly all four, that manned this position, supported by artillery, repulsed all the attacks and managed to hold the position.

According to a published letter of Queen Louise Marie's secretary, Pierre des Noyers, on the other side of the river, at about this time the Queen commanded her attendants to use the horses of her carriage to move two cannon along the bank of the Vistula, and she then took charge of the artillery's fire.[8] However this incident is more likely to have taken place on the second day of battle, not on the first (which was the conclusion in a recent study of the war),[9] as discussed below.

Over and beyond the threat from the Commonwealth artillery, any frontal attack on the Commonwealth lines would also have to take into account the

---

6 *Diary of General Patrick Gordon of Auchleuchries 1635–1699,* vol. 1, p.110.

7 Nagielski, *Bitwa pod Warszawą 1656*, p.224.

8 Noyers, *Lettres*, pp.213–214.

9 Michael Fredholm von Essen, *Charles X's War: vol. 2 – The Wars in the East. 1655–1657* (Warwick: Helion & Company, 2022), pp.127–129.

Tatar camp, which was located at Białołęka, and from which the Tatars easily could fall into the rear of the Allies.

Once the vanguard was pushed back and pursued by Lithuanian banners, King Charles who had arrived at the fighting and was observing the battle, attempted a new attack, this time spearheaded by the Uppland Cavalry Regiment under command of Lieutenant Colonel Erik Planting. The fresh cavalry managed to push back a few banners of Lithuanian cavalry, and King John Casimir also tried a counter-attack. One regiment of Lithuanian cavalry under the command of Połubiński – probably the Royal one, with the monarch's hussar banner – was to attempt to cut off the Swedish cavalry by charging from between the hill fort and Białołęka Forest. Those units marched too slowly however, and it seems that their arrival was soon noticed by the Swedes. Robert Douglas led four squadrons of Swedish cavalry and hit the flank of Połubiński's force, repulsing the poorly prepared attack.

Under cover of the cavalry screen, the main body of Allied infantry (nine Brandenburg and three Swedish battalions) were deployed in the corridor and reinforced with the artillery. There were no further attempts to disrupt the deployment of Swedish and Brandenburg units by Commonwealth soldiers, although the Polish artillery continued its fire against the Allies.

On the Swedish side, Colonel David Sinclair suffered a fatal wound (having lost an arm to the artillery fire, he died the following day, but not before toasting the anticipated victory with his remaining hand and asking King Charles to take care of his family).[10]

With sunset at 7:34 p.m., the Allied army retreated outside of the range of the Polish cannon and started to set up their overnight camp on the field between the villages of Żerań and Świdry. The centre was covered by infantry and artillery, Swedish cavalry and dragoons were stationed next to the Vistula, while Brandenburg cavalry and dragoons were covering the flank next to wooded dunes. Field fortifications with artillery emplacements at their end as well were built, to provide protection for troops and to continue the exchange of fire with the Polish positions.

Nightfall did not totally stop the troop movements. Regiment of Polish cavalry, followed by their long tabor wagons, crossed to the right bank of the Vistula in preparation for the next day's battle. Large numbers of the Polish levy of nobility followed them, although these travelled without tabor, which remained on the left bank of the river.[11] It was probably a rather chaotic scene, with many thousands of men and horses moving throughout the night, finding an improvised camp site to rest for a few hours and then to be ready to deploy in the morning. It is likely that for many in the Allied camp it was also a sleepless night, as strong pickets were set up in case of surprise night attacks, while Swedish and Brandenburg commanders had to think about a new course of action.

As discussed above, the first day of the battle brought surprises for both sides. The Commonwealth army had had to abandon plans for an offensive

10 Wolrad von Waldeck, *Relation oder wahrhafftiger Bericht* [in:] Droysen, *Die Schlacht von Warschau 1656*, p.124.

11 Jemiołowski, *Pamiętnik dzieje Polski zawierający (1648–1679)*, p.208.

towards Nowy Dwór but managed to react in time to the changed situation. After their crossing, the Allies were marching very slowly, through the narrow corridor between the dunes and the Vistula, further hampered by the need to repair the bridge. It provided the Poles with enough time to prepare field fortifications and deploy infantry and artillery there. However, the cavalry counterattacks attempted by John Casimir's forces were poorly prepared, so unsurprisingly, these half-hearted attacks were easily repulsed by the Swedes. It was clear to both sides that the next day of the battle would be crucial and that again the fighting would take part on the right bank of the Vistula. The Allies had their whole army gathered here, except a strong guard left to protect the old camp at Nowy Dwór.

It was slightly different for the Commonwealth forces. Lithuanian Field Hetman Gosiewski and his men were too far away and their participation in the battle was out of the equation. Stefan Czarniecki with his large contingent of Polish cavalry (probably 2,000 men) was at Zakroczym. King John Casimir sent him messengers with orders to return quickly and to re-join the main army. However, Czarniecki and his men were too far away and only arrived at the battlefield in the evening of 29 July, after the fighting of the second day of the battle had ended. In the Polish camp there were high hopes about the presence of the Tatars, as it was believed that they would be able and well-placed to harass the rear of the Allied army. Their contingent was despatched to Białołęka, from which they were to use their hit-and-run attacks against the Swedish-Brandenburg Army. The plan was to continue the defence of the field fortification, in order to bleed out the attackers, then counter-attack with the cavalry. It was correctly believed that the Allies had just a few days of food supplies and, with their only access to fresh water being from the River Vistula, that they would be vulnerable to harassing attacks and their morale would quickly begin to erode.

First day of battle, 28 July 1656. (Theatrum Europaeum 7, 1663; National Library, Warsaw)

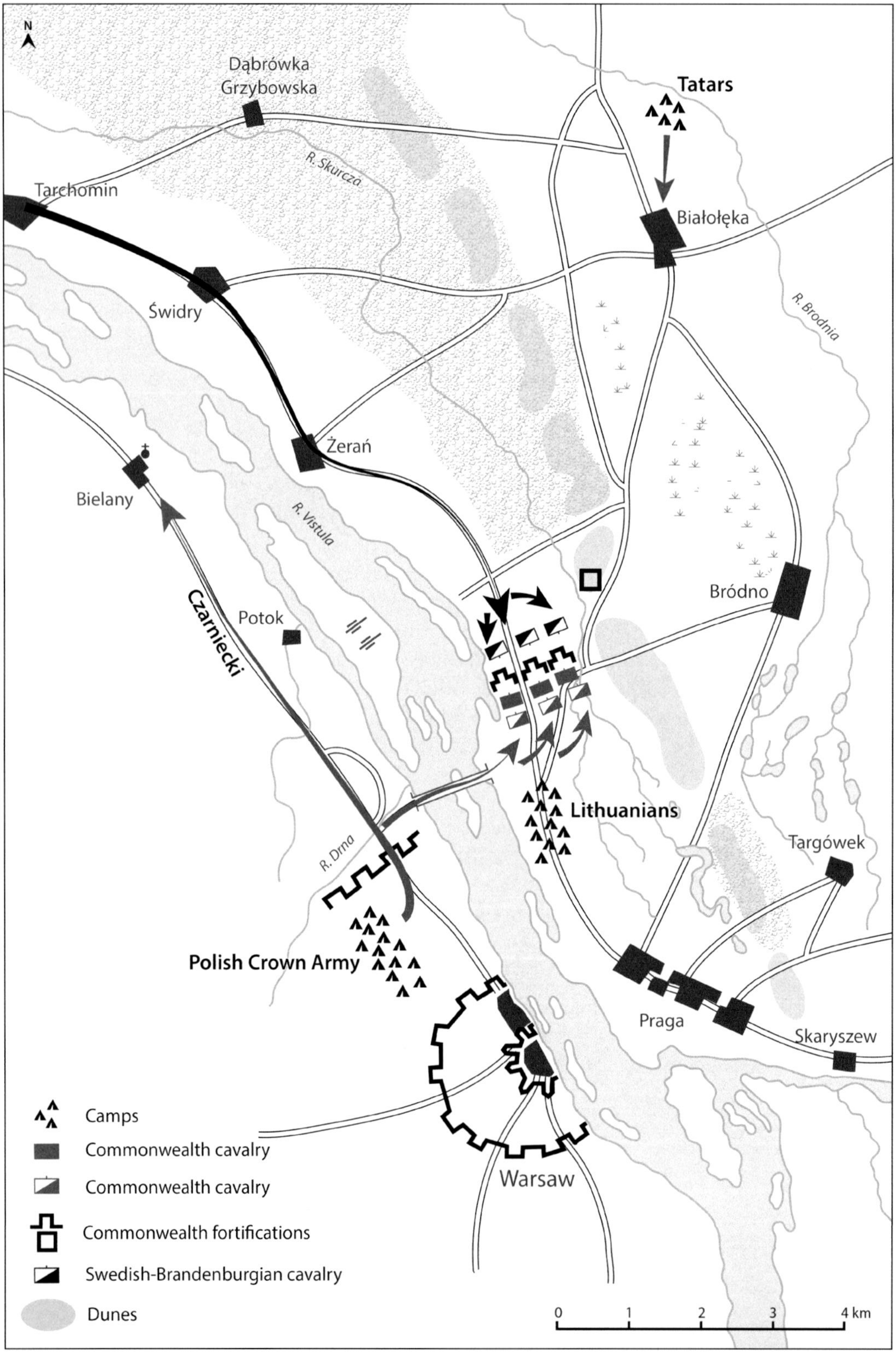

The Battle of Warsaw, 28 July 1656

When the fighting ended for the evening, the Commonwealth commanders were accordingly confident of victory, due to their superior strength and the prepared positions. The Swedish and Brandenburg commanders, however, did not share the King's optimism – there appeared to be a lot of Commonwealth soldiers opposite them. King Charles's own feelings at the time remain unknown, but in front of his men he downplayed their worries, stating that he was confident of a victory.

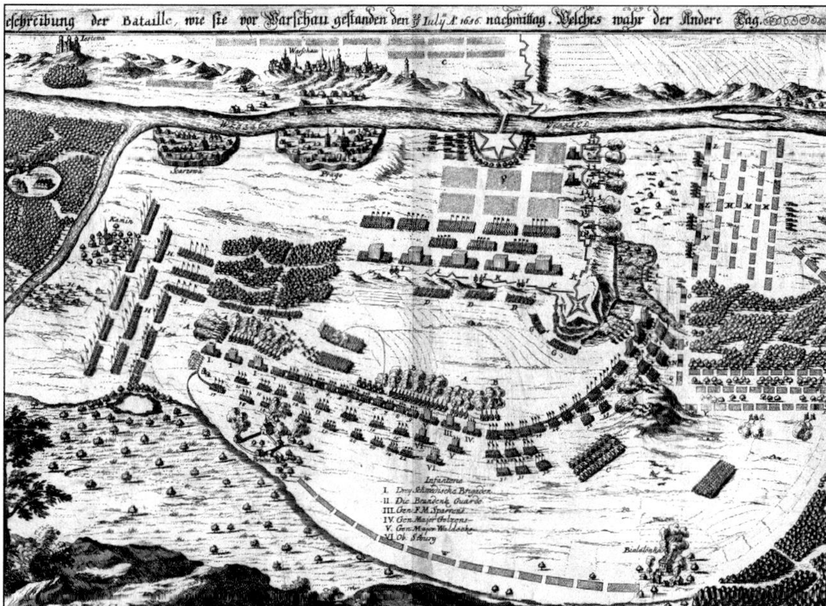

Second day of battle, 29 July 1656. (Theatrum Europaeum 7, 1663; National Library, Warsaw)

Erik Dahlbergh's illustration of the second day of battle, 28 July 1656. (Erik Dahlbergh)

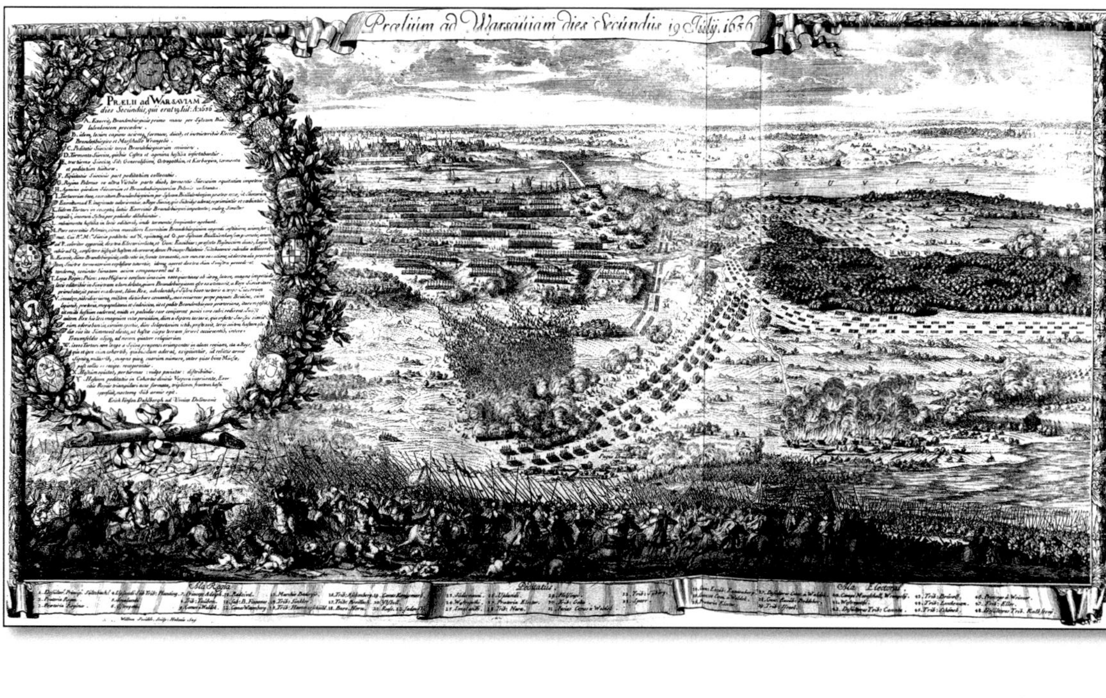

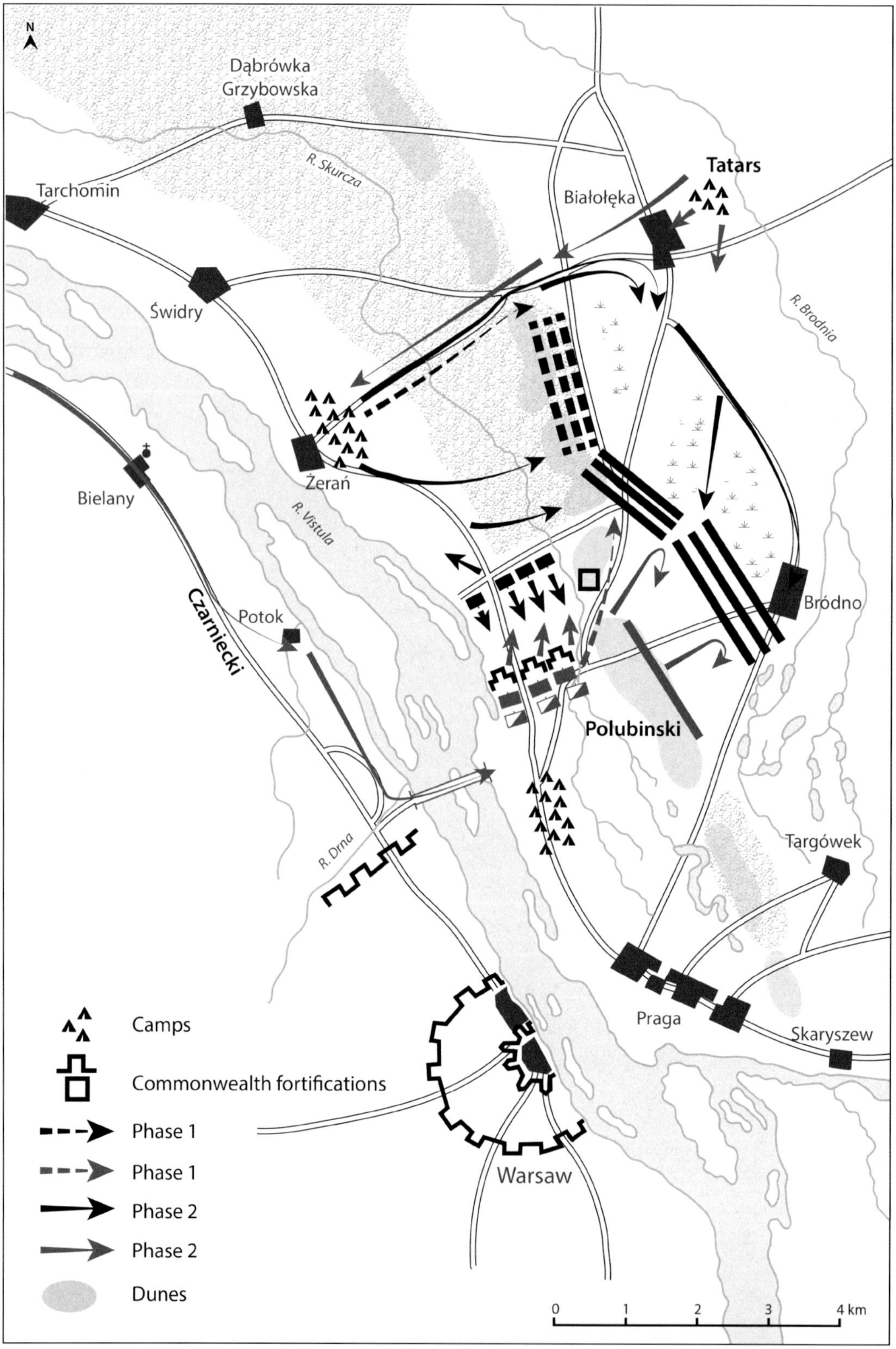

The Battle of Warsaw, 29 July 1656

The Second Day of Battle: 29 July 1656

The Battle of Warsaw took place at the height of summer, and the sun had risen at 3:52 a.m. on the second day. Early in the morning, King Charles, together with Frederick William, Carl Gustav Wrangel, and the Elector's commander, Otto Christoph von Sparr with a cavalry unit for protection, set off to reconnoitre the enemy deployment.

Arriving near the Białołęka Forest, they realised that their army could not succeed with further attacks against the field fortifications. The narrow corridor in which they had to fight, combined with difficult terrain around it, made it extremely difficult to continue with the same type of attacks as on the previous day.

Realising that the Commonwealth lines were too strong to be attacked from the front, King Charles needed to find more open terrain to deploy his units in proper order to enable full use of their firepower and manoeuvrability. All of this could be had east of the Commonwealth lines.

King Charles devised a bold plan. With his cavalry, he would ignore the Tatar camp in that area, and send the army on a flank march so that the eventual battle line would face the Commonwealth units not from the north but from the north-east. He would deploy the Allied army on the dunes between Białołęka and Bródno, opening the way for the attack against the Polish-Lithuanian camp, and push towards the River Vistula. The King knew that this meant that the Tatar camp would then be in his rear, but was willing to take that risk. The army would march and deploy in its ordinary manner, with the few infantry units in the centre. The Brandenburgers, already on the left wing, would lead the way under the Elector's personal command, and would strike against Białołęka, to push back the Commonwealth troops from there. At the same time, the Swedes would continue engaging the Polish units manning the fortifications, to keep them occupied and to cover the movement of the Brandenburgers. Once the Elector's units set up in the new position, the Swedes would disengage from the Poles and move all of their troops to the new battlefield. This redeployment was not without risk since, as already mentioned, it meant that the Allied army would have a Tatar contingent (deployed near Białołęka) in their rear. King Charles was, however, confident in his men and the deep battle formation of the Allied troops would provide better protection against the harassing attacks.

At around 9:00 a.m., the Allied army began its march. As on the previous day, King Charles led the right wing, with Duke Adolph John as his deputy, and Frederick William, with Wrangel as his deputy, led the left wing, Sparr commanded the centre. We have seen that in the appointment of the experienced Wrangel as Frederick William's deputy, King Charles followed the Swedish practice in the Thirty Years' War, during which allied commanders were provided with Swedish deputies to ensure that overall strategic objectives and policies were followed. Even so, Frederick William and Wrangel got on well and over time became close friends, a friendship which survived the two future wars between Brandenburg and Sweden.

The Swedish infantry, supported by artillery, began to exchange fire with the Polish positions before 9:00 a.m. A strong battery was set up near the river, to fire against the Polish camp and the bridge over the Vistula. The Swedish cavalry, formed in three lines, were placed in support behind the infantry. Using the Swedes as cover and distraction, the Elector and his men left the camp and started the slow march towards Białołęka. The Brandenburg vanguard pushed away the Lithuanian pickets defending the small hill next to the southern edge of the Białołęka Forest. Seeing it as good vantage point, the Elector's soldiers managed, after a lot of trouble, to drag two 12pdr cannon onto the hill; the position was now defended by two battalions of infantry and some dragoons. The initial phase of this Brandenburg redeployment reached its conclusion around 11:00. The masses of men and horses took two hours to cross 4km along a muddy road and over the Skurcza Stream, but they were now in the planned positions. The cavalry was deployed in three echelon lines, with the first line stationed across the road on the edge of the forest, and the two furthers lines behind it, across the woody dunes. Alarmed Lithuanians started to move towards Białołęka, while the Tatars were despatched to harass the northern part of the Allied lines.

The Swedes continued to engage the Poles, very effectively drawing their attention to this part of the battlefield. It was probably during this day that the episode with Queen Louise Marie taking control of the small Polish artillery battery took place. When observing the fight from the safety of the Polish field fortifications, she noticed that the fire from a two-cannon battery set up on the left bank of the Vistula River was not hitting the Swedish and Brandenburg troops. She gave an order for the horses from her carriage to be used to move the cannons to Kępa Potocka, on the bank of the river, from which they began a much more successful fire. Patrick Gordon, who placed this event on 29 July, described her actions in a heroic way:

> Ane houre after this the Queen of Polland came in her coach to the other syde of the bridge, and seeing the Sweds to have the use of the river, she caused two cannon be brought with her owne coach horses downe the banke of the river, walking downe her self on foot, Amazonian-lyke, and caused plant and secure them for annoying the Sweds on the other syde of the river and hindring them from watering, which tooke the wished effect.[12]

So, on which day did the event take place? The Swedish historian Johan Levin Carlbom, who in the early 1900s made a detailed study of the battle, dated this event to the second day. Unfortunately, he did not explain his reasons for this, so his conclusion had little impact on future research.[13] Modern Polish researchers tend to rely on the description provided by Aleksander Przeździecki (1814–1871), who in 1851 translated some of Noyers's letters.[14] In his account of the battle, he additionally relied on the seventeenth century French gazettes that were compiled by Louis-René-Antoine Grangier de La

12 *Diary of General Patrick Gordon of Auchleuchries 1635–1699,* vol. 1, p.112.

13 Carlbom, *Tre dagars slaget vid Warschau,* p.159.

14 Aleksander Przeździecki (ed.), 'Zdobycie Warszawy przez Szwedów w 1656 r. opisane w listach królowej polskiej Marii Ludwiki,' [in:] *Biblioteka Warszawska* (Warszawa: Drukarnia Stanisława Strąbskiego, 1851), vol. III, pp.189–210.

Marinièr (1814–1882). They are a very interesting source of information, most likely based on the correspondence from the French courtiers of the Queen – thus not just Noyers himself – and contain information missing in works of seventeenth century historians like Kochowski and Rudawski. According to those accounts, Louise Marie was initially observing the battle from her palace but, due to the large distance, she could not see it in detail so decided to travel to the bridgehead, from where she would have a much better view. After ordering her horses to be used to move two heavy cannons to a better position, she remained there to witness the fighting. The account described her sitting on a drum, with a Tatar *burka* overcoat protecting her from the summer heat, while having her dinner.[15]

One therefore has to ask where did the idea of placing this event during the first day of the battle come from? There are three contemporary sources that place the event on the first day of battle. It is mentioned by Jemiołowski in his diary but there are many problems with his account.[16] Serving under Czarniecki, he was not present at Warsaw during the first two days of the battle. He seems to confuse actions of the Polish and Lithuanian troops, placing Połubiński's hussar charge during the first day of battle. As such, it is easy to hypothesise that, as he based it on what he heard from the others present during the event, he mistook the days when the Queen played her part as General of Ordnance. The second contemporary source that places the event on the first day of the battle is that of Georg Barkmann, the aforementioned envoy of the city of Danzig. On the map of the battle he drew and attached to his report to the City Council, he pointed out the place where the Queen and her entourage of ladies-in-waiting were observing the battle and from where horses from her carriage were used to redeploy the cannon.[17] One could definitely argue, that he *should* be a good source of the information, being close to the court. He provided interesting insights into the situation in the Polish camp but often exaggerated the numbers and disposition of the Polish troops. What is even worse, his manuscript reports do not survive, as they burnt during the Second World War. We only have the materials quoted by Droysen, who seems to often have had issues with deciphering Barkmann's handwriting, leading to errors in the published version of this source. As such, while very interesting, he needs to be used with caution. Finally, the third source, and on first sight much stronger than the others, is the description of the Queen's involvement provided in the edition of her secretary Noyers's letters.[18] As he was Louise Marie's secretary, he was part of her entourage, and most likely witnessed the Queen ordering the moving

15 Przeździecki, 'Zdobycie Warszawy przez Szwedów w 1656 r. opisane w listach królowej polskiej Marii Ludwiki,' p.204. In Polish, a *burka*, from the Persian *berek/berk*, signified an overcoat, usually made from camel fur or wool. This garment was used by Crimean Tatars as protection against rain and became very popular amongst the Polish cavalry, especially in the second half of the seventeenth century. They were very sought after and were purchased from Tatar merchants or exchanged from Tatars horsemen.

16 Jemiołowski, *Pamiętnik dzieje Polski zawierający*, p.210.

17 Droysen, *Die Schlacht von Warschau 1656*, p.147.

18 Noyers, *Lettres*, pp.213–14 (his actual letter) and p.222 (summary of the battle, prepared by Wojciech Chrzanowski).

of the cannon. Noyers described the event in a letter written on 11 August, 12 days after the battle. In this letter, he first describes various events on 28 July, after which he relates the story of the Queen's action beginning with the words 'Meanwhile' (*En ce temps*). However, a definite attribution of the event to a certain date appears only in the more comprehensive description of the battle, written by another hand, that follows this particular letter in the published edition. The other hand was Wojciech Chrzanowski (1793–1861), a Polish general and cartographer. It appears that in 1859 the publisher asked Chrzanowski to write a detailed narrative of the battle for inclusion in the published edition of Noyers's letters, based on the available Polish sources and Pufendorf's work.[19] This is why his depiction of the Queen's redeploying the cannon is so similar to that of Jemiołowski, as he seems to have based it on the diary. As such, it appears that Gordon is the more reliable source of the information and for this reason we agree with his turn of the events, placing Louise Marie's action during the second day of the battle.

While the Queen's two cannons could not influence the outcome, her initiative forms the only known case of an active redeployment of the Commonwealth artillery during the battle. While the Swedish and Brandenburg artillery, in the manner of the Thirty Years' War, remained mobile and frequently redeployed, their Commonwealth counterparts essentially remained in fixed positions throughout the action. Perhaps this can be explained by the fact that most of the experienced Commonwealth artillery officers by this time remained loyal to their oath to the Swedish Crown.

The Commonwealth commanders seemed to be surprised by the turn of events. In the early morning, King John Casimir, with his senior officers, senators, and entourage travelled to the Bernardine monastery at Praga, to take part in Holy Mass. Afterwards, he toured the Polish positions, visiting the infantry deployed in the field fortifications. The regular Polish and part of the Lithuanian cavalry, divided into regiments, was stationed behind the line of fortifications, ready for counter charges against Swedes. The levy of nobility was stationed here as well, adding to the overall number of available men. It seems that Polish cavalry was used for some small-scale attacks against Swedes, clashing with cavalry on a few occasions but every time forced to retreat behind the safety of fortifications because of the heavy Swedish firepower. However, there was no attempt to utilise them in larger charges, as the Polish command did not coordinate their actions.

The Tatars Attack

Meanwhile, the Tatars attacked the Swedish rear, not just once but twice. It is possible they were also supported by some Lithuanian cavalry banners. Both attempts were repulsed, but the fighting was desperate. King Charles reacted quickly to this threat, despatching units of his third line which constituted the

19 Noyers, *Lettres*, p.219.

reserve, under the command of Henrik Horn. These units were spearheaded by the Tavastehus Cavalry Regiment. The Tatars were finally driven off by Horn's Swedish cavalry. As usual, King Charles led from the front. On one occasion, he became separated from his men, except for his personal aide, Lieutenant Colonel Bengt Trafvenfelt.[20] According to Pufendorf:

> But at the same time a very fierce fight broke out, in which the King [Charles X] became so entangled with the enemy that he had no other man with him than Cavalry Captain [Bengt] Trafvenfelt. Seven Tatars, armed with arrows and spears, descended on him at once. The King immediately shot two of them with his pistols, and the third one, who had tangled his spear in the bridle of the King's horse, he struck so hard in the head with his sword that the man fell off his horse. Then the King hastened to the aid of Trafvenfelt, who also shot two of them and fought with the rest, so that the other two escaped. In this way the King was saved from obvious danger.[21]

King Charles and Bengt Trafvenfelt fighting off the Tatars. (Johann Philip Lemke; National Museum, Stockholm)

20 Bengt Trafvenfelt (b. 1601), before he was ennobled in late 1650 (1651 N.S.) known as Trafvare, was an experienced soldier who had accompanied Charles as aide ever since Charles, then a mere captain, had served in the Thirty Years' War in 1642–1645.

21 Pufendorf, *Sieben Bücher* vol. 3, p.179.

King Charles on horseback, as he customarily appeared in combat. Note the breastplate barely visible under his French coat. (Author's collection)

Black felt hat with plume, attributed to King Charles. Diameter 505mm, height 190mm. (Royal Armoury, Stockholm; Photo: Göran Schmidt)

Boots, attributed to King Charles. (Royal Armoury, Stockholm; Photo: Göran Schmidt)

Swedish or Brandenburg cavalry fight Tatar or (less likely) Lithuanian cavalry at the Battle of Warsaw. (Erik Dahlbergh)

The Tatars were pushed back, taking some losses, including many horses, abandoned when they got stuck in the mud. The swift horsemen retreated, ending up at the rear of the redeployed Brandenburg units. They may have succeeded in capturing some of the Swedish supply wagons, although it was very small consolation when compared with the overall failure of their attack.

The Lithuanian, and eventually also the Polish, units began to attack the marching army. The Crimean Tatars repeated their attacks from the north. However, these attacks were also beaten off by superior firepower, and the Brandenburgers and Swedes continued their flank march. The Swedes and Brandenburgers then deployed on and in front of several sandy hills overlooking the Commonwealth army. The disciplined and rapid redeployment of the army took the defenders by surprise. By lunchtime, the Commonwealth commanders felt confident, and they considered that all was going well and between noon and 1:00, the commanders departed for an extended lunch break. They were happy with the situation so far, relying on the Tatars sowing confusion in the enemy's rear. Jan Leszczyński, who was present, later wrote in a letter that 'we thought that we were already victorious and so the elders [commanders] left for an early dinner, deciding that they will do some more [fighting] after the meal.'[22]

The Swedes and Brandenburgers, however, did not stop to eat, instead moving forwards into the newly captured positions, with King Charles joining the Elector. From the Brandenburg-held hill, the Swedish King could see the Polish positions near the village of Bródno. From then on, the next phase of the Allied plan was activated. More Brandenburg units, three infantry battalions and some artillery, under the command of Wolrad von Waldeck, were slowly crossing the Skórcza Stream, to reinforce the lines of Brandenburg horse. The Swedes began their own retreat from the front of the Polish fortifications and redeployed on the plain between Białołęka and Bródno. From there, the Allied army would be in a position overlooking the Commonwealth camp, with only the Tatars at the rear of the now redeployed

22 Jan Leszczyński; cited in Nagielski, *Warszawa*, p.172.

battle line. The Lithuanians tried a poorly prepared attack against the Brandenburgers but were repulsed thanks to the well-placed artillery from Wolrad von Waldeck's contingent. It was at this point that the Tatars tried their second attack on the Swedish rear but were again repulsed.

While the Commonwealth soldiers were resting, the Swedes began their move. The first line of their cavalry was still covering the front of the Polish fortifications, while the third line under Horn was protecting the rear against the Tatars. The main force, under Adolph John, in a few hours managed to move from the previously occupied corridor and deploy towards Bródno. At the same time, the Elector's units marched parallel to the Swedes, moving units so far hidden behind the previously captured hill. By 3:00 p.m. the Allied vanguard appeared about 1km from Bródno and on the edge of the Białołęka Forest. The Tatars tried to harass the marching troops, setting fire to both Białołęka and Bródno.

Returning from their lunch, the Commonwealth commanders finally discovered what was happening. Alarmed, they despatched a series of orders to different units, with Polish and Lithuanian cavalry redeploying to face the newly-arrived enemy. It is surprising that, despite having such an advantage in light cavalry, King John Casimir did not deploy a reconnaissance and was not aware of the movement of the masses of Swedish and Brandenburg units. There was no attempt to attack and disrupt the Allied redeployment, instead the Commonwealth army had to execute a difficult turning of its front through 90 degrees and prepare a new battle line. The main force of foreign infantry and 12 cannon abandoned the field fortifications and moved to the line of wooded dunes. The Poles also manned a fort protecting their flank, where another six cannon were set up. Large numbers of cavalry were deployed near the eastern side of the dunes, with Lithuanians under Połubiński on the right wing and Polish cavalry in the centre and on the left wing. King John Casimir was hoping to break the enemy line with a cavalry charge on the Allied (Swedish) left wing, to push the Swedes into nearby marshes.

At 4:00 p.m., the Commonwealth army was ordered to charge. The King of Poland was hoping to catch the Allies while they were still deploying into their line of battle, when they did not have all their troops available and without units being drawn up in lines supporting each other.

The Hussars Attack

The charge was to take part on the right wing of the Commonwealth army, where the Lithuanian units were deployed. At around 4:00 p.m., Lithuanian hussars under Aleksander Hilary Połubiński charged the flanking units. Their target was the Swedish cavalry regiments of the left wing.

For many years, Polish authors have varied in their estimates of both the units and the numbers taking part in the charge, with the suggested strength being between 800 and 1200 horses. Stanisław Herbst in 1973 mentioned no more than 900 men, with the main force composed of Polish hussars (the banners of Grand Hetman Potocki, Field Hetman Lanckoroński,

Myszkowski, and Zamoyski), supported by the Lithuanian Royal banner under Połubiński and possibly by Grand Hetman Sapieha's unit.[23] Mirosław Nagielski assumed that there were eight banners of hussars taking part in the charge. To the six mentioned by Herbst, he added two more Lithuanian ones: the unit of Michał Kazimierz Radziwiłł and a former unit of Janusz Radziwiłł, under Władysław Jerzy Chalecki. Połubiński was leading the Royal banner, while Hrehory Kruniewicz was supposedly in charge of Grand Hetman Sapieha's hussars. In total, Nagielski assumed Połubiński's units consisted of approximately 800 horses.[24] Most up-to-date research, published by Andrzej Adam Majewski, lowered these numbers significantly as it seems that only two Lithuanian banners, with a real strength of approximately 300 men, took part in the attack – the Royal banner under Połubiński (who led the charge) and Hetman Sapieha's banner (the former banner of Hetman Janusz Radziwiłł) under Lieutenant Władysław Jerzy Chalecki.[25] Each had a paper strength of 200 horses but their muster strength (which included 'dead pays' for officers) was smaller: the Royal banner had 147 and Sapieha's banner 193 horses.

Majewski's theory is very plausible, for a number of reasons.[26] Firstly, it would be highly unlikely that in an already chaotic situation on the battlefield, units of Polish hussars would be moved from their own regiments to join with the Lithuanians. It was a matter of both practicality and pride – Polish commanders would not want to send their banners to serve under the command of a Lithuanian officer. There was really no time to prepare a well-coordinated attack of several regiments (or parts thereof), so instead the order was sent to Połubiński, who was fiercely loyal to the King. Then there is matter of available weapons: Łoś wrote that only the Lithuanian banners were equipped with lances, while none of the Polish banners had them.[27] Wolrad von Waldeck also mentioned that the hussars had *kopia* lances and that they 'attacked with such fury, that more than half of them managed to break through our first line.'[28] Karl Ernst von Platen, who as a part of the Elector's Privy Council accompanied him during the campaign, recorded in his letter written after the battle that the hussars fought bravely and made a good effort but were forced to retreat.[29] The charging hussars first took casualties from the musketry fire of the infantry in the Swedish-Brandenburg centre. Then, although they broke through the first line of

23 Stanisław Herbst, 'Trzydniowa bitwa pod Warszawa 28–30 VII 1656' in Jan Wimmer (ed.), *Wojna polsko-szwedzka 1655–1660* (Warszawa: Wydawnictwo Ministerstwa Obrony Narodowej, 1973), p.321.

24 Nagielski, *Bitwa pod Warszawą 1656*, pp.140–142.

25 Nagielski incorrectly assumed that Hetman Sapieha had two banners, and the unit of Michał Kazimierz Radziwiłł was disbanded in 1655 and could not participate in the Battle of Warsaw. Radziwiłł's banner was created in autumn 1654 and disbanded after just one quarter of service at the beginning of 1655.

26 Andrzej A. Majewski, *Marszałek wielki litewski Aleksander Hilary Połubiński (1626–1679)* (Warszawa: Instytut Historyczny Uniwersytetu Warszawskiego, 2014), pp.112–114.

27 Łoś, *Pamiętnik towarzysza chorągwi pancernej*, p.68.

28 Wolrad von Waldeck, *Relation oder wahrhafftiger Bericht* [in:] Droysen, *Die Schlacht von Warschau 1656*, p.126.

29 Droysen, *Die Schlacht von Warschau 1656*, p.133.

Aleksander Hilary Połubiński, artist unknown. (Collection of the Library of University of Warsaw)

the Swedish cavalry – consisting of Her Royal Majesty the Queen's Life Regiment of Horse, Uppland Cavalry Regiment, and Småland Cavalry Regiment, two squadrons of the latter whom reportedly fired their pistols too early to make an impact – and also penetrated the second, they failed to reach the third line, which repulsed the hussars without any particular difficulty. Moreover, the hussars failed to inflict many casualties (see below). Nor did the Commonwealth cavalry, in the face of musket and artillery fire, make an impact on the infantry in the centre or on the Brandenburgers in the now right wing. Under the heavy fire of Swedish cavalry from the third line and infantry from the centre and without the support of the rest of the Polish and Lithuanian cavalry, the hussars were forced to retreat, taking heavy losses.[30]

Characteristically, King Charles entered the fray against the hussars. Taking command of the Åbo Cavalry Regiment, whose Colonel, Berndes, had fallen ill on the previous day and could not participate, he charged leading one Åbo squadron, with Lieutenant Colonel Carl Bäck in command of the other. King Charles rode a dapple-grey English horse.

Two hussars, Wojciech Lipski and Jakub Kowalewski, attacked King Charles.[31] One of them hit the King in the chest, dangerously near the throat, with his lance. The King's bullet-proof cuirass turned the lance, and he was

Clash between Polish and Swedish cavalry. Detail from Erik Dahlbergh's drawing for Samuel Pufendorf's *De rebus a Carolo Gustavo Sueciae rege gestis*, published in 1696. (National Library, Warsaw)

30 Majewski, *Marszałek wielki litewski Aleksander Hilary Połubiński (1626–1679)*, pp.114–117.
31 Majewski, *Marszałek wielki litewski Aleksander Hilary Połubiński*, pp.114–116.

not wounded, and one of the King's companions then shot the hussar – the second hussar suffered the same fate. The attendant (or attendants, since there were two hussars) who saved King Charles on this occasion was either the indefatigable Trafvenfelt or, with regard to at least one assailant, Prince Bogusław Radziwiłł.

Multiple sources give different testimonies about the identity of the hussar who hit King Charles. The accounts give different names and even different details of the event itself. The Polish soldier and historian Wespazjan Kochowski named the hussar as Jakub Kowalowski, companion of the Royal hussar banner. Kochowski says that Kowalowski recognised King Charles from his splendid armour (which is unlikely, given that King Charles only wore a hat and had a coat over his utilitarian back and breast plates) and the standard carried next to him (which is far more likely). Kowalowski managed to get close to the King, aimed his lance at Charles's chest but just before he was able to hit the Swedish monarch, the hussar was shot in the head by someone from the King's entourage. Kochowski mentioned, that 'many attributed it to [Prince] Bogusław Radziwiłł'. According to the rather anecdotal description by the Polish historian, King Charles asked who the brave soldier was and added that 'even though his name is unknown, I myself give witness that the bravery of this soldier, whoever he is, will certainly earn him eternal glory'. Kochowski even had King Charles give the (unlikely) comment that 'if I would have ten thousand of such soldiers, I would not only have easily conquered Turkey but the whole world'.[32] Łoś does not name the hussar but specified that it was Prince Bogusław Radziwiłł who killed him. He also added that King Charles ordered his men to give the hussar a burial with full honours.[33] This ceremony, which took place in the Benedictine monastery in Praga, is also mentioned by Kochowski.[34] The Polish historian also quoted Johannes Loccenius's *Historiae Suecanae*, according to which the King was able to parry the lance with his sword and then shot the attacker with his pistol.[35] On this occasion Gordon is not much help, as he only wrote that during the fight against hussars the 'King himself with his guards charged them, even to the endangering of his owne person.'[36] Gordon does not mention the event of the individual charge against the Swedish monarch. What is more, he mistook the name of the commander of the charge, claiming that 'the Swedish King commanded only Sapiha [Sapieha], the commander of the husars, out of a singular respect to his valour, to be buryed.'[37]

Another seventeenth century historian and poet, Samuel Twardowski, wrote that the hussar's name was Kowalewski and that he managed to 'hit the King' with his lance but was then killed by the soldiers of the Life Guard.[38] Jemiołowski introduced yet another name, as according to him a

32 Kochowski, *Lata Potopu 1655–1657*, p.203.

33 Łoś, *Pamiętnik towarzysza chorągwi pancernej*, p.68.

34 Kochowski, *Lata Potopu 1655–1657*, pp.203–204.

35 Kochowski, *Lata Potopu 1655–1657*, p.204.

36 *Diary of General Patrick Gordon of Auchleuchries 1635–1699*, vol. 1, p.114.

37 *Diary of General Patrick Gordon of Auchleuchries 1635–1699*, p.115.

38 Samuel Twardowski, *Woyna Domowa z Kozaki i Tatary, Moskwą, potym Szwedami i z Węgry Przez lat Dwanaście za Panowania Nayjaśnieyszego Jana Kazimierza Króla Polskiego tocząca się*

hussar named Dąbrowski attacked the King's entourage, was able to hit one of the Swedes with his lance, and then safely returned to his own lines.[39] The specialist in heraldry, Kasper Niesiecki (1682–1744), added another name to the list: in his description of the Lipski family, he mentioned that Wojciech Lipski 'almost struck [Charles] Gustav, the Swedish King [but] was mortally wounded by Prince [Radziwiłł].' He referenced the so-called *Lament Muzy Polskiej*, currently unidentified and presumably a lost seventeenth century account.[40] Those three surnames: Kowalewski/Kowalowski, Lipski, and Dąbrowski, led modern Polish researcher Mirosław Nagielski to suggest that it could actually be the same man. The father of Wojciech Lipski, Kasper Zygmunt, at that time held the office of the *starosta* of Kowalew or Dąbrowa, so documents would often name him and his son after this title, which was common practice of the era. On the other hand, in 1661, during the Sejm in Warsaw, one of the nobles – very likely Adam Kowalewski – accused Prince Bogusław Radziwiłł of killing his son during the Battle of Warsaw, thus supporting those accounts that mention the hussar's death at the hand of the Prince.[41]

A crucial element in the puzzle of the identity of the hussar that attacked the Swedish King was published in 2014. Polish researchers Zbigniew Hunder and Andrzej A. Majewski found a document from 1672, which revealed the identity of the attackers. It is a so-called *laudum* (published resolution) of the district assembly of the nobility from Warsaw Land (*ziemia warszawska*) from 27 April 1672. It mentioned two Mazovian nobles, [Wojciech] Lipski and [Jakub] Kowalewski, both of the same coat of arms (known as *Łada*), who during the Battle of Warsaw bravely charged the King of Sweden with their lances and who both died during the attempt.[42] The presence of Polish nobles in the ranks of the Lithuanian hussar banner is not surprising, as the unit was recruiting in Mazovia during the spring and summer of 1656, to replenish its ranks. This process continued after the Battle of Warsaw to recover from the losses incurred during the fight against the Swedes.[43] Of course it is still possible that even more hussars arrived in the vicinity of the Swedish King but these documents definitively confirm the identity of the two main attackers, linking it with other sources mentioned before.

It is estimated that the Royal banner lost, in killed and wounded companions and retainers, up to one-third of its strength.[44] Sapieha's banner suffered 18 companions killed but the number of companions wounded, and

(Calissi: Collegis Calliensis, 1681), p.198.

39 Jemiołowski, *Pamiętnik dzieje Polski zawierający (1648–1679)*, p.208.

40 Kasper Niesiecki, *Herbarz polski Kaspra Niesieckiego powiększony dodatkami z późniejszych autorów, rękopismów, dowodów urzędowych i wydany przez Jana Nep. Bobrowicza*, vol. 51, (Lipsk: Breitkopf i Haertel, 1841), p.122.

41 Nagielski, *Bitwa pod Warszawą 1656*, pp.150–151.

42 Zbigniew Hundert, Andrzej A. Majewski, 'O dwóch Rochach Kowalskich (najsłynniejszy epizod bitwy warszawskiej 1656 roku w świetle nowego źródła)', *Przegląd Historyczny*, 2014, vol. IICV, issue 2 (Warszawa: Wydawnictwo DiG, 2014), pp.283–286; Majewski, *Marszałek wielki litewski Aleksander Hilary Połubiński (1626–1679)*, pp.114–116.

43 Mirosław Nagielski, 'Chorągwie husarskie Aleksandra Hilarego Połubińskiego i króla Jana Kazimierza w latach 1648–1666', *Acta Baltico-Slavica*, 15 (1983), pp.86–88.

44 Nagielski, *Bitwa pod Warszawą 1656*, p.149.

retainers killed or wounded, is unknown.[45] Wolrad von Waldeck's statement that practically all attackers, including their commander, were shot and killed, is however a clear exaggeration.[46] Both units also lost many horses, including some that were captured by Swedes, as shown on Dahlbergh's drawings.

So, what was the impact of the hussar charge on the Swedes? According to Patrick Gordon, King Charles in anticipation of the attack from the famous Polish-Lithuanian cavalry 'gave orders to all commanders of battalions and regiments that when the hussars or lancers should charge them, they should open [ranks] and give way to their fury, which he knew was not to be withstood with any force of other policy at that tyme'.[47] Such tactics could explain what Polish sources assumed to be breaking through the first line of Swedish cavalry, when in fact they followed the King's orders and retreated towards the second line. Holsten claimed that the 'hussars harmed us the most' but he was not present at the battlefield.[48] Pufendorf mentioned that two Swedish squadrons 'gave fire too early' and were broken by the hussars' charge and pushed towards the second line.[49] Polish researchers always assumed that Swedish cavalry from the Uppland and Småland Cavalry Regiments took the highest losses, as they were facing the hussars in the first line, which was broken by the charge.[50] Also badly affected, in their estimate, were Her Royal Majesty the Queen's Life Regiment of Horse also known as Duke John George of Anhalt-Dessau's Cavalry Regiment and Count Palatine Philip von Sulzbach's Cavalry Regiment.[51] However, the main problem with this theory is that it is not supported by any written evidence. We lack post-battle muster rolls of those regiments that would allow us to confirm if they took heavy losses. Certainly, some muster rolls and casualty lists of the Uppland and Småland Cavalry Regiments, although not from the Queen's Life Regiment, have survived and a summary of these is given below. The primary difficulty for the task of assessing Swedish casualties in the hussar charge is that the surviving muster rolls usually do not specify when and where the losses took place during a campaign. In short, the surviving muster rolls can tell us that the hussars likely did make an impact, but we cannot express that impact in figures. All evidence taken into consideration, it seems that the hussars failed in their task, although their opponents certainly did not escape unscathed.

45 Majewski, *Marszałek wielki litewski Aleksander Hilary Połubiński*, p.117.

46 Wolrad von Waldeck, *Relation oder wahrhafftiger Bericht* [in:] Droysen, *Die Schlacht von Warschau 1656*, p.126.

47 *Diary of General Patrick Gordon of Auchleuchries 1635–1699,* vol. 1, p.113.

48 Holsten, *Przygody wojenne 1655–1666*, 36.

49 Pufendorf, *Sieben Bücher* vol. 3, p.179.

50 The Småland Cavalry Regiment was probably commanded by Major Zacharias Sabelfelt. Some historians mention Johann von Rosen (1623–1657) as the commander of the regiment. However, Rosen was in the Livonian Retinue of Nobles at the time and, as far as is known, not present at Warsaw.

51 Nagielski, *Bitwa pod Warszawą 1656*, p.146.

Roll Calls of the Swedish Regiments that had Faced the Charge of The Hussars[52]

Uppland Cavalry Regiment

12 June 1656: 80 dead since the campaign began. (Source: SE/KrA/0022/1656/3, pp.43–45)
1 September 1656: 201 dead since the campaign began. At least a dozen names, but far from all, are annotated 'died at Warsaw'. (Source: SE/KrA/0022/1656/3, pp.34–38)
This suggests that the Uppland Cavalry Regiment suffered some notable losses in the Battle of Warsaw, although the exact figure is impossible to determine.

Småland Cavalry Regiment

17 April 1656: 158 dead and wounded since the campaign began, including some at Warsaw before the three-day battle. (Source: SE/KrA/0022/1656/3, pp.53–56)
This was presumably the muster roll read by an earlier Swedish researcher, Lars-Olof Larsson who noted only four men lost in the Battle of Warsaw (Larsson, *På marsch mot evigheten*, p.66). If so, Larsson must have missed the date on the list.
12–13 July 1656: A total of 600 men fit for duty across six of the eight companies. Roll calls for the other two companies appear to be missing; details are included but they are date-lined Kalmar, Sweden, 1655. (Source: SE/KrA/0022/1656/3, pp.153–73)
13 September 1656: A total of 770 or possibly 776 men on duty across all eight companies. The figures for the six companies listed in July produce a total of 545 men. (Source: SE/KrA/0022/1656/3, pp.129–152)
This suggests a number of dead at the Battle of Warsaw, but the total is impossible to determine.

Her Royal Majesty the Queen's Life Regiment of Horse

No records found.

Count Palatine Philip von Sulzbach's Cavalry Regiment

No records found.

52 All sources are in the Swedish National Archives; exact details are as given. NB all dates are O.S.

Lithuanian hussars breaking through the left wing of Swedish-Brandenburg army during the Battle of Warsaw. Detail from Erik Dahlbergh's drawing for Samuel Pufendorf's *De rebus a Carolo Gustavo Sueciae rege gestis*, published in 1696. (National Museum, Cracow)

Polish standards and horses of winged hussars captured by Swedes during Battle of Warsaw. Detail from Erik Dahlbergh's drawing for Samuel Pufendorf's *De rebus a Carolo Gustavo Sueciae rege gestis*, published in 1696. (National Library, Warsaw)

Further units of cavalry were supposed to follow up the charge, in support of the hussars. Unfortunately, none of this took place, and not a single banner followed Połubiński's men, which shows the clear lack of proper leadership amongst the Commonwealth ranks. Neither Grand Hetman Potocki nor Field Hetman Lanckoroński played any part in the battle and they were not seen encouraging their men. Czarniecki and Lubomirski, the two most active Polish commanders, were not present on the battlefield. Nor did any Lithuanian officers step forward to lead their soldiers in support of the hussars. King John Casimir tried to encourage his army to action, 'with fire in his eye and voice (it was heard that he was giving orders with "In God's name" on his lips).'[53] Noyers mentioned that the King 'was taking [at the same time] the role of sergeant, quartermaster, and ordinary soldier, running everywhere with sabre in his hand, asking some, threatening others, and at a times talking to them in such affectionate way, that some of them shed a tear.'[54] The unique structure of the Polish-Lithuanian army was its undoing on this occasion: noble soldiers refused to follow orders and simply watched the bloody charge of the Lithuanian hussars. Without support, scattered remains of the two hussar banners disengaged from the Swedes and returned to their own lines. Łoś commented that 'our men were just [watching it] surprised, instead [of sending] reinforcements, while if just a few banners had followed the [hussar] banners, they would have prevented the Swedes from putting

53 Kochowski, *Lata Potopu 1655–1657*, p.198.

54 *Portfolio królowej Maryi Ludwiki*, vol. 2, p.67.

[their ranks] in order.'[55] Gordon also pointed out the lack of support, 'These few but gallant and resolute men, being as in a hose nett, attracted on all hands, were as dry fuell with a violent fyre in a short tyme consumed, few fynding the way back againe, the great body of the reserve, as the voluntiers also, not giveing them any help or offering any reall engadgment or charge, but upon the plaine appearance of the losse of these gallant husars, retired confusedly.'[56] Wierzbowski summarised it in a very religious tone, 'Our men did not support them. For [our] sins, God took away clear mind and bravery [from us].'[57]

The lack of the follow-up charge allowed the Swedes to re-order their ranks and get their battle line in order.

The Tatars again attacked the rear of the Swedish line, however, they had no effect on the outcome of the fighting. This time, Duke Adolph John led Duke Charles of Mecklenburg-Schwerin's Cavalry Regiment, Colonel Jacob Johan Taube's Cavalry Regiment, and Christian von Pretlach's Cavalry Regiment against the Tatars, soon followed by some dragoons who could easier deal with the broken ground into which the Tatars were pushed, terrain that both hampered their movements and shielded them until the dragoons arrived.

Meanwhile, Major General Kannenberg was badly wounded by fragments of a falconet shot, although he miraculously survived the wound. The Allies lost another senior officer – Böddeker, who was not wounded, but being elderly simply fell ill during the day.

The final stage of the battle was a half-hearted attempt by the Polish regular cavalry to charge the Brandenburg cavalry. It seems that a group of cossack cavalry (and probably some *pancerni* as well) attacked the Elector's troops but was greeted with infantry salvoes and quickly retreated after giving fire from their pistols. Knowing the typical equipment of Polish cavalry, it is very likely that companions and retainers alike used their carbines and bows as well – all without much success. It is worthwhile to note that according to Brandenburg accounts, the Polish cavalry tried another charge and was involved in hand-to-hand combat with the Elector's cavalry. The second attack is not confirmed by any available Polish sources, so it was possibly an exaggeration designed to show the Brandenburgers in a heroic light. This episode – whether there was one or two charges – did not take long, probably no more than an hour. Around 6:00 p.m., the Polish units were back in their original positions, waiting for the next move by the Allied army. Around this time, the foreign infantry regiment of Ernst Magnus Grothusen, supported by some dragoons (a few companies?) and two small cannon redeployed to the left wing and into the Praga Forest to better support the Lithuanians, who lacked infantry and dragoons, against the expected Swedish offensive. Czarniecki and his cavalry regiments, who at this point finally re-joined the army, were moved near to the line of dunes in front of Bródno, to defend against the Swedes.

---

55 Łoś, *Pamiętnik towarzysza chorągwi pancernej*, p.70.

56 *Diary of General Patrick Gordon of Auchleuchries 1635–1699*, vol. 1, p.114.

57 Wierzbowski, *Konnotata wypadków w domu i w kraju zaszłych od 1634 do 1689 r*, p.103.

King Charles deployed the army for the night in what has been described as a triangle, with three defensive fronts so that he could meet attacks from any direction. It was difficult for the men, who now had spent most of four days on the march and, in some cases, had got little opportunity to eat and to feed their horses for the last two days, and had barely found any time for sleep.

By the evening of the second day of battle, the mood had changed in both armies. Those Swedish and Brandenburg commanders who had previously doubted the audacious plan (and many had, since they knew they were outnumbered) were now confident of success. However, the Commonwealth commanders who had earlier paid more attention to their lunch than to their enemies had lost confidence. Some Commonwealth units deserted, and the rest, under King John Casimir, began to retreat across the River Vistula, on the one available bridge.

Despite having ample time to try their own attack – dusk did not take place until 7:30 p.m. – King Charles and the Elector were happy to stop and not attempt any further action. They had clearly won the day, safely moving their army out from a dangerous corridor, redeploying all their units and shattering the morale of the Polish-Lithuanian troops. While Polish researchers tend to explain the inactivity of the Allied army at the final phase by heavy losses taken during Połubiński's charge and the need to rest their men, it seems to be more wishful thinking than a proper assessment of the situation. After all it was the Commonwealth units that were now in disarray: their commanders did not react quickly enough to the surprising change in the situation, while their own attacks were poorly executed and ended, in case of the hussars, in heavy losses. The initiative was now fully in Allied hands, and they were to dictate how the next day of the battle would be shaped.

The Swedish and Brandenburg armies set up a makeshift camp near the village of Bródno, torched during the day by Tatars. In the meantime, the Commonwealth troops were on the move. King John Casimir ordered the majority of his infantry, artillery, and the whole of his supply train to start crossing to the left bank of the River Vistula. On the right (Praga) side, he was to leave a strong contingent of his cavalry, and Grothusen's infantry in the forest, as a delaying force. A long line of wagons and the masses of the levy of the nobility – not very eager to fight – were milling around next to the only bridge, trying to cross as soon as possible. As this blocked the route of evacuation of the regular troops, for the time being infantry regiments were kept on the line of dunes, to defend them until they could finally cross. Some nobles sent their wagons towards Okuniew in the east, along the one road not blocked by the Allied forces. It was another problem affecting Polish plans, as this was the planned escape route for the regular cavalry if it had to disengage from the next day's fight. Chaos was spreading and morale was very low. Grand Hetman Potocki was providing the worst example, as he was one of the first to send away his supply wagons. King John Casimir remained with the main army on the Praga side, where he was joined by Czarniecki but it was clear that the Commonwealth's plans for the battle had failed.

Elsewhere, fighting continued until around 10 p.m. When darkness fell, King Charles and Frederick William agreed to attack again on the following day. Despite the day's victories, the night provided little rest for the Swedish-Brandenburg army. During the night they were harassed by Tatars, who tried to keep them awake by shouting and keeping sentries on constant alert. The Tatars made repeated approaches against the camp, attempting to catch stragglers or take plunder.

King Charles and Duke Adolph John spent the night resting in the King's coach, and shared a meal of cold food.

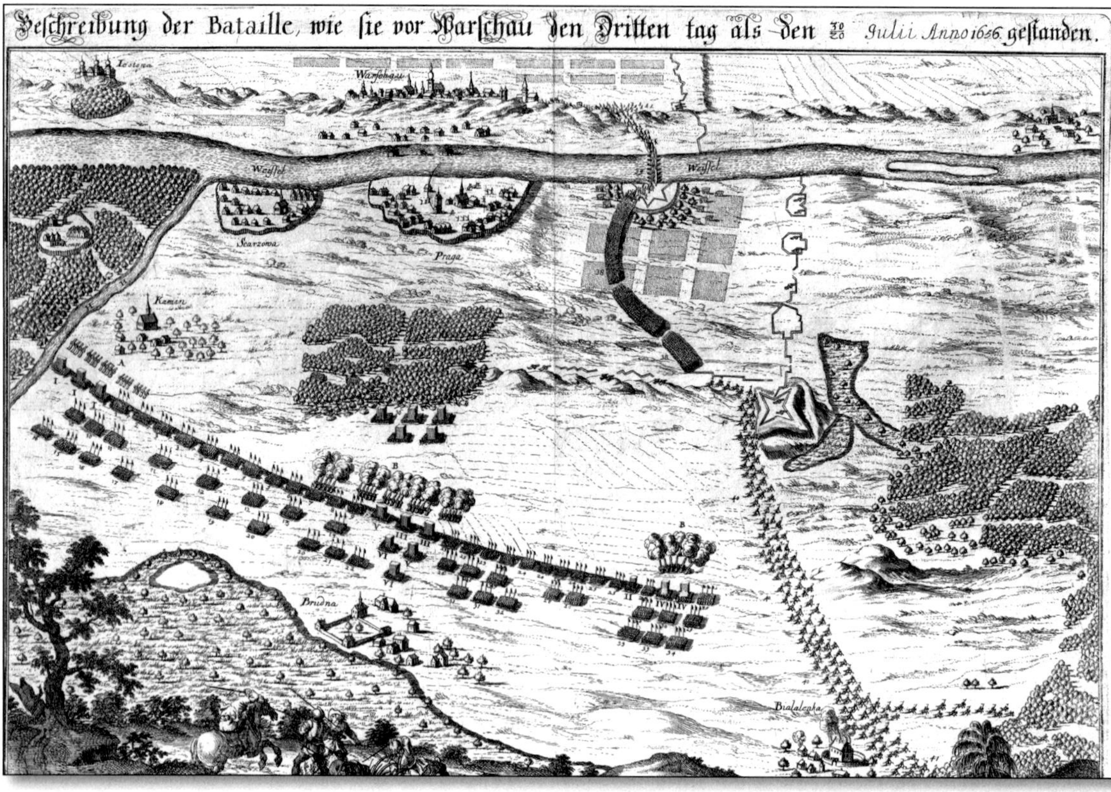

The third day of battle, 30 July 1656. (Theatrum Europaeum 7, 1663; National Library, Warsaw)

The Third day of Battle: 30 July

On 30 July, just before dawn, King Charles ordered the firing of a Swedish salute (two cannon shots in rapid succession). The Poles responded with a Polish salute (three cannon shots). A Polish salute was identical to the Imperial salute, an old German practice incidentally also followed by Denmark.

The sun rose very early, at 4:54 a.m., but the morning was misty and the thick fog did not disappear until around 8:00 a.m. Both armies used the time to prepare their battle lines, except for the Polish levy of nobility which focused on retreating across the bridge. Only men from three voivodeships: Bełż, Lublin and Sandomierz, stayed and were ready to fight. King Charles wanted to strike towards the line of dunes and the Praga Forest. Capturing those positions would push the Polish-Lithuanian army towards its only

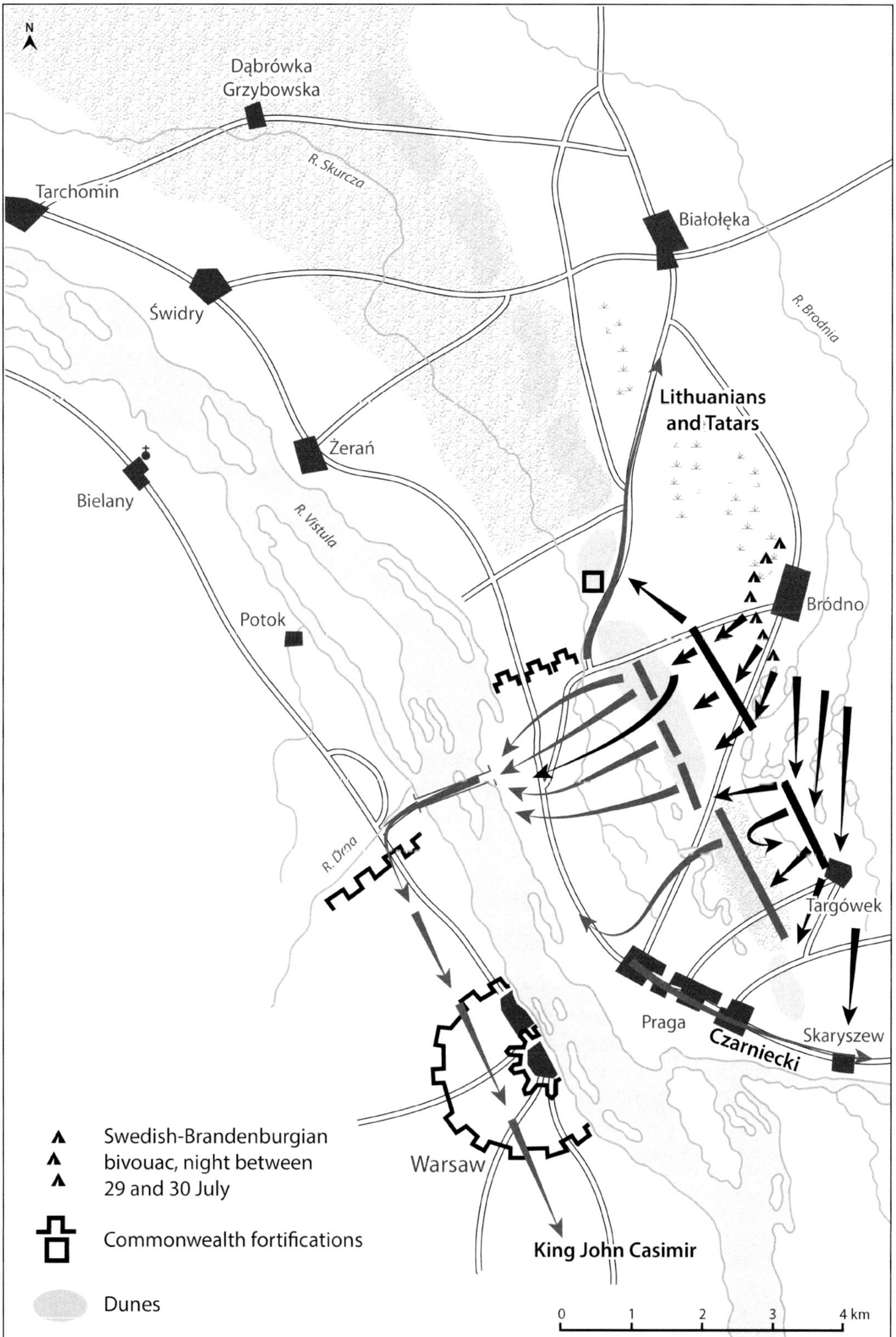

The Battle of Warsaw, 30 July 1656

bridge over the Vistula, giving the Allied army the chance to destroy its opponents next to the crossing, but such a plan was not without risk. As discussed above, the Allies had brought supplies for only three days, with no chance of resupply in the area. Behind their deployment area, they had difficult terrain, full of marshes, which would severely impede their retreat in case of defeat. Though considering the events of the second day of the battle, both King Charles and Frederick William could be optimistic.

Leaving the supply train, the sick, and the wounded in the remains of Bródno, under cover of the fog the Allies formed up for battle. Brandenburger cavalry, supported by dragoons, were on the right wing, from which they were to attack against the dunes. The centre, with battalions mostly of Brandenburg troops with some Swedish infantry, was to march by the road from Bródno towards Praga. Swedish cavalry and dragoons, probably with some infantry as well, were to attack on the left wing against Praga Forest. The centre, which was at least six battalions, was deployed in two lines, and both wings were deployed in three.

The Commonwealth units were deployed in several groups. The left flank, under the command of Połubiński, was composed of Lithuanian cavalry, supported by some Tatars. At the left edge of this flank was a fort, still held by Polish infantry or dragoons; on the right was Praga Forest, held by infantry and dragoons under Grothusen. The main force of the Polish regular cavalry, supported by some of the levy of nobility and the main force of Tatars, was deployed in the front of the dunes, covering both the centre and the right flank. The majority of the Polish infantry, of three foreign regiments, and artillery was set up on the dunes, although they were preparing to retreat across the bridge. King John Casimir, possibly with both Potocki and Lanckoroński (who again did not play any part in the events), was on the Lithuanian wing. The Polish cavalry was under the command of Stefan Czarniecki and Aleksander Koniecpolski. While the infantry was busy building earthworks on both dunes and at the edge of Praga Forest, it seems that they did not manage to finish them. Morale was low and many thought only of how to safely escape towards Warsaw. The Commonwealth forces were not showing any initiative, simply waiting for the Allies to start their attack.

The Swedish-Brandenburg army again attacked across the open plain as the fog disappeared around 8:00 a.m. and they easily penetrated the remaining Commonwealth defences.

Their close battle line advanced rapidly, with the infantry centre under Otto Christoph von Sparr marching towards Praga Forest, both cavalry wings moving faster than their foot. The Poles and Lithuanians were completely immobile and there was no attempt to interrupt this move with cavalry charges. The Swedish and Brandenburg artillery quickly opened fire against the Polish positions at the edge of the forest. According to Wolrad von Waldeck, the Poles resisted with heavy fire of their cannon and muskets for close to an hour. About 500 Brandenburg musketeers under Colonel

Sieberg spearheaded the attack, outflanking the Polish position.[58] Clearly outnumbered by Sparr's infantry, and seeing that his cavalry was unwilling to engage the enemy, Grothusen ordered his men to abandon their positions at the forest. His soldiers 'retreated moving slowly [in order]', although due to the lack of available horses they had to abandon their guns.[59] At 09:00 a.m., Sparr's men entered the position, capturing two field pieces left behind by the Poles. Foot regiments from the centre of the Allied line continued the pursuit of the Polish infantry, while the cavalry on the right wing turned towards the Lithuanians. The rest of the army continued the attack against the Polish positions. The regiments of regular Polish cavalry fled without fight, abandoning three infantry regiments stationed on the dunes. Colonels Wilhelm Butler and Krzysztof Grodzicki, cut off from any other command, decided to retreat as well. Again, as in Praga Forest, some cannon (7 of the 12 available) were abandoned and soon captured by the Brandenburgers. Yet worse for the Commonwealth soldiers, was that the Elector's troops turned them and used them to fire against the retreating Poles. Regiments were slowly crossing the muddy area around the small river Skurcza, now also under fire by both artillery and the Brandenburg infantry. It seems that Jan Zamoyski's regiment was in the rearguard, as according to Łoś this unit took the heaviest losses.

The Commonwealth army was saved by two fortunate events. Firstly, the Swedish-Brandenburg soldiers and horses had now fought for three days, and for that time barely had anything to eat, and were now exhausted and quite unable to pursue effectively. Secondly, and here sheer luck played a role, the retreat of so many Commonwealth units was facilitated by a misunderstanding on the Allied side. Several Polish infantry units asked to surrender. They laid down their weapons, raised their hats in surrender, and shouted for 'accord'. This caused the Elector's men to stop their cannonade, giving the Poles time to re-order their ranks and safely continue their retreat. The Brandenburgers lost precious time while waiting for the Polish surrender and thus they ended up well behind the retreating Poles.

Most accounts describe how Frederick William still wanted to push on against the retreating Polish infantry, and ordered his men to engage with musket and artillery fire. At this point, Duke Adolph John rode up to the Brandenburg Lieutenant Colonel Polenz, in Waldeck's command, and told him that the Poles already had surrendered, and that he should not advance further. After a while, Frederick William arrived on the scene, asking the unfortunate Polenz why he was not engaging the Polish infantry. As Polenz prepared to do so, Duke Adolph John returned, ordering him to desist. The Duke had, in the past, accepted the surrender of Polish units that might otherwise have been destroyed, so it was perhaps not out of character for him to do so again. The situation then turned into a heated argument between Frederick William and Duke Adolph John. The misunderstanding, which surely saved some Commonwealth units, turned into a major embarrassment for the Elector and the Duke. In fact, this was such an embarrassment that

58 Droysen, *Die Schlacht von Warschau 1656*, p.127.

59 Nagielski, *Bitwa pod Warszawą 1656*, pp.168–169.

the two soon accused each other over who had wanted to push on, and who had wanted to abandon the pursuit.[60] The conflicting stories are not easier to disentangle when taking into account that Duke Adolph John on the previous day had suffered a further bad wound to his already damaged knee and must have been in serious pain at the time.

Meanwhile, many Commonwealth units fled, and in the process, they abandoned 13 cannon. At this point, chaos broke out among the retreating Commonwealth units. The plan was to evacuate the Commonwealth supply train and infantry across the Vistula but because of poor discipline and management, parts of the supply train and infantry ended up blocking the bridge, causing considerable confusion in the Commonwealth lines.

At this stage the battle was already lost, even without much fighting and resistance from the Polish-Lithuanian troops. The Polish regular cavalry was either trying to get across the bridge or moving towards Okuniew in the east. Połubiński's men were quickly pushed back by Brandenburg cavalry and began to retreat towards Białołęka. Masses of men and camp servants were trying to force their way across the bridge, in scenes of total chaos. Hetman Potocki was thrown from his horse and ended up in the river, saved only by the timely intervention of Andrzej Modrzejewski, a companion from the *pancerni*/cossack cavalry banner of Zygmunt Karol Przerembski. Jan Zamoyski was also thrown into the water but survived. King John Casimir, with his guard dragoons and cavalry, was trying to calm the situation but no one heeded him. Then, the already overcrowded bridge collapsed. Although hurriedly repaired so that the rest of the artillery and infantry could continue the withdrawal, this aggravated the chaotic situation further. The Royal secretary, Mikołaj Szulga, in his post-battle letter to Zygmunt Stanisław Koniecpolski complained about the Polish regulars, who did not follow orders, 'They stand [fought] without virtue, one of their standard bearers almost lost his head to the King's palash, when he was fleeing from the battlefield.'[61] It appears that one of the groups that continued with a fairly orderly retreat was, quite surprisingly, the levy of nobility from Sandomierz Voivodeship. Those men fought bravely during the final stage of the battle, their standard bearer Marcin Dembicki even saved Hetman Potocki's life but the levy lost 19 companions who fell in the struggle.[62]

According to Noyers, during the retreat the King was mistaken by one Brandenburg officer formerly in Polish service, and reportedly named 'Valcrot', for 'some German officer' and was called out with the words 'come over my friend, come over to us, you will be welcomed here and you will find better [service] here than amongst those cowardly Poles.'[63] The enraged King, recognising the officer from his court, answered 'Traitor! One day I will see you hang!' After the battle the Brandenburg officer allegedly made

60 Carlbom, pp.187–188 & pp.203–206 (reprinted relation by an unknown writer).

61 AGAD, AR II, 21, p.90.

62 Kochowski, *Lata Potopu 1655–1657*, pp.206–207.

63 'Valcrot' was most likely a member of the Wallenrodt family, several of whom served in the Polish Army in 1655, with at least three: Henrich/Henryk, Martin/Marcin, and Friedrich/Fryderyk, in the King's Guard regiment which was disbanded in the summer of 1655, while returning from an attempt to support the Lithuanians against the Muscovite invasion.

the comment that he did not recognise the King; if he had, he would have made a courtly bow to him.[64]

The Allies, at this point seemingly caught by surprise at their own success, advanced rather steadily, wary of possible counter attacks from the Polish cavalry.

According to Andrzej Leszczyński, Archbishop of Gniezno and Primate of Poland, who watched the events from Warsaw, King John Casimir ordered the bridge across the Vistula to be burnt after he and Stanisław 'Rewera' Potocki had crossed.[65] Indeed, as soon as King John Casimir, with his guard units, and regiments of infantry had crossed, the bridge was then set on fire from the Warsaw side. While this prevented the Brandenburg forces from crossing, it allowed them to capture all the wagons abandoned on the Praga side.

In the meantime, the main body of the Swedish army, led by King Charles himself, was dealing with the Polish cavalry of the right wing, both regular and the levy of nobility – the main group of Tatars was there as well. The masses of horsemen could not reach the bridge, so decided to retreat towards Okuniew, via Kamion, Goróch and Grzybów. While Stefan Czarniecki, Aleksander Koniecpolski, and Jan Sapieha were present with those troops, it is very unlikely they had much control over what was happening. There was no attempt to put the units in order, and no one tried to counter-attack the Swedes. The thousands of horses raised such a dust cloud that the Swedes did not realise that those men were retreating. Instead, King Charles halted his advance, probably thinking that the Polish cavalry was getting ready to attack. Once he realised that the enemy was fleeing, he sent Robert Douglas with several regiments in pursuit, but without much success.

A final, rather bloody episode of the battle took place in the muddy fields near Kamion: when the levy of nobility from Bełż Voivodeship paused, wanting to avoid marching alongside Tatars, the Swedes and Brandenburgers caught them in difficult terrain and inflicted very heavy losses. Almost 80 high-ranking nobles were lost, some taken prisoner, others '[stuck] in the mud and the bog were shot like ducks with pistols and carbines.'[66]

King John Casimir ordered his cavalry to delay the Swedes and Brandenburgers as long as possible, and then to retreat south. The King then abandoned his capital for the second time in 12 months, retreating south along the Vistula. On the eastern side of the river, the Lithuanians and Tatars dispersed to the north, while Czarniecki's Polish army fled south. Yet, the Swedes and Brandenburgers were too few to take full advantage as the Commonwealth armies retreated. As a result, King John Casimir's defeated army managed to extricate itself, although it took several days to reassemble – on the right bank of the Vistula, south of the lower River Wieprz.

Warsaw again fell into Swedish hands.

---

64 Noyers, *Lettres*, 217.

65 Andrzej Leszczyński, Archbishop of Gniezno and Primate of Poland, to the Commonwealth Ambassador in Vienna, 31 July 1656; reprinted in Carlbom, pp.206–207.

66 Mikołaj Jemiołowski, *Pamiętnik dzieje Polski zawierający (1648–1679)*, p.11.

Losses in the Battle

The Commonwealth's total losses in the battle remain unclear, although they were not great. Gordon noted that 'The Polls in this battell lost about 2,000 men and above 40 cannon of different syzes.'[67] Modern historians tend to offer similar (or even lower) figures. Cavalry losses are believed not to have exceeded 1,000 men, while known losses in the infantry were 600.[68] Such losses were unremarkable for three days of fighting, however, we might also assume that not all casualties were recorded. There is, for instance, no surviving information on Tatar losses, and these have tended to be ignored by historians, since the Tatars formed an independent contingent.

The losses incurred by all of the armies involved are very difficult to assess, primarily due to a lack of detailed information. It is clear that the victorious Swedish-Brandenburg army suffered far lower losses than their enemy. Patrick Gordon mentioned 'not above 700', which seems to include both dead and wounded.[69] An anonymous Brandenburg account, dated 31 July 1656 and written in Warsaw, stated that the Allies lost no more than 300 killed.[70] Karl Ernst von Platen, writing in the Brandenburg camp on 31 July, estimated Allied losses as 300 to 400 men.[71] Pufendorf stated that approximately 400 rank and file were killed or wounded, with losses amongst officers being very low.[72] The modern Swedish military historian Lars Ericson Wolke suggests that Swedes and Brandenburgers lost some 1,300 men.[73] Among senior officers, losses were minimal, too. Colonel Sinclair was mortally wounded on the first day of battle and died soon afterwards. Duke Adolph John was badly wounded on the second day, in the same knee as his wound during the Battle of Gołąb, and was sent to The Netherlands for treatment, returning only a year later.[74] Lieutenant Colonel Johan Printzenskiöld of Count Palatine Philip of Sulzbach's Cavalry Regiment suffered seven wounds, but survived. Major General Christoph von Kannenberg, as noted, was hit by a fragment of a falconet bullet but it was miraculously stopped by the coins in his purse. Some Polish sources, in order to play down the scale of their defeat, unsurprisingly exaggerated the losses of the Allied armies. Kochowski went to so far as to write of 3,000 Swedes killed, including Colonel Horn's cavalry regiment being completely wiped out (he was presumably referring to the Tavastehus Cavalry Regiment which until recently had been known as Henrik Henriksson Horn's Cavalry Regiment – but there are no casualty

67 *Diary of General Patrick Gordon of Auchleuchries 1635–1699*, volume 1, p.115.

68 Herbst, 'Tredagarsslaget', p.287; Nagielski, *Warszawa*, p.241.

69 *Diary of General Patrick Gordon of Auchleuchries 1635–1699*, volume 1, p.115.

70 Droysen, *Die Schlacht von Warschau 1656*, p.129.

71 Droysen, *Die Schlacht von Warschau 1656*, p.133.

72 Pufendorf, *Sieben Bücher* 3, p.181.

73 Lars Ericson, 'Warszawa 1656', Lars Ericson et al., *Svenska slagfält* (np: Wahlström & Widstrand, 2003), pp.189–197, on pp.189 & 196.

74 Ulrich Lange, *Karl X Gustavs bror Adolf Johan: Stormaktstidens enfant terrible* (Stockholm: Medström, 2019), pp.127–129.

figures to support this very unlikely claim).[75] Noyers, basing his account on the information from captured troops, claimed that the Swedes suffered more than 2,000 dead.[76]

With the losses of the Polish-Lithuanian Commonwealth army, the situation is even more complicated. Łoś did not mention the overall number of Commonwealth losses but added that during the last day of the battle both the foreign infantry regiment of Jan Zamoyski and the regular cavalry regiment under nominal command of the magnate were 'beaten badly', which suggests serious losses.[77] Jan Chryzostom Pasek did not take a direct part in the Battle of Warsaw and his description of the struggle is very short, and he blamed the Tatars for the loss, writing that 'first the auxiliary Tatars fled from us'. According to him, the Poles 'lost many good men' but 'many Swedes [died] too'.[78] According to Royal secretary Mikołaj Szulga, the Poles lost 12 cannon (2 large and 10 smaller pieces) and during the retreat 200 infantry were cut off and had to surrender.[79] Noyers, basing his comment on the accounts of the officers reporting to the royal couple, wrote in his post-battle letter that 'no more than 400 [of ours] were killed.'[80] It is more than likely though that it was part of 'damage control', with commanders reporting lower losses to downplay the scale of the defeat. Kochowski wrote that the Polish cavalry lost 'no more than 1,000 killed', also adding that much higher losses were amongst the foreign infantry. He incorrectly stated that three regiments were 'all captured alongside their colours', also mentioning that many men were lost during the retreat across the bridge, when during the crowded passage soldiers were pushing each other into the water.[81] Pufendorf was fairly cautious with his estimates, stating that 'it is unknown how many enemy were killed, as many of them perished in the swamps.' He added that up to 4,000 bodies were counted on the battlefield.[82] However, even if one is to believe such high losses, these could be both soldiers and camp servants (and additionally those Tatars driven into the swamp and then allegedly wiped out by dragoons). The same number of 4,000 killed is mentioned in the anonymous Brandenburg account written in Warsaw on 31 July 1656, although it also adds that the exact number of Polish losses is as yet unknown.[83]

The Swedes and Brandenburgers took only 18 prisoners. The small war and religiously inspired murders had caused considerable enmity, and the army was angry over the many Swedish soldiers that the Poles had massacred after the surrender of Warsaw. As a result, the men were not inclined to show

75 Kochowski, *Lata Potopu 1655–1657*, p.207. Kochowski is known for often inventing 'facts', from the size of losses to fancy quotes from kings and generals, and in this case, his claim is unlikely to correspond to reality.

76 *Portfolio królowej Maryi Ludwiki*, volume 2, p.68.

77 Łoś, *Pamiętnik towarzysza chorągwi pancernej*, p.70.

78 Jan Chryzostom Pasek, *Pamiętniki* (Warszawa: Państwowy Instytut Wydawniczy, 1963), p.69.

79 AGAD, AR II, 21, p.190.

80 *Portfolio królowej Maryi Ludwiki*, volume 2, p.67.

81 Kochowski, *Lata Potopu 1655–1657*, pp.206–207.

82 Pufendorf, *Sieben Bücher* 3, p.181.

83 Droysen, *Die Schlacht von Warschau 1656*, p.129.

mercy. When Poles attempted to surrender, some Swedes merely shouted *Warschauer Accord* ('Warsaw agreement') and slaughtered them.

Comparing the paper strength of regular units of the Polish army before and after the battle, based on the surviving documents of the military treasury, Mirosław Nagielski concluded that infantry – mostly the regiments of Grodzicki, Butler (Guard), and Zamoyski – lost 600 killed, wounded and captured. Of course, using such data to estimate the losses is far from being 100 percent accurate, as it does not take into consideration factors like the real strength of the units, possible post-battle recruitment or, most serious of all, accuracy of figures given by officers to the treasury officials to receive pay for their regiments. Nagielski took the figure of the cavalry losses as provided by Kochowski, so no more than 1,000 casualties, although he specified it was for both Poles and Lithuanians. Altogether, adding losses of the regular troops, levy of nobility, and camp servants, he gave a total figure of more than 2,000, which seems to include both those killed and taken prisoner. A total of 12 cannon and one mortar were captured by the Allies on the battlefield, with a further 27 guns and another mortar abandoned in Warsaw because of a lack of horses.[84] Interestingly, none of the sources mentioned the number of flags captured by Swedish and Brandenburg units. This was an important measurement of success in battle but, rather surprisingly, the figure is missing from the accounts written by the victors nor is it mentioned by the defeated Commonwealth's diarists and politicians. Some indication could be provided from Erik Dahlbergh's drawing of the third day of the battle for Pufendorf's work. There are 20 standards of all type – both cavalry and infantry – in the hands of Swedish soldiers, with a few more laid down by Polish nobles in front of King Charles. Polish researcher Franciszek Viscardi, who is currently working on the Polish and Lithuanian flags from the seventeenth century held in the trophy collection of the Army Museum in Stockholm, identified 15 flags that can be associated with the Battle of Warsaw. Seven of them belonged to cavalry, and the rest to infantry units.[85]

As was highlighted by Michael Fredholm von Essen in a previous study, historians tend to ignore the issue of Tatar losses, mostly due to the lack of available information and their status as an independent contingent.[86] Only Pufendorf wrote a about Tatar casualties, with some exaggeration describing their defeated attack during the second day of the battle, when facing four squadrons of Swedish cavalry under Duke Adolph John. The charging Tatars were repulsed with heavy losses, with most of those fleeing getting stuck in the swamp and killed.[87] It is impossible to even estimate what the real losses were in the Tatar contingent. Considering that the same Tatars were very active post-battle, taking part in actions against Swedish and Brandenburg units in Prussia, their loss in manpower and horses had to be fairly low.

---

84 Nagielski, *Bitwa pod Warszawą 1656*, pp.181–182.

85 Michał Paradowski would like to thanks Franciszek Viscardi for sharing with him his research in this field.

86 Fredholm von Essen, *Charles X's Wars* pp.3 & 136.

87 Pufendorf, *Sieben Bücher* pp.3, 179 & 180.-

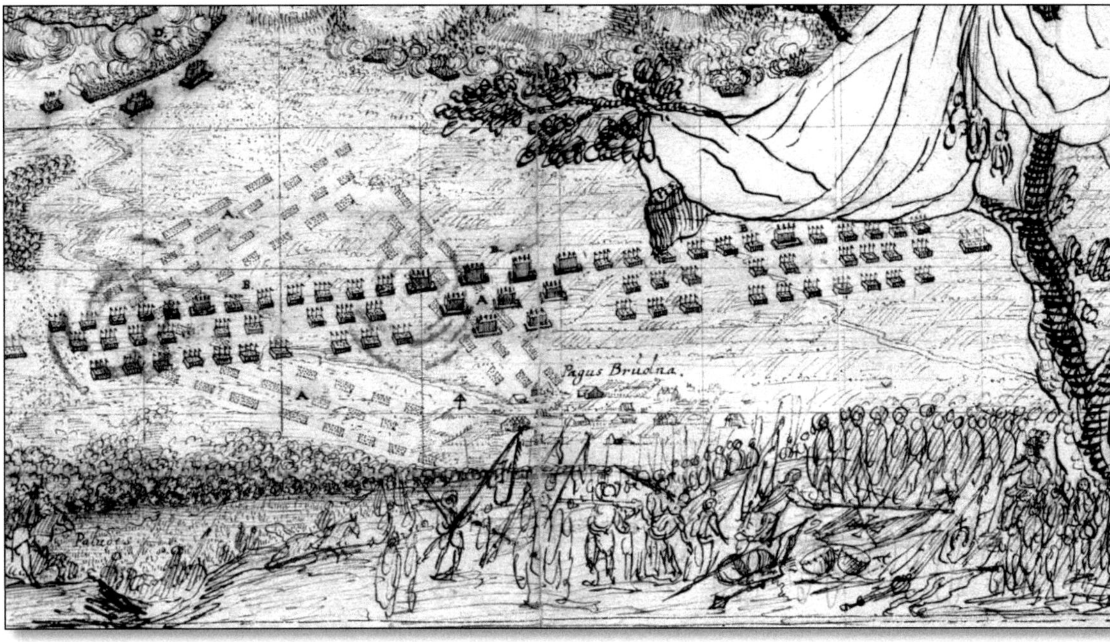

Erik Dahlbergh's early sketch of the third day of the Battle of Warsaw, with Polish units surrendering to King Charles. (National Archives, Stockholm)

Sabre of Ottoman origin owned by Jan Zamoyski with a hilt covered in silver gilt and decorated with turquoise. Total length 102cm, blade length 88.5cm, and blade width 3.9cm. Captured by Carl Gustav Wrangel from Jan Zamoyski during the disengagement of Zamoyski's Regiment of Foot on the third day of the 1656 Battle of Warsaw. When too many Poles attempted to cross the only available bridge over the River Vistula at the same time, part of the bridge collapsed and Zamoyski, together with Crown Grand Hetman Stanisław 'Rewera' Potocki, almost drowned. (Skokloster Castle; photo: Erik Lernestål)

8

Aftermath

Despite the victory, King Charles did not stay long in Warsaw. He soon set out, leaving Major General Barthold Hartwig von Bülow in charge of the garrison. However, it was now clear that Warsaw could not be held. In mid-August, Bülow had already begun to move archive documents relating to taxation and land ownership out of the city. This was standard Swedish procedure in conquered capitals, since such documents were useful for administering the new territories. Bülow also moved out the captured artillery as well as valuable books, and other treasures, since Swedish Kings considered such items were more needed in Stockholm than in territories exposed to hostile powers. King Charles ordered Warsaw's fortifications to be demolished, so that they could not be used by an aggressor – or by the Elector, whose intentions he had good reason to distrust.

Nonetheless, in late August King Charles sent a proposal for peace negotiations to King John Casimir. He again floated the possibility of an alliance against Muscovy, which by this time had declared war on Sweden and invaded Swedish territory. King Charles demanded certain lands for his Allies, chiefly Frederick William who had certain territorial requirements. As for the future of Prussia, the King seems deliberately to have left the issue open until proper negotiations got underway. However, King John Casimir rejected the Swedish proposal out of hand. He was also unwilling to jeopardise his present understanding with Muscovy (the two parties had just commenced negotiations in Wilno for an armistice) – despite the fact that Tsar Alexis occupied the major part of Lithuania and had no intention of leaving it. At the time, the King of Poland was engaged in canvassing support elsewhere in Europe through diplomatic means. He had already received vaguely positive messages from several European rulers, as well as significant support from The Netherlands and Denmark. Presumably, King John Casimir expected that he could eventually negotiate from a position of strength if he only waited for these contacts to mature. The war was far from over.

For these reasons, the short-term importance of the three-day Battle of Warsaw was slight. The outcome had no real strategic impact on the hostilities between Sweden and the Commonwealth. King John Casimir and the Commonwealth armies again abandoned the capital to fight another day, while the Swedes realised that it made no difference whatsoever who held Warsaw. Yet, the Battle of Warsaw carried significant long-term consequences. It was the first battle fought by a Brandenburg-Prussian Army. The Battle of Warsaw thus proved an important stepping stone on Prussia's path to independence and, ultimately, great power status.

Colour Plate Commentaries

Plate A.

1.King Charles X of Sweden

King Charles X Gustavus of Sweden thrived at war and was physically brave. He was a very experienced soldier with years of experience of battle during the Thirty Years' War behind him. Trusting in God and his good fortune, the King led from the front, often at considerable personal risk. He was a lucky soldier, on numerous occasions surviving personal combat against seemingly impossible odds. Despite a lifetime of war, he seems never to have suffered a wound – even though his hat, coat, and shirt often were shot through and once he even lost a lock of hair from enemy fire.

King Charles did not wear the obsolete cuirassier armour that still was common among senior officers. Instead, he wore a simple shot-proof breast- and backplate. When posing for a portrait, he might also wear pauldrons that covered the shoulder areas to show status, as depicted in this plate. However, when riding out on the battlefield, like most soldiers he would discard pauldrons and any other nonessential gear. The King would retain the breast- and backplate, but it might well be hidden under a coat in French style. In addition, he would wear a black wide-brimmed felt hat which apparently (based on a surviving specimen) was adorned with red and orange plumes and high riding boots. Here King Charles carries a marshal's baton to represent his rank, and a rapier as a sidearm. In battle, he would leave the baton behind as well, instead trusting in God, his two pistols, and utilitarian rapier.

2. Frederick William, Elector of Brandenburg and Duke of Prussia

Frederick William, Elector of Brandenburg and Duke of Prussia, had seen war take its toll on his territories during the Thirty Years' War, but he personally had little experience of command. He wears the traditional three-quarter armour of a cuirassier. This style, which covered the entire upper body and both arms as well as the front half of the legs down to and including the knee, was already obsolete among fighting men but remained in use among some senior officers. It was always worn with high riding boots. Cuirassier armour was often blackened. Not even senior officers any longer wore the old visored close helmet or burgonet that had characterised earlier times. Instead, they would commonly wear a wide-brimmed felt hat. Frederick William carries a marshal's baton to represent his rank, and a rapier as a sidearm.

Plate B.

1 Swedish Cavalryman, Uppland Cavalry Regiment

A Swedish cavalryman was expected to wear a helmet and cuirass, consisting of a shot-proof breastplate and backplate. However, most cavalrymen seem to have dispensed with the helmet, even though they continued to rely on the shot-proof cuirass. Many cavalrymen would also wear a buff coat, either below the cuirass (as shown here) or instead of a cuirass. Perhaps for this reason, cavalry units seem not yet to have dressed in garments of uniform colour. The colour of the clothing was simply not much visible under the cuirass and buff coat. This trooper is armed with a rapier with a hand guard for added protection, which was the most common type of rapier at the time of the wars of the Deluge. He would also carry two pistols, in saddle holsters.

2 Swedish Dragoon, Count Palatine Philip von Sulzbach's Dragoon Regiment

At the outbreak of war, most Swedish dragoon units, including Count Palatine Philip von Sulzbach's Dragoon Regiment, were enlisted on the Continent. Dragoons were mounted musketeers who moved on horseback but fought on foot. They were armed with muskets, in this case a standard matchlock, with a rapier as sidearm. This dragoon carries a rapier of the old type with quillons, still serviceable but by this time regarded as near obsolete. No doubt, remaining stock was used to arm newly raised dragoon units. Pistols were not distributed to Swedish dragoons at this time. Swedish dragoons wore supposed to be issued helmets but no breastplates. This man either never received a helmet or simply prefers his wide-brimmed felt hat. Newly raised dragoons wore shoes, not riding boots, and did not use spurs.

Plate C.

1 Swedish Musketeer, Hälsinge Regiment

Like most other Swedish national infantry and dragoon units, the soldiers of the Hälsinge Regiment were issued uniforms, in their case a blue coat and breeches. This soldier is armed with the standard 10 bore matchlock musket. He belongs to one of the many units which at this time were in the process of replacing the old-style bandolier, which had wooden bottles for gunpowder, with paper cartridges, each containing a measured charge of gunpowder. A soldier would carry his paper cartridges in a cartridge box of leather. As a sidearm, this musketeer relies on a modern-style rapier with hand guard. He has discarded the regulation issue musket fork rest, either for good or because he is engaged in a siege operation, when fork rests were less useful.

2 Brandenburg Musketeer, Johann Georg von Sieberg's Regiment of Foot

The arms, equipment, and dress of the Brandenburgian army were essentially identical to those in the Swedish army. A musketeer carried a matchlock musket and a fork rest or swinefeather of the Swedish type. A pikeman was expected to wear a helmet and breastplate and backplate. Both were issued rapiers as sidearms. This musketeer employs a fork rest and wears the oldstyle bandolier with wooden bottles for gunpowder. There is little surviving information on Brandenburgian uniforms. However, we do know from the French envoy to Brandenburg, Jean (Johann) Frischmann, that the infantry was 'all dressed in blue cloth'. Not all units may have worn blue uniforms, but his remark suggests that several regiments certainly did so.

Plate D.

1 King John II Casimir of the Polish-Lithuanian Commonwealth

While there are some paintings depicting King John Casimir in Polish attire, we decided to present him with Western-style clothing and armour in the way he would have fought at Warsaw in 1656. In this battle, he had to look like the many Swedish, Brandenburg or foreign officers in the Polish service, with blackened armour of very good quality and long leather cavalry boots. According to de Noyers, during the retreat of the Polish and Lithuanian armies on the third day of the battle (30 July 1656), the King was mistaken by some Brandenburg officer (ex-Polish soldier) for 'some German officer' and was shouted at, 'come over my friend, come over to us, you will be welcomed here and you will find here better [service] than amongst those cowardly Poles'. The enraged King, recognising the officer from his court, was to answer, 'Traitor! One day I will see you hang!'. After the battle, the Brandenburg officer allegedly made the comment that he did not recognised the King; otherwise, he would have courtly bowed to him.

King John Casimir showed on many occasions his personal bravery on the battlefield, at both Zborow and Beresteczko calming down waving troops and restoring order. At Warsaw, he tried to organise the support of the other cavalry for the hussars' charge, ordering banners 'as sergeant, quartermaster and ordinary soldier', but, despite his requests and even tears, the other soldiers were not willing to take part in the charge. On the final day of the battle, with his sword in hand, the King was leading the retreat of the infantry regiments. We presented him with the so-called 'regiment', a baton used as a symbol of rank of an important officer not only in Western-European armies but also in foreign *autorament* in the Commonwealth's armies.

2 Queen Louise Marie of the Polish-Lithuanian Commonwealth

Queen Ludwika Maria (as Marie Louise Gonzaga was known in Poland) had a keen interest not only in the Commonwealth's politics but also in the military matters, supporting King King John Casimir on many occasions and raising the morale of the soldiers during siege operations. We decided to present her in the most famous episode of her 'military career', from the second day of the Battle of Warsaw (29 July 1656). When observing the fight from the safety of the Polish field fortifications, she noticed that the fire from a two-cannon battery set up on the left bank of the Vistula river did not hit the Swedish and Brandenburg forces. She ordered for the horses from her own carriage to be used to move the cannons to Kępa Potocka, on the bank of the river, from which they started a much more successful fire. Her haircut, dress and jewellery are based on the period paintings. Additional parts of the Queen's attire presented here are based on a source describing the event, as she is covered with a Tatar *burka*, an overcoat normally made from camel fur or (like here) from wool. She is sitting on the infantry drum, holding a scope with which she was checking the progress of the fight. It is possible that she looked very similar in 1658, while, on many occasions, she was inspecting the siege lines at Toruń.

Plate E.

1 Polish hussar, Jan Zamoyski's Banner

A Polish hussar was ostensibly well protected by half-armour and helmet, commonly of the *szyszak* type which is illustrated here. However, the armour was not shot-proof and thus vulnerable to Swedish musket fire. The hussar's main weapon was a long, lightweight lance for melee combat supplemented by either a palash or an armour-piercing sword hung on the horse under the left side of the saddle. As an additional sidearm, the hussar customarily carried a curved sabre. Many hussars, including this man, also brought a couple of wheellock pistols in saddle holsters. This is obvious from the wheellock spanner suspended from his belt. Quite a few added the traditional composite bow and arrows as well. This man carries a war hammer, which was the sign of a noble or somebody in command. Judging from his serviceable but non-spectacular armour, this hussar perhaps serves as a junior officer.

Like other hussars, this man wears civilian dress under his armour, of a style which to a significant degree derived from Inner Asian patterns. Wealthy hussars wore a fur of a wild animal, preferably a leopard or wolf, over his armour. In battle, this hussar would have added a wing made of a line of feathers inserted into a wooden frame which was affixed either to his armour backplate or saddle. While the proud winged hussars were regarded as the primary Polish arm, they were rapidly becoming obsolete in comparison to modern types of soldiers, whether fielded by Swedes, Prussians, or Muscovites.

2 Polish *Pancerny*, Crown Grand Hetman Stanisław Rewera Potocki's Banner

Here is a very well-equipped companion from a *pancerni* banner, although, at the same time, he could be serving in cossack cavalry or even levy of nobility. He has long chainmail (*kolczuga*) worn over a red *żupan*, while his head is protected by a *misiurka* helmet; there are also *karwasze* arm-guards. The Eastern-style *kałkan* shield was not required as a part of the equipment mentioned in recruitment letters, although it seems to have been common enough amongst Polish cavalry. The soldier should be equipped with 'three firearms'. In fact, we can see a spanner-like tool on his belt used for wheellock pistols kept at the horse's saddle in holsters. Instead of a long firearm, though, he has a bow, often used by companions as a symbol of status and an efficient weapon on its own. For hand-to-hand combat, he has not only a sabre but also a *czekan* warhammer.

Plate F.

1 Unarmoured Noble, Levy of the Nobility from Sandomierz Voivodeship

Presented figure, based on a few drawings of Polish horsemen from the period, could be used as a representation of many more types: levy of nobility, retainers (or even poorer companions) from cossack cavalry banners, and both companions and retainers of the light horse (Tatar and Wallachian). His clothing consists of the common combination: he wears a red *kontusz* outer garment, worn over a blue *żupan* (bottom of it is visible, as it is slightly longer than the *kontusz*). He had brown long boots, as he was not able to afford more expensive saffian ones. On his head we can see fur-brimmed cap; many types of those were worn by soldiers and civilians alike. He is lacking any sort of armour, while his weapons are sabre and wheellock pistol. Of course, depends on availability and his own wealth, such cavalryman could be equipped with other weapons as well: bow, *bandolet* carbine and additional hand-to-hand weapons like the backsword or palash, *nadziak* or *czekan*.

2 Wallachian Cavalry Officer, Franciszek Dziewanowski's Wallachian Banner

Wallachians and Transylvanians fundamentally dressed alike, in Hungarian style, although Wallachians often wore large fur hats. Wallachian cavalry were primarily armed with composite bow and sometimes spear, and only those of some means and a traditional outlook wore mail armour. Wallachians used the curved sabre as sidearm. This officer would, no doubt, also carry a pair of wheellock pistols in saddle holsters. It is the quality fur-lined coat and, even more so, the *nadziak* warhammer, long enough to be utilised as a walking stick, which identify him as an officer in Commonwealth service.
While the Wallachian banners initially were enlisted in Wallachia, over time the numbers were invariably filled out by men from the Commonwealth. Based on contemporary illustrations, most Wallachians wore full beards. This officer is either of Commonwealth origin or has adopted a more up-to-date hairstyle because of his years in Commonwealth service.

Plate G.

Lithuanian Cossack Cavalryman, Jerzy Karol Hlebowicz's Banner

This Lithuanian cossack cavalryman wears a *misiurka* helmet. The most common subtype of this helmet in the Commonwealth was a low variant characterised by the small, round metal plate which only covered the crown of the skull (a style known in Persian as *kulah-zirah*). This type of helmet came with a long mail coif or neck guard, which the soldier fastened under the chin when preparing for battle (which this man has neglected to do). As usual, the helmet includes a significant layer of padding underneath the round metal plate, which incidentally also makes it look taller.

Like other cossack cavalrymen, this soldier would typically be armed with carbine or harquebus, known in Polish as *bandolet*. Many noble companions, like the soldier shown here, preferred – as both weapon and a symbol of their status – to use a composite bow instead, carried in a bowcase on the left side and a quiver on the right. However, this man also brings a wheellock pistol (or two), which he would carry in saddle holsters. He carries a curved sabre as a sidearm.

Some Lithuanians sported a full beard in the manner of northern Ruthenians and Muscovites. This cavalryman, however, primarily wears Polish-style dress, and this has also influenced his hairstyle. His main garment is red *żupan*, with tight black trousers and yellow saffian boots. His outer garment is called *delia* and it is another piece of clothing influenced by the Ottoman origin.

Plate H.

1 Polish Dragoon, Private Company of Konstanty Lubomirski

Despite dragoons having been a part of the foreign *autorament*, they were at least partially recruited from amongst local – Polish and Lithuanian – populations and so often combined Western and Eastern influence into their clothing. This dragoon is based on Patrick's Gordon depiction of the private company of Konstanty Lubomirski. The unit, being composed of Polish soldiers, was led by a Dutch captain and had 'blue cloaks after the Dutch manner and fashion'. He has infantry boots with garters and buckles. The dragoon obtained a more local fur-brimmed cap instead of a Westernstyle hat. He is armed with a matchlock musket, as he was not trained (or expected) to shoot when mounted. As a sidearm, this dragoon is equipped with a locally obtained Polish sabre. Other units that we know of would have had Western-style swords, described in sources as *szpady*. Dragoons were not required to use pistols, although some soldiers managed to get one or a pair as a useful additional weapon when fighting mounted. His clothing is based on the painting, 'The Dance of Death', from Bernardine Monastery in Cracow, dated circa 1670.

2 Polish Haiduk, Crown Field Hetman Stanisław Lanckoroński's Banner

Here is a haiduk with a *żupan* in typical 'infantry colour' – blue with yellow lining. Over it, he is wearing a *delia* coat, with the same combination of colours. Red trousers and good-quality yellow leather shoes could indicate a soldier from a hetman's banner or some well-funded private unit. The headgear is a Hungarian *magierka* cap, very popular in Poland since Bathory's reign; as it was a common theme, it had some feathers attached to it. While his side weapons are typical for that type of infantry – a sabre and axe – his firearm is not. He is armed with a *cieszynka* rifle, a hunter gun named after the town of Cieszyn in Silesia. Patrick Gordon had a chance to see them being used during one attack against the Swedes: 'Their ryfled gunnes, being heavy and takeing a very little bulletnot much bigger as a good pease, and not much powder, shoot very just without making a loud report'. As such, it was not a weapon used by regular army haiduks and would be more likely found to be used by privately raised haiduks or some local units.

Plate I.

Crimean Tatar

Few Tatars wore full beards, unless they were of high rank, so this cavalryman is perhaps a tribal chief. But there is another possibility as well. Although there was a Turco-Mongol strand among the Crimean Tatars, the inhabitants of the Crimea due to the Peninsula's long, settled history included many of Mediterranean and even distant Germanic origin. The full beard of this cavalryman suggests that his ancestors might be found among the latter, perhaps the Crimean Goths, who in the late Middle Ages gradually adopted Tatar customs. The rest of this man's hairstyle is hidden by the fur-lined cap. We do know that Tatars generally shaved their heads, but they commonly wore moustaches.

Otherwise, this Tatar cavalryman is dressed in the customary Tatar fashion, with a caftan, a fur-lined coat, high, soft riding boots, and a fur-lined cap. His armaments include a composite bow in a bowcase on his left side (not visible from this angle), a curved sabre as a sidearm, and no doubt a curved dagger as well (in this illustration carried out of sight). On his right side, the Tatar cavalryman carries a quiver of arrows, which he has protected from poor weather with a cloth. Some Tatars also carried pistols, arquebuses, or muskets. Firearms and gunpowder were Ottoman in style. Tatars rode in the Mongol manner, with a saddle and short stirrups, and guided their horses with a short whip, in the same manner as other easterners who based their military on the Mongol system. They did not use spurs.

Tatar horses were small but hardly. The saddle was placed over a felt horsecloth which also could be used as a blanket, or even as a simple tent.

Plate J.

1. Commonwealth: Cavalry Standard or Dragoon Guidon

Cavalry standard or dragoon guidon, very likely captured during the battle of Warsaw in 1656. The large white Knight's Cross was a common motif on both Polish and Lithuanian flags in the seventeenth century. A seventeenth-century drawing by Olof Hoffman, from the collection of the Army Museum, Stockholm. In the years 1677-1709, Hoffman carefully copied thousands of trophy standards taken by the Swedish army and stored in Stockholm. His paintings give a unique view of the copied standards since they, unlike most of the original flags, preserve the original colours. Dimensions: 251 x 187 cm. Stave length: 230 cm. (Army Museum, Stockholm; AM.084141)
Artist: Olof Hoffman

2. Commonwealth: Cavalry Standard or Dragoon Guidon

Cavalry standard or dragoon guidon, captured by the Swedish army in 1655. Dimensions: 230 x 175 cm. Stave length: 230 cm. (Army Museum, Stockholm; AM.083904)
Artist: Olof Hoffman

3. Commonwealth: Infantry Colour

Large colour, adorned with the Burgundian Cross, often used on the infantry flags. Captured in 1655 or 1656, possibly during the battle of Warsaw. Dimensions: 235 x 180 cm. Stave length: 180 cm. (Army Museum, Stockholm; AM.084023)
Artist: Olof Hoffman

4. Commonwealth: Light Cavalry Standard

Standard associated with the light cavalry, possibly Tatars in the Polish or Lithuanian army. Captured in 1655 or 1656. Dimensions: 140 x 70 cm. Stave length: 332 cm. (Army Museum, Stockholm; AM.083906)
Artist: Olof Hoffman

Plate K.

1. Commonwealth: Cavalry Standard

Well preserved example of the cavalry flag with the white Knight's Cross, most likely from a *pancerni* or cossack cavalry unit. The museum's attribution is fairly wide, from the 1620s to 1657. This motif was very common in the Commonwealth cavalry throughout the seventeenth century, so it is very likely that units in 1650s would use it. Dimensions: 229 x 138.0 cm. Stave length: 200 cm. (Army Museum, Stockholm; AM.083784/ST 26:153,2)

2. Commonwealth: Infantry Colour

Another infantry colour, captured between 1655 and 1660. Very simple design, with the Burgundian Cross – most likely from one of the foreign infantry regiments. Dimensions: 205 x 185 cm. Stave length: 290 cm. (Army Museum, Stockholm; AM.084028)
Artist: Olof Hoffman

3. Commonwealth: Cavalry Standard

Smaller standard, possibly of the cossack cavalry or light horse. Next to the the Knight's Cross there is the acronym INRI, from the Latin *Iesus Nazarenus Rex Iudaeorum* ('Jesus, King of the Jews'). Dimensions: 177.6 x 34.3 cm. Stave length: 263.2 cm. (Army Museum, Stockholm; AM.083730/ST 25:108a)
Artist: Olof Hoffman

4. Commonwealth: Cavalry Standard

Standard that could possibly be linked to a winged hussars or *pancerni* unit, as indicated by the motif of the White Eagle and size of the standard, much larger than the other cavalry standards. Captured in 1655 or possibly in 1656. Dimensions: 320 x 159 cm. Stave length: 245 cm. (Army Museum, Stockholm; AM:084076/ST 28:58)
Artist: Olof Hoffman

Plate L.

1. Sweden: Life Company Colour

The colour of the Life Company, that is, 1st Company, of a Swedish regiment was white. The colours of the other companies of the regiment were similar, but with fields in different colour and with different text. There are hardly any remaining Swedish colours that can definitely be linked to the battle of Warsaw. This company colour, which nonetheless is typical of those in use at the time, was made by Peter Blom in Hamburg in 1658. Although the regiment has not been positively identified, several of its company colours remain in the Army Museum, Stockholm. This is the colour of the Life (1st) Company. The cypher of King Charles (C G R S, Carolus Gustavus Rex Sueciae) is painted on one side of each colour. The breadth is 185.0 cm and the length 165.0 cm. The colour of the Life Company carries the text CAROLO DUCE, while the other preserved colours of the series, as far as can be determined, carry the respective texts ARMIS [ÆQVISSI]MI[S], [ROBORE JUSTO], and OMINE FA[U]ST[O]. The colours of the other companies are of similar but not identical size. (Army Museum, Stockholm; AM.067877)
Artist: Tomasz Nowojewski

2. Sweden: Company Colour

Swedish infantry company colour made by Peter Blom in Hamburg in 1658 for the 4th company of the same unknown regiment illustrated above. Although the regiment has not been positively identified, several of its company colours remain in the Army Museum, Stockholm. The cypher of King Charles (C G R S, Carolus Gustavus Rex Sueciae) is painted on a yellow field. The painted device is a golden crown with red, surrounded by a golden laurel wreath. Swedish colours were flown even with battle damages, at times being reduced to little more than broken rags yet remaining in service. The colour has a breadth of 187.0 cm and a length of 170.5 cm. (Army Museum, Stockholm; AM.068006)
Artist: Anderson Subtil

3. Brandenburg: Guidon of Georg Friedrich von Canitz's Dragoon Regiment

Brandenburgian colours and standards followed the same stylistic traditions as their Swedish and Continental equivalents. Several Brandenburgian dragoon guidons were captured by Czarniecki's units at Bromberg in February 1657. Based on contemporary published descriptions, the guidons were four in number (Daniel Schorr, *The Bromberg Trophies 1657*, Northern Wars web site (defunct), 2007). There is no consensus on which unit they belonged to. However, assuming that Georg Friedrich von Canitz's Regiment of Horse originally consisted of dragoons, it seems likely that these dragoon guidons were the original ones fielded by the unit, and that they remained in storage in the supply train even though the regiment had received new cornets when it was upgraded to cavalry status. Alternatively, the guidons belonged to dragoon companies which were attached to the cavalry regiment – a common practice during the Deluge.
Artist: Tomasz Nowojewski

4. Brandenburg: Guidon of Georg Friedrich von Canitz's Dragoon Regiment

One of several Brandenburgian dragoon guidons captured by Czarniecki's units at Bromberg in February 1657, on the same occasion as the one illustrated above. Based on contemporary published descriptions, the guidons were four in number (Daniel Schorr, *The Bromberg Trophies 1657*, Northern Wars web site (defunct), 2007). There is no consensus on which unit they belonged to. However, they are believed to have belonged to the same unit of dragoons. For the reasons mentioned above, we have identified it as Georg Friedrich von Canitz's Dragoon Regiment.
Artist: Anderson Subtil

Further Reading

Possibly the most important contemporary source is Samuel von Pufendorf's *History of the deeds of King Charles*, the official Swedish history of the wars, first published in Latin so as to get the maximum international exposure. It is perhaps most easily accessible to the modern-day reader in its German translation, published in 1697 as *Sieben bücher von denen Thaten Carl Gustavs Königs in Schweden*. Pufendorf worked with primary sources and eyewitness accounts. Naturally, a large number of source documents are also available in the national archives of the countries which participated in the wars. For the researcher who knows Swedish or Polish, most relevant sources are summarised and analysed in the Swedish Military Academy's series of studies on the wars of King Charles (*Carl X Gustaf-studier*) carried out by leading military historians of Sweden, Finland, Denmark, Norway, and Poland under the leadership of Arne Stade. The eight volumes, published between 1965 and 1979, provide detailed descriptions of most aspects of the campaigns. They also provide extensive archival citations, which make the volumes of the series invaluable sources as to what is already known about the Wars of The Deluge as well as the location of relevant archival documents. While all volumes were published in a form understandable to Swedish readers, several were also translated into Polish, and at least one into Finnish.

With regard to earlier Swedish histories of the wars, Johan Levin Carlbom's several works (1905–1910) are very detailed but suffer from some errors in details, which because of the lack of footnotes are sometimes difficult to identify. Among Swedish regimental histories, *Kungl. Svea livgardes historia* 3:2 by Bertil C:son Barkman, Sven Lundkvist, and Lars Tersmeden (1966) remains a solid study. Intended to form part of the Swedish Military Academy project, it was published earlier and gives a, for its time, up-to-date interpretation of the battles in Poland in which the Life Guard took part, based on Swedish sources which can profitably be read in conjunction with the Polish studies published later within the project. Another important regimental history, an early version of which formed part of the Swedish Military Academy project, is Jonas Hedberg's *Kungl. artilleriet: Carl X Gustafs tid* (1982), which presents later research on the artillery not included in the project's volumes.

In the nineteenth century, Polish historians started to show more interest in the history of the Battle of Warsaw, following in the footsteps of works published by Julius Mankell (1859), Gustav Droysen (1863) and August

Riese (1870). For a long time, the main Polish work about the battle was the one published by Konstanty Górski (1887). More articles and books were published after the Second World War, written by Stanisław Herbst (1973), Jan Wimmer (1973), and Wiesław Majewski (1998). The most detailed study on the topic was the monograph on the battle by Mirosław Nagielski, published in 1990 and with a number of later editions, including an updated version in 2007. Certain aspects of the battle were covered by other authors in their articles and books. Andrzej Adam Majewski wrote a biography of Aleksander Hilary Połubiński (2014), Mirosław Nagielski researched some of the hussar banners taking part in the battle (1983), Radosław Sikora wrote about Połubiński's charge and the hussar banners taking part in it (2011), while Zbigniew Hundert and Andrzej Adam Majewski looked into the identification of the hussars that directly attacked the Swedish King (2014).

For the Brandenburg Army, the works by Curt Jany (published 1901–1906 and 1928–1933) are invaluable. In comparison, much less research has been devoted to those states which participated in the wars but either lack modern successors or find themselves represented by less formidable entities. Lithuania's part in the story is to some extent covered by Polish research, but it seems that more could be done. The far greater geographical extent of Lithuania in the seventeenth century than in the present means that this part of the Grand Duchy's history does not fit easily into the historiography of either modern-day Poland or modern-day Lithuania. Major parts of the territory in question now belong to Belarus, which of course has a historiography of its own and which is seldom consulted by historians elsewhere. Moreover, one voice is conspicuously lacking. The Crimean Khanate ceased to exist in the eighteenth century, and there is little current research on its military history. In part, this is because the Khanate's records were destroyed or dispersed, but perhaps even more so, because the Khanate has no successor state. When researching the history of the wars involving the Crimean Khanate, the historian must remember that the Khanate is the silent partner in the records.

There are numerous popular and academic books, in various languages, which describe the Wars of The Deluge. Among modern works in Swedish, Peter Englund's *Ofredsår* (1993) and, in particular, *Den oövervinnerlige* (2000) should be mentioned, since both, and in particular the last, cover events during the Wars of The Deluge in considerable detail and have also been translated into Polish. Sadly, both are written in the style of extended literary essays, lack a system of notation, and add little to the results of the Swedish Military Academy project.

Since most works on the Wars of The Deluge are published in languages other than English, the following bibliography is limited to the works most frequently referenced in notes and most useful for continued research. Many other works are only mentioned in the notes.

Bibliography

Contemporary Sources and Compilations

Abduzhemilev, Refat R. (ed.), *Dokumenty krymskogo khanstva iz sobraniya khuseyna feyzkhanova*. Simferopol': Akademiya nauk Respubliki Tatarstan, 2017

Anonymous [Pierre Chevalier], *Histoire de la Guerre des Cosaques contre la Pologne, avec un discours de leur origine, païs, mœurs, gouvernement & religion: Et un autre des Tartares Précopites* (Paris: Thomas Iolly, 1668). *A Discourse of the Original, Countrey, Manners, Government and Religion of the Cossacks, With Another of the Precopian Tartars, and the History of the Wars of the Cossacks against Poland* (London: Hobart Kemp, 1672, translation of the French edition)

Beauplan, Guillaume Le Vasseur, Chevalier de. *Description de l'Ukranie depuis les confins de la Moscovie jusqu'aux limites de la Transylvanie* (Paris: J. Techener, 1861). First published in 1651, the 1861 edition reproduces the revised and enlarged text of the 1660 edition. (Andrew B. Pernal and Dennis F. Esar trans), *A Description of Ukraine*. Cambridge, Massachusetts: Harvard Ukrainian Research Institute, 1993.

Bennigsen, Alexandre, Pertev Naili Boratav, Dilek Desaive, and Chantal Lemercier-Quelquejay, *Le Khanat de Crimée dans les Archives du Musée du Palais de Topkapi* (Paris and Den Haag: Mouton, 1978)

Chrapowicki, Jan Antoni, *Diariusz. Część pierwsza: lata 1656–1664* (Warszawa: Instytut Wydawniczy Pax, 1978)

Dahlbergh, Erik (Herman Lundström ed.), *Erik Dahlberghs dagbok (1625–1699)* (Uppsala: Almqvist & Wiksell, 1912)

Erdmannsdörffer, Bernhard, et al. (eds). *Urkunden und Actenstücke zur Geschichte des Kurfürsten Friedrich Wilhelm von Brandenburg* (Berlin: Georg Reimer, 23 vols, 1864–1930)

Evliya Efendi [Evliya Çelebi] (Joseph Hammer-Purgstall tr.), *Narrative of Travels in Europe, Asia, and Africa, in the Seventeenth Century* (London: Oriental Translation Fund of Great Britain and Ireland, 1834 and 1850)

Gordon, Patrick (Dmitry Fedosov ed.), *Diary of General Patrick Gordon of Auchleuchries 1635–1699* (Aberdeen: AHRC Centre for Irish and Scottish Studies/Aberdeen University Press, 2009–2016)

Gramont, Antoine de. *Iz istorii moskovskogo pokhoda Yana Kazimira, 1663–1664 g.g.* (Yuriev: Tipografiya *K. Mattisena, 1929)*
Holsten, Hieronim Chrystian. *Przygody wojenne 1655–1666* (Warszawa: Instytut Wydawniczy Pax, 1980)
Jany, Curt. *Urkundliche Beiträge und Forschungen zur Geschichte des Preussischen Heeres* (Berlin: Grosser Generalstab, Kriegsgeschichtliche Abteilung II / Ernst Siegfried Mittler und Sohn, 1901–1906). (NB Jany's work has been described as the most comprehensive treatise of the subject not only of its time but of all times, since many of the original army records he worked with were destroyed in an air raid on Potsdam in 1945)
Jemiołowski, Mikołaj. *Pamiętnik dzieje Polski zawierający (1648–1679)* (Warszawa: Wydawnictwo DiG, 2000)
Jerlicz, Joachim. *Latopisiec albo kroniczka*, volume 1 (Warszawa: Kazimierz Władysław Wóycicki, 1853)
Kochowski, Wespazjan. *Lata potopu 1655–1657* (Warszawa: Wydawnictwo Ministerstwa Obrony Narodowej, 1967)
Korespondencja wojskowa hetmana Janusza Radziwiłła w latach 1646–1655, vol. I, *Diariusz kancelaryjny 1649–1653* (Warszawa: Wydawnictwo Neriton, 2019)
Księga podróży Ewliji Czelebiego (wybór) (Warszawa: Książka i Wiedza, 1969)
Łoś, Jakub, *Pamiętnik towarzysza chorągwi pancernej* (Warszawa: Wydawnictwo DiG, 2000)
Montecuccoli, Raimondo (Alois Veltzé ed.), *Ausgewählte Schriften des Raimund Fürsten Montecuccoli* (Vienna: Kriegs-Archiv/W. Braumüller, 4 vols, 1899–1901)
Niesiecki, Kasper. *Herbarz polski Kaspra Niesieckiego powiększony dodatkami z późniejszych autorów, rękopismów, dowodów urzędowych i wydany przez jana nep. bobrowicza*, vol. 51 (Lipsk: Breitkopf i Haertel, 1841)
Noyers, Pierre des. *Lettres de Pierre des Noyers* (Berlin: B. Behr, 1859)
Pasek, Jan Chryzostom, *Pamiętniki: Całość* (Cracow: Polska Akademja Umiejętności, 1929)
Pasek, Jan Chryzostom (Catherine S. Leach tr.), *Memoirs of the Polish Baroque: The Writings of Jan Chryzostom Pasek, a Squire of the Commonwealth of Poland and Lithuania* (Berkeley: University of California Press, 1976)
Pasek, Jan Chryzostom, *Pamiętniki* (Warszawa: Państwowy Instytut Wydawniczy, 1963)
Pisma polityczne z czasów panowania Jana Kazimierza Wazy, 1648–1668. Publicystyka, eksorbitancje, projekty, memoriały. Volume 1. 1648–1660 (Wrocław-Warszawa-Kraków-Gdańsk-Łódź: Wydawnictwo Polskiej Akademii Nauk, 1989)
Portfolio królowej Maryi Ludwiki, volume 2. (Poznań: Drukarnia i księgarnia Nowa, 1844)
Przeździecki, Aleksander (ed.), 'Zdobycie Warszawy przez Szwedów w 1656 r. opisane w listach królowej polskiej Marii Ludwiki,' in *Biblioteka Warszawska*, volume 3 (Warszawa: Drukarnia Stanisława Strąbskiego, 1851)

Pufendorf, Samuel von, *Sieben Bücher von denen thaten Carl Gustavs Königs in Schweden* (Nuremberg: Christoph Riegel, 1697). A translation of *De rebus a Carolo Gustavo, Suecia̧ rege, gestis commentariorum libri septem* (Nuremberg: Christophor Riegel, 1696)

Rudawski, Wawrzyniec Jan, *Historja Polska od smierci Władysława IV aż do pokoju oliwskiego*, volume 2 (Petersburg-Mohylew: Nakładem Bolesława Maurycego Wolffa, 1855)

Stanisława Oświęcima Dyarusz 1643–1651 (Kraków: Akademia Umiejętności, 1907)

Troupitzen, Lorentz von, *Kriegs Kunst: Nach Königlicher Schwedischer Manier eine Compagny zu richten, in Regiment, Zug- vnd Schlacht-Ordnung zu bringen, zum Ernst anzuführen, zu gebrauchen, vnd in esse würcklich, zu unterhalten*. (Frankfurt-am-Main: Matthaeus Merian, 1633)

Twardowski, Samuel, *Woyna domowa z kozaki i Tatary, Moskwą, potym Szwedami i z Węgry przez lat dwanaście za panowania nayjaśnieyszego Jana Kazimierza króla Polskiego tocząca się* (Calissi: Collegis Calliensis, 1681)

Wierzbowski, Stanisław, *Konnotata wypadków w domu i w kraju zaszłych od 1634 do 1689 r.* (Lipsk: Księgarnia Zagraniczna, 1858)

Zetterstéen, Karl Vilhelm, *Türkische, Tatarische und Persische Urkunden im Schwedischen Reichsarchiv* (Uppsala: Almqvist and Wiksell, 1945)

Published Works

Augusiewicz, Sławomir, *Prostki 1656* (Warsaw: Bellona, 2001)

Augusiewicz, Sławomir, *Przebudowa wojska pruskiego w latach 1655–1660. U źródeł nowożytnej armii* (Oświęcim: Wydawnictwo Napoleon V, 2014)

Baranowski, Bohdan, 'Tatarszczyzna wobec wojny polsko-szwedzkiej w latach 1655–1660', *Polska w okresie Drugiej Wojny Północnej 1655–1660. Volume 1. Rozprawy* (Warszawa: Państwowe Wydawnictwo Naukowe, 1957)

Barkman, G. Bertil C:son, Sven Lundkvist, and Lars Tersmeden, *Kungl. Svea livgardes historia* 3:2: *1632 (1611)–1660* (Stockholm: Stiftelsen för Svea livgardes historia, 1966)

Bobiatyński, Konrad, *Od Smoleńska do Wilna: wojna Rzeczypospolitej z Moskwą 1654–655.* (Zabrze: Inforteditions, 2004)

Carlbom, Johan Levin, *Tre dagars slaget vid Warschau den 18, 19 och 20 juli 1656: Samt de föregående mindre fältslagen 1655 och 1656 – Ett tvåhundrafemtioårigt minne* (Stockholm: Varia, 1906)

Dzieszyński, Ryszard, *Kraków 1655–1657* (Warsaw: Bellona, 2019)

Englund, Peter, *Ofredsår: Om den svenska stormaktstiden och en man i dess mitt* (Stockholm: Atlantis, 1993)

Englund, Peter, *Den oövervinnerlige: Om den svenska stormaktstiden och en man i dess mitt* (Stockholm: Atlantis, 2000)

Fredholm von Essen, Michael, *Muscovy's Soldiers: The Emergence of the Russian Army 1462–1689* (Warwick: Helion & Co., 2018)

Fredholm von Essen, Michael, *The Lion from the North*, 2 volumes (Warwick: Helion, 2020)
Fredholm von Essen, Michael, *Charles X's Wars*, 3 volumes (Warwick: Helion, 2021–2023)
Frost, Robert I, *The Northern Wars: War, State and Society in Northeastern Europe, 1558–1721* (Harlow: Pearson Education. 2000)
Frost, Robert I, *After the Deluge: Poland-Lithuania and the Second Northern War, 1655–1660.* (Cambridge: Cambridge University Press, 2003)
Gawęda, Marcin, *Od Beresteczka do Cudnowa. Działalność wojskowa Jerzego Sebastiana Lubomirskiego w latach 1651–1660* (Zabrze-Tarnowskie Góry: Wydawnictwo Inforteditions, 2013)
Gembarzewski, Bronisław, *Husarze: ubiór. Oporządzenie i uzbrojenie, 1500–1775* (Warsaw: Nakładem "Broni i Barwy", 1939)
Gembarzewski, Bronisław, *Żołnierz polski:* 1: *ubiór, uzbrojenie i oporządzenie od wieku XI do roku 1960* (Warsaw: Wydawnictwo Ministerstwa Obrony Narodowej, 1960)
Hedberg, Jonas (ed.), *Kungl. artilleriet: Yngre vasatiden* (Stockholm: Militärhistoriska Förlaget, 1985)
Hedberg, Jonas, *Kungl. artilleriet: Carl X Gustafs tid* (Stockholm: Militärhistoriska Förlaget, 1982, 1995 edn)
Jany, Curt. *Geschichte der Königlich Preußischen Armee bis zum Jahre 1807* (Berlin: Karl Siegismund, 4 vols, 1928–1933)
Kersten, Adam, *Stefan Czarniecki 1599–1665* (Lublin: Wydawnictwo Uniwersytetu Marii Curie-Skłodowskiej, 2006)
Kubala, Ludwik, *Wojna Brandenburska i najazd Rakoczego w roku 1656 i 1657* (Lwów: H. Altenberg, G. Seyfarth, E. Wende i Sp, 1914)
Lange, Ulrich, *Karl X Gustavs Bror Adolf Johan: Stormaktstidens Enfant Terrible* (Stockholm: Medström, 2019)
Larsson, Lars-Olof, *På marsch mot evigheten: Svensk stormaktstid i släkten stålhammars spegel* (Stockholm: Prisma, 2007)
Majewski, Andrzej A., *Marszałek wielki litewski Aleksander Hilary Połubiński (1626–1679)* (Warszawa: Instytut Historyczny Uniwersytetu Warszawskiego, 2014)
Nagielski, Mirosław (ed.), *Relacje wojenne z pierwszych lat walk polsko-kozackich powstania Bohdana Chmielnickiego okresu "Ogniem i Mieczem" (1648–1651)* (Warszawa: Wydawnictwo VIKING, 1999)
Nagielski, Mirosław, *Bitwa pod Warszawą 1656* (Warszawa: Bellona, 2007)
Nagielski, Mirosław, *Warszawa 1656* (Warszawa: Bellona, 2009)
Paradowski, Michał, *Against the Deluge: Polish and Lithuanian Armies during the War against Sweden 1655–1660* (Warwick: Helion & Co., 2022)
Paradowski, Michał, *The Khotyn Campaign 1621: Polish, Lithuania and Cossack Armies Against the Ottoman Empire* (Warwick: Helion & Co., 2023)
Stade, Arne (ed.), *Carl X Gustafs armé* (Stockholm: Militärhögskolan, Carl X Gustaf-studier 8, 1979)
Stade, Arne; and Jan Wimmer (eds). *Polens krig med Sverige 1655–1660: Krigshistoriska studier* (Stockholm: Kungl. Militärhögskolan, Carl X Gustaf-studier 5, 1973) [Published in Polish as Wimmer, Jan (ed.), *Wojna*

polsko-szwedzka, 1655–1660 (Warsaw: Wydawnictwo Ministerstwa Obrony Narodowej, 1973)]

Szejchumierow, Amet-chan A., *Armia chanatu krymskiego. Organizacja i taktyka (XV-XVIII w.)* (Zabrze-Tarnowskie Góry: Wydawnictwo Inforteditions, 2021.)

Tessin, Georg. D*ie Deutschen Regimenter der Krone Schweden 1: Unter Karl X. Gustav (1654–1660)* (Cologne: Böhlau, 1965)

Ulfhielm, Hans, and Granefelt, Eric (eds), *Kungl. Artilleriet: Svenska Artilleriet i Östersjöprovinserna 1561–1721* (np: Militärhistoriska Förlaget, 2005)

Wimmer, Jan. *Wojsko polskie w drugiej połowie XVII wieku* (Warsaw: Wojskowy Instytut Historyczny, Ministerstwo Obrony Narodowej, 1965)

Essays, Chapters, Journal Articles

Augusiewicz, Sławomir, 'Skład i liczebność stałej armii w Prusach Książęcych w latach 1656–1660' in *Komunikaty Mazursko-Warmińskie* 243 (1/2004), pp.27–47

Collins, Leslie J. D., 'The Military Organization and Tactics of the Crimean Tatars During the Sixteenth and Seventeenth Centuries' in Vernon J. Parry and Malcolm Edward Yapp (eds). *War, Technology and Society in the Middle East* (London: Oxford University Press, 1975), pp.257–276.

Danielsson, Arne. 'Polska baner och gardesfanor i Statens Trofésamling' in *Meddelande 41–42 Armémuseum 1980–1982* (Stockholm: Armémuseum, 1984), pp.35–51

Herbst, Stanisław. 'Tredagarsslaget vid Warszawa 1656' in Arne Stade and Jan Wimmer (eds). *Polens krig med Sverige 1655–1660: Krigshistoriska studier* (Stockholm: Kungl. Militärhögskolan, Carl X Gustaf-studier 5, 1973), pp.255–293

Herbst, Stanisław, 'Trzydniowa bitwa pod Warszawa 28–30 VII 1656' in Jan Wimmer (ed.), *Wojna Polsko-Szwedzka 1655–1660.* (Warszawa: Wydawnictwo Ministerstwa Obrony Narodowej, 1973)

Hundert, Zbigniew & Majewski, Andrzej A., 'O dwóch Rochach Kowalskich (najsłynniejszy epizod bitwy warszawskiej 1656 roku w świetle nowego źródła)' in *Przegląd Historyczny*, 2014, volume CV, issue 2 (Warszawa: Wydawnictwo DiG, 2014)

İnalcık, Halil, 'The Khan and the Tribal Aristocracy: The Crimean Khanate under Sahib Giray I' in *Harvard Ukrainian Studies* 3/4, Part 1: Eucharisterion: Essays presented to Omeljan Pritsak on his Sixtieth Birthday by his Colleagues and Students (1979–1980), pp.445–466

Küpeli, Özer, 'Campaigns of the Crimean Tatars and Ottomans against Iran' in *Zolotoordynskoye Obozreniye (Golden Horde Review)* 2: 4 (2014), pp.226–242

Łopatecki, Karol, '"Szwedzkie napoje" czyli rzecz o wysadzeniu zamku w Sandomierzu w świetle grafiki *Gesta ad Sandomiriam* Erika Dahlbergha' in W. Walczak and K. Łopatecki (eds), *Stan Badań nad Wielokulturowym Dziedzictwem Dawnej Rzeczypospolitej* 7 (Białystok: Instytut Badań nad Dziedzictwem Kulturowym Europy, 2017), pp.151–179

Majewski, Wiesław, 'Działania wojenne w Prusach Książęcych, wrzesień 1656-luty 1657' in *Komunikaty Mazursko-Warmińskie,* no.4 (Olsztyn: Ośrodek Badań Naukowych im. Wojciecha Kętrzyńskiego, 1997)

Manz, Beatrice Forbes, 'The Clans of the Crimean Khanate, 1466–1532' in *Harvard Ukrainian Studies* 2: 3 (1978), pp.282–309

Nagielski, Mirosław, 'Chorągwie husarskie Aleksandra Hilarego Połubińskiego i króla Jana Kazimierza w latach 1648–1666' in *Acta Baltico-Slavica,* 15 (1983)

Ostapchuk, Victor. 'Crimean Tatar Long-Range Campaigns: The View from Remmal Khoja's *History of Sahib Gerey Khan*' in Brian J. Davies (ed.). *Warfare in Eastern Europe, 1500–1800.* (Leiden: Brill, 2012), pp.147–171.

Penskoy, V. V., 'Voyennyy potentsial krymskogo khanstva vo kontse XV – nachale XVII v.' in *Vostok (Oriens)* 2 (2010), pp.56–66

Rachuba, Andrzej. 'Wysiłek mobilizacyjny Wielkiego Księstwa Litewskiego w latach 1654–1667' in *Studia i materiały do Historii Wojskowości,* XLIII (2007)

Stolicki, Jarosław. 'Oblężenie Krakowa przez Jerzego Lubomirskiego w latach 1656–1657', *Studia i materiały do Historii Wojskowości,* volume 40. Białystok: Ośrodek Badań Historii Wojskowej Muzeum Wojska w Białymstoku, 2003.

Syroyechkovskiy, V. E., 'Mukhammed-Geray i yego vassaly' in *Uchenyye zapiski Moskovskogo gosudarstvennogo universiteta* 61 (1940), pp.3–71

Tepkeyev, V. T., '"Ot nego, krymskogo khana, pravdy i postoyanstva net": Nabegi kalmytskikh otryadov na Krym vo vremya Russko-pol'skoy voyny 1654–1667 rr.' In *Novyy Istoricheskiy Vestnik* 4, 38 (2013), pp.9–28

Tersmeden, Lars, 'Carl X Gustafs Armé: En konturteckning mot bakgrund av kriget mot Polen' in Arne Stade (ed.), *Carl X Gustafs armé* (Stockholm: Militärhögskolan, Carl X Gustaf-studier 8, 1979), pp.9–48

Tersmeden, Lars. "Manskapsersättningsproblematiken' vid det inhemska infanteriet under Carl X Gustafs krig' in Arne Stade (ed.). *Carl X Gustafs armé* (Stockholm: Militärhögskolan, Carl X Gustaf-studier 8, 1979), pp.77–115

Tersmeden, Lars. 'Värvningskampanjen 1655' in Arne Stade (ed.), *Carl X Gustafs armé* (Stockholm: Militärhögskolan, Carl X Gustaf-studier 8, 1979), pp.117–162

Tersmeden, Lars, 'Carl X Gustafs armé 1654–1657' in Arne Stade (ed.), *Carl X Gustafs armé.* (Stockholm: Militärhögskolan, Carl X Gustaf-studier 8, 1979), pp.163–276

Wimmer, Jan. 'Polens krig med Sverige 1655–1660: Operativ översikt' in Arne Stade and Jan Wimmer (eds). *Polens krig med Sverige 1655–1660: Krigshistoriska studier* (Stockholm: Kungl. Militärhögskolan, Carl X Gustaf-studier 5, 1973), pp.325–417

Unpublished Theses

Kotljarchuk, Andrej, *In the Shadows of Poland and Russia: The Grand Duchy of Lithuania and Sweden in the European Crisis of the mid-17th Century* (Södertörn University College, dissertation, 2006)

Ocakli, Sait. *The Relations of the Crimean Khanate with the Ukrainian Cossacks, the Polish-Lithuanian Commonwealth and Muscovy during the Reign of Khan Islam Giray III (1644–1654)* (University of Toronto, dissertation, 2017)

Sikora, Radosław. *Taktyka walki, uzbrojenie i wyposażenie husarii w latach 1576–1710* (Siedlce: Uniwersytet Przyrodniczo Humanistyczny, dissertation, 2010)

About the Authors

Professor **Michael Fredholm von Essen** is an historian and former military analyst who has published extensively on the history of Eurasia and has lectured, during conferences and as a visiting professor, around the world, both at conferences and as a visiting professor. He has published a large number of books, including *The Goths* 1–2 (Society of Ancients, 2021–2022); *Afghanistan Beyond the Fog of War* (NIAS Press, 2018); *Transnational Organized Crime and Jihadist Terrorism: Russian-Speaking Networks in Western Europe* (Routledge, 2017); numerous articles in *Slingshot*, the journal of the Society of Ancients, and *Arquebusier*, the journal of the Pike and Shot Society; as well as a number of books for Helion Press.

Michał Paradowski is a Polish independent researcher who lives in Scotland. While he is interested in all aspects of early modern warfare, his principal field of study is the Polish-Swedish Wars waged between 1621 and 1635. To date, he has published four books in the 'Century of the Soldier' series and several historical articles in Polish, English, Russian and French. In his spare time when he is not writing on his historical blogs (in Polish and in English), he helps as an historical consultant for the *By Fire and Sword* miniature game produced by Wargamer.

About the Artist

Sergiy Shamenkov graduated from the Academy of Arts in Lviv. He lives and works in Odessa, Ukraine. He is the author of a number of articles, books, and scientific, graphic reconstructions on the subject of the clothing, material and military culture of the Ukrainian Cossacks, the material and military culture of the Polish-Lithuanian Commonwealth, the army of Sweden, and of other European armies. He has also produced the illustrations for many books from the Helion publishing house.

Other titles in the Century of the Soldier series

No 35 ***The Battle Of Glenshiel:*** *The Jacobite Rising in 1719*

No 36 ***Armies And Enemies Of Louis XIV:*** *Volume 1 - Western Europe 1688–1714: France, Britain, Holland*

No 37 ***William III's Italian Ally:*** *Piedmont and the War of the League of Augsburg 1683–1697*

No 38 ***Wars and Soldiers in the Early Reign of Louis XIV:*** *Volume 1 - The Army of the United Provinces of the Netherlands, 1660–1687*

No 39 ***In The Emperor's Service:*** *Wallenstein's Army, 1625–1634*

No 40 ***Charles XI's War:*** *The Scanian War Between Sweden and Denmark, 1675–1679*

No 41 ***The Armies and Wars of The Sun King 1643–1715:*** *Volume 1: The Guard of Louis XIV*

No 42 ***The Armies Of Philip IV Of Spain 1621–1665:*** *The Fight For European Supremacy*

No 43 ***Marlborough's Other Army:*** *The British Army and the Campaigns of the First Peninsular War, 1702–1712*

No 44 ***The Last Spanish Armada:*** *Britain And The War Of The Quadruple Alliance, 1718–1720*

No 45 ***Essential Agony:*** *The Battle of Dunbar 1650*

No 46 ***The Campaigns of Sir William Waller***

No 47 ***Wars and Soldiers in the Early Reign of Louis XIV:*** *Volume 2 - The Imperial Army, 1660–1689*

No 48 ***The Saxon Mars and His Force:*** *The Saxon Army During The Reign Of John George III 1680–1691*

No 49 ***The King's Irish:*** *The Royalist Anglo-Irish Foot of the English Civil War*

No 50 ***The Armies and Wars of the Sun King 1643-1715:*** *Volume 2: The Infantry of Louis XIV*

No 51 ***More Like Lions Than Men:*** *Sir William Brereton and the Cheshire Army of Parliament, 1642–46*

No 52 ***I Am Minded to Rise:*** *The Clothing, Weapons and Accoutrements of the Jacobites from 1689 to 1719*

No 53 ***The Perfection of Military Discipline:*** *The Plug Bayonet and the English Army 1660–1705*

No 54 ***The Lion From the North:*** *The Swedish Army During the Thirty Years War: Volume 1, 1618–1632*

No 55 ***Wars and Soldiers in the Early Reign of Louis XIV:*** *Volume 3 - The Armies of the Ottoman Empire 1645–1718*

No 56 ***St. Ruth's Fatal Gamble:*** *The Battle of Aughrim 1691 and the Fall Of Jacobite Ireland*

No 57 ***Fighting for Liberty:*** *Argyll & Monmouth's Military Campaigns against the Government of King James, 1685*

No 58 ***The Armies and Wars of the Sun King 1643-1715:*** *Volume 3: The Cavalry of Louis XIV*

No 59 ***The Lion From the North:*** *The Swedish Army During the Thirty Years War: Volume 2, 1632–1648*

No 60 ***By Defeating My Enemies:*** *Charles XII of Sweden and the Great Northern War 1682–1721*

No 61 ***Despite Destruction, Misery and Privations..:*** *The Polish Army in Prussia during the war against Sweden 1626–1629*

No 62 ***The Armies of Sir Ralph Hopton:*** *The Royalist Armies of the West 1642–46*

No 63 ***Italy, Piedmont, and the War of the Spanish Succession 1701–1712***

No 64 ***'Cannon played from the great fort':*** *Sieges in the Severn Valley during the English Civil War 1642–1646*

No 65 ***Carl Gustav Armfelt*** *and the Struggle for Finland During the Great Northern War*

No 66 ***In the Midst of the Kingdom:*** *The Royalist War Effort in the North Midlands 1642–1646*

No 67 ***The Anglo-Spanish War 1655–1660:*** *Volume 1: The War in the West Indies*

No 68 ***For a Parliament Freely Chosen:*** *The Rebellion of Sir George Booth, 1659*

No 69 ***The Bavarian Army During the Thirty Years War 1618–1648:*** *The Backbone of the Catholic League (revised second edition)*

No 70 ***The Armies and Wars of the Sun King 1643–1715:*** *Volume 4: The War of the Spanish Succession, Artillery, Engineers and Militias*

No 71 ***No Armour But Courage:*** *Colonel Sir George Lisle, 1615–1648 (Paperback reprint)*

No 72 ***The New Knights:*** *The Development of Cavalry in Western Europe, 1562–1700*

No 73 ***Cavalier Capital:*** *Oxford in the English Civil War 1642–1646 (Paperback reprint)*

No 74 ***The Anglo-Spanish War 1655–1660:*** *Volume 2: War in Jamaica*

No 75 ***The Perfect Militia:*** *The Stuart Trained Bands of England and Wales 1603–1642*

No 76 ***Wars and Soldiers in the Early Reign of Louis XIV:*** *Volume 4 - The Armies of Spain 1659–1688*

No 77 ***The Battle of Nördlingen 1634:*** *The Bloody Fight Between Tercios and Brigades*

No 78 ***Wars and Soldiers in the Early Reign of Louis XIV:*** *Volume 5 - The Portuguese Army 1659–1690*

No 79 ***We Came, We Saw, God Conquered:*** *The Polish-Lithuanian Commonwealth's military effort in the relief of Vienna, 1683*

No 80 ***Charles X's Wars:*** *Volume 1 - Armies of the Swedish Deluge, 1655–1660*

No 81 ***Cromwell's Buffoon:*** *The Life and Career of the Regicide, Thomas Pride (Paperback reprint)*

No 82 ***The Colonial Ironsides:*** *English Expeditions under the Commonwealth and Protectorate, 1650–1660*

No 83 ***The English Garrison of Tangier:*** *Charles II's Colonial Venture in the Mediterranean, 1661–1684*

No 84 ***The Second Battle of Preston, 1715:*** *The Last Battle on English Soil*

No 85 ***To Settle the Crown:*** *Waging Civil War in Shropshire, 1642–1648 (Paperback reprint)*

No 86 ***A Very Gallant Gentleman:*** *Colonel Francis Thornhagh (1617–1648) and the Nottinghamshire Horse*

No 87 ***Charles X's Wars:*** *Volume 2 - The Wars in the East, 1655–1657*

No 88 ***The Shōgun's Soldiers:*** *The Daily Life of Samurai and Soldiers in Edo Period Japan, 1603–1721 Volume 1*

No 89 ***Campaigns of the Eastern Association:*** *The Rise of Oliver Cromwell, 1642–1645*

No 90 ***The Army of Occupation in Ireland 1603–42:*** *Defending the Protestant Hegemony*

No 91 ***The Armies and Wars of the Sun King 1643–1715:*** *Volume 5: Buccaneers and Soldiers in the Americas*

No 92 ***New Worlds, Old Wars:*** *The Anglo-American Indian Wars 1607–1678*

No 93 ***Against the Deluge:*** *Polish and Lithuanian Armies During the War Against Sweden 1655–1660*

No 94 ***The Battle of Rocroi:*** *The Battle, the Myth and the Success of Propaganda*

No 95 ***The Shōgun's Soldiers:*** *The Daily Life of Samurai and Soldiers in Edo Period Japan, 1603–1721 Volume 2*

No 96 ***Science of Arms: the Art of War in the Century of the Soldier 1672–1699:*** *Volume 1: Preparation for War and the Infantry*

No 97 ***Charles X's Wars:*** *Volume 3 - The Danish Wars 1657–1660*

No 98 ***Wars and Soldiers in the Early Reign of Louis XIV:*** *Volume 6 - Armies of the Italian States 1660–1690 Part 1*

No 99 ***Dragoons and Dragoon Operations in the British Civil Wars, 1638–1653***

No 100 ***Wars and Soldiers in the Early Reign of Louis XIV:*** *Volume 6 - Armies of the Italian States 1660–1690 Part 2*

No 101 ***1648 and All That:*** *The Scottish Invasions of England, 1648 and 1651: Proceedings of the 2022 Helion and Company 'Century of the Soldier' Conference*

No 102 ***John Hampden and the Battle of Chalgrove:*** *The Political and Military Life of Hampden and his Legacy*

No 103 ***The City Horse:*** *London's militia cavalry during the English Civil War, 1642–1660*

No 104 ***The Battle of Lützen 1632:*** *A Reassessment*

No 105 ***Monmouth's First Rebellion:*** *The Later Covenanter Risings, 1660–1685*

No 106 ***Raw Generals and Green Soldiers:*** *Catholic Armies in Ireland 1641–1643*

No 107 Polish, Lithuanian and Cossack armies versus the might of the Ottoman Empire

No 108 ***Soldiers and Civilians, Transport and Provisions:*** *Early Modern Military Logistics and Supply Systems During The British Civil Wars, 1638-1653*

No 109 ***Batter their walls, gates and Forts:*** *The Proceedings of the 2022 English Civil War Fortress Symposium*

No 110 ***The Town Well Fortified:*** *The Fortresses of the Civil Wars in Britain, 1639-1660*

No 111 ***Crucible of the Jacobite '15:*** *The Battle of Sheriffmuir 1715*

No 112 ***Charles XII's Karoliners Volume 2 -*** *The Swedish Cavalry of the Great Northern War 1700-1721*

No 113 ***Wars and Soldiers in the Early Reign of Louis XIV:*** *Volume 7 - Armies of the German States 1655–1690 Part 1*

No 114 ***The First British Army 1624–1628:*** *The Army of the Duke of Buckingham (Revised Edition)*

No 115 ***The Army of Transylvania (1613–1690):*** *War and military organization from the 'golden age' of the Principality to the Habsburg conquest*

No 116 ***The Army of the Manchu Empire:*** *The Conquest Army and the Imperial Army of Qing China, 1600–1727*

No 117 ***French Armies of The Thirty Years' War 1618–48***

No 118 ***Soldiers' Clothing of the Early 17th Century:*** *Britain and Western Europe 1618–1660*

No 119 ***Novelty and Change:*** *Proceedings of the 2023 Helion and ompany 'Century of the Soldier' Conference*

No 120 ***Peter The Great's Disastrous Defeat:*** *The Swedish Victory at Narva, 1700*

No 121 ***Royalist Newark 1642-1646:*** *Sieges and Siege Works*

No 122 ***The Battle of Fribourg 1644:*** *Eughien and Turenne at War*

No 123 ***Science of Arms: the Art of War in the Century of the Soldier 1672–1699:*** *Volume 2: Cavalry, Artillery & the Conduct of War*

No 124 ***Supplying the New Model Army:*** *Logistics, arms, ammunition, clothing, victuals and the matériel of war, 1645–1646*

No 125 ***Wars and Soldiers in the Early Reign of Louis XIV:*** *Volume 7 - Armies of the German States 1655–1690 Part 2*

No 126 ***Wars and Soldiers in the Early Reign of Louis XIV:*** *Volume 7 - Armies of the German States 1655–1690 Part 3*

No 127 ***Confrontation of Kings, 1656:*** *The Three-Day Battle of Warsaw in the Swedish Deluge, 1655-1660*

SERIES SPECIALS:

No 1 ***Charles XII's Karoliners:*** *Volume 1: The Swedish Infantry & Artillery of the Great Northern War 1700–1721*